KU-266-951

of Northu

Harassment, Bullying and Violence at Work

K

Harassment, Bullying and Violence at Work

A practical guide to combating employee abuse

Angela Ishmael with Bunmi Alemoru

First published in 1999 by
The Industrial Society
Robert Hyde House
48 Bryanston Square
London W1H 7LN
Telephone: 0171 479 2000

© The Industrial Society 1999

ISBN 1 85835 104 9

British Library Cataloguing-in-Publication Data.
A catalogue record for this book is available from the
British Library.

All rights reserved. No part of this publication may be reproduced, stored in a retrieval system or transmitted, in any form or by any means, electronic, mechanical, photocopying, recording and/or otherwise without the prior written permission of the publishers. This book may not be lent, resold, hired out or otherwise disposed of by way of trade in any form, binding or cover other than that in which it is published, without the prior consent of the publishers.

Typeset by: Wyvern 21 Ltd
Printed by: J W Arrowsmith
Cover by: Sign Design

The Industrial Society is a Registered Charity No. 290003

UNIVERSITY OF
NORTHUMBRIA AT NEWCASTLE
LIBRARY

ITEM No.	CLASS No.
20 033 371 72	331·4 ISH

Acknowledgements

My thanks go to Bunmi Alemoru for her contributions and tolerance whilst working with me on this project. Also to Sarah Gilmore, who contributed greatly to and edited Chapters 4 and 5. Without her expertise, knowledge, friendship and support this book would probably have taken another three years to write! Thanks Sarah, and to her partner Frank Clune who supplied us with pasta and wine while we were working! Mr Lawrence Davies who helped Bunmi with the updates, and the North Lambeth Law Centre for the use of their library and other facilities!

My thanks also goes to numerous people connected to The Industrial Society, including Susannah Lear for giving me the encouragement to finish (Susannah and Sheridan Maguire are patience personified); Ingrid Adams, for co-ordinating vast amounts of typing, telephone calls and diary arrangements and for her and Samantha Barnard's continued support of my work; Viv Holt, Patricia Adams, Rhiannon Chapman, Linda Clarke, Nigel Strange, Jo Gardiner, Eleanor Niles, Julie Amber and Jacquie Bamborough for talking through ideas and commenting on chapters; Brendan McDonagh in the Information Service for scouring and sifting through the library at the drop of a hat and without a word of complaint – thanks for your help.

To individuals and organisations that have contributed to the content of the book: Jenny Price at Royal Mail, Rachael Ross of Schneider-Ross, James Partridge at Changing Faces, Sarah Simpson at the Suzy Lamplugh Trust, Emma Murray at the Consumer Association, Ann Gibson of MSF, Rights of Women (ROW), Lesbian and Gay Employment Rights, thank you for help and advice.

To all of my family and friends who have tolerated my absences, not returning phone calls or attending social events when they needed me to be there, and who have waited diligently for me to finish this book, including my parents Harry Ishmael and Elsie Ishmael, Philip, Kellie and Max Ishmael, Ado, Yvonne Bentley, and Colin Croney. To Wilbert Maxwell and Anthea Maxwell for encouragement and support, Erville Maxwell for his advice on education and learning, Peter Alleyne, Felicité Lynton, Stephen Lewis and Cathie Louis for commenting on chapters, thank you for your guidance, faith and patience.

Contents

Foreword

This important book signifies how far we have come in our understanding of the problem of harassment and bullying at work.

It is easy to forget that ours is the first generation that has recognised the phenomenon of harassment in the workplace. In 1987, when
I prepared my report "The dignity of women at work" for the
Commission of the European Communities, sexual harassment was
widely regarded in British industry as a joke. "My problem is that I'm
not being harassed enough" would be a common first reaction from
male managers when confronted with the issue. Those days are long
gone. Virtually all public sector, and most medium-sized and large private sector, employers now have detailed policies and procedures to
deal with sexual harassment.

A generation ago racial harassment was often part of the workplace
culture. Ethnic minority people were expected to have to put up with
insulting racial epithets and demeaning stereotypes in order to "fit in".
That too is on the wane, though deep-seated racism, and sexism for
that matter, remains widespread. Nevertheless, employers now realise
that to allow a workplace culture which tolerates racist remarks and
jokes is to invite legal proceedings for unlawful discrimination. There
have been similar developments in respect of harassment of disabled
people and in terms of sectarian harassment in Northern Ireland.

This does not represent some sort of triumph for political correctness or the so-called "discrimination industry". The truth is that harassment and bullying represent behaviour that the victim would walk
away from if it took place in a social setting but which they are forced
to endure in a work context because of the power of the harasser or
because of their economic dependence.

That we now understand this is due to a major change in both attitudes and in the interpretation of the law. Which came first is a mat-

ter for speculation, but each feeds off the other to create a better climate. So far as attitudes are concerned, we now place little weight on the traditional defence of the harasser that he/she "didn't mean anything by it" and now focus on the effect the behaviour has on the person experiencing it. This has been accompanied by a series of largely sympathetic decisions from the courts, which have given an expansive definition to unlawful sexual and racial harassment and to the circumstances in which an employer will be legally liable for the harassment of its employees.

Yet much remains to be done. Anti-harassment policies and procedures which look good on paper often do not work in practice. There is no effective legal remedy against bullying, short of leaving the job. Violence at the workplace is often not addressed. The links between harassment, bullying and violence are rarely recognised. The challenge now is to devise effective policies. This book will be of enormous assistance to those who are attempting to grapple with these problems, and to find solutions for them.

Michael Rubenstein

Editor of Industrial Relations Law Reports. Co-Editor of Equal Opportunities Review. Author of the European Commission expert report on sexual harassment and the law and consultant to the Commission on its Code of Practice on measures to combat sexual harassment at work.

Introduction

Almost everyone would agree that harassment, bullying and violence have no place in the work environment and society in general. They are forms of behaviour which are discriminatory and have a negative impact on individuals and organisations alike.

Harassment, bullying and violence in the workplace are not new phenomena; they have been around for years.

However, as we become less tolerant of discrimination at work there is a growing need to comprehend the nature of harassment, bullying and violence in order to eliminate these behaviours and their negative effects.

Prejudice and power are the roots from which these behaviours spring. An appreciation of the nature of prejudice and how it evolves may lead to a greater understanding of the reasons why harassment, bullying and violence manifest themselves in the way they do.

Figure 1.
Discrimination
model

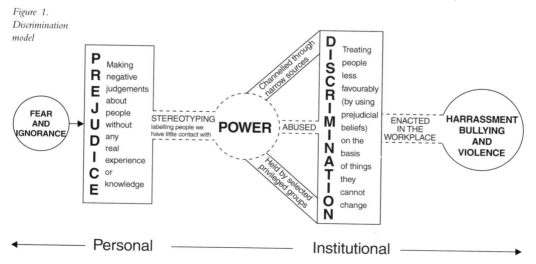

Much has been written about harassment, bullying and violence as separate topics; however, very little has been written about the connections between all three and the impact they have on organisations, and, unfortunately, what exists only scratches the surface.

This leaves those who experience discriminatory behaviours wanting to know more about why it is happening to them and how they can stop it, and those who mete out the behaviour needing to understand why it is unacceptable. Those whose responsibility it is to manage these issues need the tools to develop strategies that will combat workplace discrimination.

It is hoped that this book will go some way towards answering these concerns, as well as raising awareness on the subject.

The extent of the problem

It happens — there must be no doubt about that. Enough statistical evidence about harassment and bullying has been gathered over the years to back this up.

Research into the extent of sexual harassment in the workplace exposes the types of behaviour experienced and the extent to which appropriate action was (or in most cases was not) taken to combat it. In 1983, a survey by the Civil and Public Services Association found that 30% of its members experienced some form of sexual harassment. Ten years later, The Industrial Society's survey on sexual harassment entitled *No Offence?* revealed that 45% of respondents experienced some form of sexual harassment in the workplace.

Similar trends have been revealed in other countries. In the United States, where the process for combating sexual harassment began, a major audit carried out by the Merit Systems Protection Board in 1987 on "Sexual Harassment in the Federal Government" found that 42% of women and 14% of men had experienced some form of sexual harassment.

In the case of violence in the workplace, it is still difficult to estimate the true size of the problem because of under reporting. In some industries, there is a tacit acceptance that threatening behaviour and violence is part of the risk employees face when undertaking certain roles, and therefore incidents are not worth reporting. Nevertheless, the few figures that exist indicate a wider, more serious problem that will explode unless organisations introduce strict procedures to reduce occurrences of violent attacks.

A survey conducted in June 1997 by UNISON, one of the UK's largest trade unions, found that two-thirds of its members had either experienced or witnessed bullying, and in over 73% of cases, management knew about the bullying but chose not to act against it.

It is clear from these statistics that harassment, bullying and violence pose a widespread problem which must be faced and tackled in every workplace. Organisations need to have strategies in place to combat discrimination which are integrated as a matter of principle, and not added on for reasons of political correctness or legislative expediency.

However, implementing strategies to combat harassment is not easy. Dealing with internal resistance to changing the organisational culture can sometimes be difficult, and getting commitment at all levels in the organisation presents a challenge. In addition, external pressures, such as negative experiences of industrial tribunals (now known as *employment* tribunals), the media hype of sexual and racial harassment cases, and the sensationalised reporting of compensation awards, force organisations into a reactive rather than a proactive mode.

It is important that organisations do not succumb to external pressures, and plan carefully to overcome internal resistance when eliminating workplace discrimination. Introducing preventative measures and taking a proactive stance against harassment, bullying and violence are vital steps in creating a positive working environment.

Whom is this book for?

As harassment in the workplace is an issue that concerns everyone, this book is written with everyone in mind. Personnel/human resource (HR) specialists will find guidelines and advice on strategy and policy development to combat harassment, and leaders and managers will gain fresh insights into how integral their roles are in shaping an organisational culture which discourages harassment, promoting a healthy working climate.

Individuals, particularly those who may be part of a group frequently discriminated against and targeted for harassment, will gain a greater understanding of the impact of these negative behaviours and how vital it is to challenge all kinds of unacceptable behaviour.

What does this book cover?

We have attempted to put into print issues that people may have only discussed verbally. To fully appreciate the extent of workplace discrimination and its effects, and to be able to implement changes that will create a more positive work environment, it is vital to take an holistic approach to the topic.

This book begins with an in-depth analysis of the issues involved. The first five chapters of the book look carefully at what constitutes harassment, bullying and violence, their effects on the target and the perpetrator, and their roots within organisational cultures.

We then go on to examine what actions organisations can take in order to adopt a proactive stance to eliminate workplace discrimination, and to encourage individuals to take responsibility for challenging it. The role of education in this process has also been explored.

Finally, we take a pragmatic view of the future, and look closely at the way forward for organisations, policy-makers and individuals.

To illustrate different experiences of harassment, we have used case studies throughout the book. All of the case studies are based on real-life experiences: some taken from interviews with individuals and organisations, others selected from well-publicised incidents in the media. There are also activities and exercises that may help you focus on aspects of harassment on a personal as well as an organisational level.

Combating harassment, bullying and violence relies mainly on the sharing of information and experiences. We have included best practice examples of organisations which have shown a full commitment to eradicating harassment, in the hope that others will learn and grow from their experiences.

To make it easy to identify key actions, activities and learning points, look for the following symbols in the margins:

Food for thought – principles, theories and points for learning.

Activity – aimed at both individuals and the organisation.

Key action – practical points for individuals and organisations.

We hope this book will give you the opportunity to reflect on you or your organisation's current position, and that you will develop a more objective view of the effects of discriminatory behaviours in the workplace.

CHAPTER 1

What is harassment?

This chapter defines the subject, and gives examples of the sort of unacceptable behaviour which constitutes harassment at work.

There are several working definitions of harassment, all of which are based on the European Commission Code of Practice on the Protection of the Dignity of Women and Men at Work, which defines sexual harassment as:

"unwanted conduct of a sexual nature, or other conduct based on sex affecting the dignity of women and men at work. This can include unwelcome physical, verbal or non-verbal conduct."

This definition has been adopted by the Equal Opportunities Commission (EOC), and the Commission for Racial Equality (CRE), in their recent guidelines on combating racial harassment which state that the definition can "usefully be extended to racial harassment". There is, however, no equivalent European code of practice on racial or religious harassment.

In the Disability Discrimination Act of 1995, as with the Sex Discrimination Act 1975 and the Race Relations Act 1976, there does not appear to be any specific definition of harassment. However, the definition outlined in the European Code of Practice would also apply in the case of people with disabilities.

Heterosexist harassment (or homophobic harassment) is discussed in the European Commission Code of Practice as behaviour which affects and undermines the dignity of lesbians and gay men. The Code continues: "it is impossible to regard such harassment as appropriate workplace behaviour".

Although these definitions are not set in stone, they all stress that harassment is measured by the effect the behaviour has on the individual, and not the intent of the person displaying the behaviour (see Chapter 7 on legislation).

What constitutes harassment?

Harassment can consist of many types of behaviour, which generally fall into the following areas:

- verbal
- non-verbal
- physical.

Verbal

This consists of unwelcome, offensive or embarrassing remarks, comments or innuendoes.

Language is an underestimated tool of power. The impact that a few simple words can have is amazing. Language can build a person's confidence and just as quickly devastate it. The role language plays in harassment is vital: the insensitive use of words and the way that they are said has been the cause of many incidents of harassment.

Discriminatory language has its origins in three distinct areas:

1. Language which excludes.
2. The need to use labels.
3. The inappropriate use of humour.

Language which excludes

How can language exclude some groups of people and lead to harassment? Words that put others down and maintain the dominant status of a majority group (for example, words that exclude women from non-traditional roles in society and reinforce male stereotypes) play a part in excluding women and different cultures, and refuse to acknowledge their contributions to our society.

A special mention about swearing: Most swear words are based on sexual innuendoes and behaviours. The list of swear words that refer to the female body is endless. Some words which refer to toilet and bedroom activities are considered socially unacceptable and not for public use.

Swearing is a form of sexual harassment because of the ingrained attitudes that persist about language and women. Many men are uncomfortable about using vulgar language in the presence of women. However, a lot of men have been brought up to believe there are two vocabularies, one for when "ladies are present" and one for the locker room with the boys.

Some swearing falls into the category of "morally unacceptable", when the words used can be defined as abusing religious and cultural values. In such cases, "Thou shalt not take the Lord's name in vain" takes on a different meaning, and can cause offence to a large group of people, leading to racial and religious harassment. The use of labels as taunts or swear words (for example, calling people "spastics" in reference to their lack of intelligence) is also a form of harassment and is highly offensive, as the case study "Extending Their Scope", later on in this chapter, highlights.

The use of swearing as a communication style can only have a negative impact on the user's professional image, and give them a reputation as someone who would not think twice about offending people. The following case study shows how excluding swearing can be.

Case Study	**Mind Your Language – There Are Ladies Present!**

"I have been in countless meetings where I am the only woman present and the other participants, seemingly oblivious to the fact that I am part of the process, lapse into what I can only describe as 'male' language. Once I heard a profanity so blue that I was embarrassed – not for myself, but for the person who uttered it. The offender then remembered I was present and said 'pardon my French', and continued his statement, which was loaded with innuendo and contained several references meaning – 'you know what I mean, chaps!'

I accept that swearing is not the domain of men. However, in most cases, I feel it is used purposely to exclude me, and undermine my role as a senior manager in the decision-making process. When I challenge this behaviour openly I am labelled as a prude, or feminist, or not being able to take a joke, or too sensitive.

I feel angry about having to deal with this behaviour – it is unacceptable. There is still a feeling amongst men that they should read from two scripts: one for the changing room after the rugby match, and one for mixed company, when 'ladies' are present.

Respect is a word that is readily used, yet rarely understood. I want

> to be respected for my ability to do my job, and not treated like a china doll who would break under pressure. I object to being singled out as a woman who is sensitive about swearing. The bad language is a smoke screen – these men don't want to accept me as an equal, that is it in a nutshell."
>
> (Margaret, senior manager)

The need to use labels

Labels reinforce stereotypes and feed into the assumptions we make about individuals. They are powerful and can have the effect of over-shadowing a person's true qualities and attributes.

The label "dumb blonde" is an example of this – conjured up is the image of a young, attractive blonde-haired woman who is dizzy, without brains and often employed as secretary by a male manager who needs an aesthetic status symbol. Any woman with blonde hair who suffers jibes and teasing in the workplace as a result of this stereo-type has to prove her worth on several levels, often before she can concentrate on the job she has been employed to do. The effects of this on her should not be underestimated – this type of harassment is rarely taken seriously and happens frequently.

Case Study

Extending Their Scope

People with disabilities often feel harassed and bullied by people who constantly use labels and stereotypes about their disability.

In November 1994, The Spastics Society changed its name to Scope. The disability organisation, which campaigns for the rights of those with cerebral palsy, had an important role in challenging people's perceptions of cerebral palsy. It is also the second largest charity providing supported employment for people with cerebral palsy. However, this role was continually undermined by the label and use of the word "spastic".

In 1952 those concerned about children with cerebral palsy needed a name that was easily remembered, a name that would appeal to the public and bring in the money. "***It may have been your child***" screamed the headline on the pamphlets. "***Please help the Spastics***". Although the slogans achieved positive results, the negative connotations left a lasting effect. The teasing of able-bodied children could be heard in the playground; the words Spastic and Spaz became popular labels for idiots or ugly people. The terms became so regularly used that people separated them from their original use: "We didn't realise The Spastics Society represented people with cerebral palsy" was a common statement.

In the workplace, the use of this offensive label as a form of harassment, not just for people with disabilities, but for able-bodied people, was difficult to challenge. "What's the fuss about? The Spastics Society haven't changed their name!" perpetrators would defend themselves. Unwittingly, the disability organisation reinforced the stereotypes that were associated with the word Spastic. However, this has changed.

Scope is an example of an organisation that helps disabled people break down barriers, achieve equality in the workplace and in society as a whole. For this goal to be achieved, it was necessary for them to look inward and reflect on the image they were projecting, and by listening to the views of others it was clear that the word Spastic was old-fashioned and out of context with the aims of the organisation. Scope reflects more than a change of name; it signifies the diversity and vision that is necessary in order to combat discrimination in the workplace.

(Adapted from a *Disability Now* special leaflet, December 1994)

The inappropriate use of humour

There are many examples of how jokes can lead to incidents of harassment, particularly sexual and racial, and research shows that they are one of the most common forms of harassment in the workplace.

Hidden behind much humour are prejudicial beliefs so ingrained that when jokes are challenged, people become defensive and find it difficult to comprehend why others object to their use.

How is humour used as a vehicle of prejudice? In their book, *The Equal Opportunities Guide*, Phil Clements and Tony Spinks explore the use of humour, researched by psychologist Hugh Foot. Humour is used in the following ways:

● **As a social asset** – Humour is used to express liking and friendship in social interactions. Jokes will often be made by someone who seeks the approval of others, because humour is valued by most groups of people. The problem with this is that those who are not normally part of the majority group will go along with jokes about themselves and try not to appear hurt. Otherwise, they fail to conform with a social asset that is valued, and therefore risk not being accepted by members of the majority group.

● **To express hostility and dislike** – Making fun of people who are different from the majority is common: Hugh Foot believes that humour may well be the only socially acceptable way of expressing hostility. The cruel humour that is used to express the dislike of minority groups is a power tool used to assert the superiority of the joker, and is aimed at perceived negative features of a person that, very often, are not in their control to change.

● **As a device to control social interactions** – Humour is often used to divert attention from issues which are uncomfortable. To change the direction or depth of a particular conversation, or to combat deep-seated attitudes which are difficult to face, it is not unusual for someone to use humour in order to make others feel comfortable. The problem with this is that avoiding issues of discomfort negates the seriousness of the issue for the minority groups concerned, and devalues their negative experiences.

● **As a way to reinforce stereotypes** – The power that dominant groups hold when using humour to reinforce stereotypes leaves those on the receiving end of it with few options to challenge it. Jokes that perpetuate myths about groups only serve to perpetuate ideologies of superiority.

Case Study

Can't Take a Joke?

A bar worker dismissed for complaining about the playing of a video recording which included racist jokes was unlawfully discriminated against, a Manchester industrial tribunal ruled.

Marie Ampadu worked part-time behind the bar at a Bolton public house. One evening, at the request of some of her customers, the publican put on a video recording by Jim Davidson. The recording included jokes with a racist element. Ms Ampadu, who was the only black person in the bar, was offended by the video and complained that she was not prepared to work under such conditions. The publican dismissed her.

Upholding the applicant's race discrimination complaint, the tribunal found her treatment "insensitive" and "inexcusable". The tribunal "did not consider that the applicant was required to listen to racist jokes, but nevertheless she worked in the bar and as the video was played she would hear them as she was working. She was therefore subject to the embarrassment of being the only black person in the room full of people who were laughing at racist jokes. Finally, and most importantly, the respondent had dismissed the applicant for refusing to work under these conditions."

(Adapted from *Equal Opportunities Review: Discrimination Case Law Digest*, Spring, 1995)

We all make mistakes – it would be unreasonable to expect everyone always to use the right words at the right time. The key is to learn from these mistakes and be aware of the effect of discriminatory language on others.

Being sensitive about using language that does not discriminate is not about learning by rote a checklist of "politically correct" words and phrases. The way to avoid using discriminatory language and therefore incidents of harassment is to develop a conscious sensitivity by:

- always being aware of the effects of language on individuals and on groups of people; and
- using words carefully and sensitively.

Non-verbal

The display and distribution of offensive materials, which includes pictures or written materials such as pin-up calendars and sexist and racist graffiti, are considered to be forms of harassment. Some people have difficulty in understanding why these forms of behaviour, which are not verbalised or meted out physically, are offensive.

However, images and words on paper can be just as threatening as physical and verbal forms of harassment. When Jewish people in Nazi Germany saw swastikas painted alongside the Star of David on the outside of their homes and businesses, it instilled terror, and represented a horrifying symbol of things to come. Racist graffiti is still evident in inner-city areas today, despite the attempts of local authorities to get rid of it.

Pin-up calendars were given to the majority of engineering and manufacturing companies as corporate gratuities and Christmas goods by sales personnel and agents trying to secure future business. This type of "soft porn" only serves to reinforce the exploitation of women, and organisations who are serious about wanting to have a positive work environment for all employees not only need to stop accepting these gifts but should use their "customer power" and refuse to trade with companies who perpetuate this form of harassment.

Case Study

Computer Pornography

Although some organisations have set guidelines for employees on the inappropriate use of E-mail and other mail systems on networked computers, few have taken seriously the impact of soft-porn (and in some cases, very hard porn) graphics and games, which are now widely available. Anna was the only woman in a department of computer technicians in a communications organisation, and relates her experience of harassment:

"One of the incidents that really upset me was the way they tampered with my machine, just to get at me. I would come into the office in the morning, log into my computer, and listen to the giggles and the jeering when, as my machine booted up, a very graphic picture of a particular sexual action appeared. The guys in the department would often change the scene when I had gone home in the evenings. I put up with this for some time, until I finally learned how to take it off my machine, and also change my password so that they could not access it."

Since soft porn is widely available on the Internet, and many organisations subscribe to its use, the inclusion of guidelines in harassment policies on the banning of computer pornography will become an important priority in the near future, and needs to be taken seriously by organisations.

Physical

This involves physically abusing or intimidating others. Unnecessary touching, pinching or brushing against bodies can be the ugliest form of harassment, and may easily escalate into violence (racial attacks are an example of this), assault and, in extreme cases of sexual harassment, rape.

There are four levels of physical harassment behaviours:

- social touching
- offensive touching
- threats
- physical abuse and force.

1. **Social touching** – This is the first level of harassment which involves physical contact. This refers to the "acceptable" touching patterns which, however innocent they may seem, are offensive to the recipient. For example, someone might touch a shoulder gently in a friendly gesture. However, in the recipient's perception, it may feel like a light, caressing touch. This poses difficulties for those who are naturally tactile, and makes the person feeling uncomfortable less likely to complain for fear of appearing over-sensitive. Cultural interpretations of what is and is not acceptable social touching often lead to misunderstandings and, although not necessarily leading to cases of harassment, can cause unease and tension amongst different cultural groups.

2. **Offensive touching** – This differs from social touching in that the harasser intends to offend. The target's personal space is often invaded by the harasser, who purposefully pushes the boundaries of acceptability. Although the harasser may claim that no offence was

intended, the nature of the touching and the number of occurrences state otherwise. An example of this in relation to sexual harassment is if a perpetrator notices that a target's blouse or shirt is undone; rather than tell them about it, he/she will button it for the target, invading their physical privacy.

3. **Threats** – The threat of physical injury or harm, or the loss of job or career opportunities, are examples of this type of harassment. Statements such as *"Do it – or else"*, *"Put up and shut up!"*, *"If you don't like it, you know where you can go or what to do"* leave the target in no doubt as to what their alternatives are if they do not succumb to the threats of the harasser.

4. **Physical abuse and force** – These actions are completely outside the bounds of socially acceptable behaviour. Unwanted physical contact is forced on the target, and these behaviours often escalate into serious criminal offences. They frequently occur when there are no witnesses around, which makes it very difficult for the target to complain.

Table 1. *A sliding scale of physical harassment behaviours*

Social touching	Offensive touching	Threats	Physical abuse and force
Invading personal space Patting	Invasion of privacy Borderline touching Using a social excuse to touch	Using position to request dates, sex, etc *Quid pro quo* (this for that) Unreasonable demands Loss of job	Grabbing Pinching Touching unacceptable zones Sexual molestation Physical assault Rape

Table 1 shows how simple actions have the potential to escalate. Not every tactile worker will naturally become an abuser, but cases of this kind of escalation, from social touching to full-scale physical force, are well documented. It is as well to recognise when behaviour becomes unacceptable, and put a stop to it before it does get out of hand. Table 2 (overleaf) summarises and gives examples of the types of behaviour that characterise different forms of harassment (sexual, racial, homophobic, able-bodiism, harassment and bullying), and is a useful learning tool to aid recognition.

Table 2. *Examples of types of behaviour that constitute harassment and bullying*

Form	Physical conduct	Verbal conduct	Non-verbal conduct
Sexual harassment	suggestive looks and gestures, staring and leering, threatening behaviour, brushing against another's body, pinching, touching or rubbing in a sexual manner, promises of job benefit in exchange for sexual favours, threat of job detriment if sexual favours are not granted	sexual remarks, jokes, catcalls, whistling and teasing, asking questions about personal or sexual life, turning discussions to sexual topics, telling sexual stories, making sexual innuendoes, sexual comments about a person's clothing, anatomy or looks, patronising, derogatory remarks or references, repeated requests for dates or sexual favours	pin-up calendars, sexually explicit materials, pornography, computer pornography, sexist graffiti
Racial harassment	repeatedly touching another's hair or clothes, physical abuse or intimidation, threatening behaviour to incite violence	racist and offensive mockery and "jokes", racist and patronising remarks, stereotypical comments, assumptions and generalisations, racial name-calling, intrusive, persistent and derogatory questioning regarding a person's racial or ethnic origin and culture	racist graffiti, segregating people from different racial groups, display or circulation of racially offensive material, exclusion from workplace functions, social events and normal conversations

Sexual orientation	stereotypical impressions of gay men and lesbians, attempts to "convert" gay men and lesbians, unnecessary, unwelcome, derogatory patting, simulating sexual acts performed by gay men and lesbians, physical abuse or intimidation	homophobic jokes and mockery, stereotypical assumptions about gay men and lesbians, heterosexist name-calling or taunts, intimate questions about a person's personal and sex life, gossip and innuendo, assumptions that all gay men and lesbians are HIV positive or have AIDS	exclusion from workplace functions or social events, exclusion from normal conversation, displaying or circulating offensive materials, sneering or whispering
People with disabilities	unnecessary, unwelcome and derogatory touching and patting of body parts, stereotypical impressions of people with disabilities, physical abuse or intimidation	asking intimate questions about a person's disability, use of offensive language, name-calling, taunts, jokes and mockery, assumptions that disabled people don't have a social or private life	assumption that physical disability equals mental disability, exclusion from workplace social events, speaking to colleagues rather than to the person with a disability, unwelcome interference in an attempt to help with work
Bullying	intimidatory, threatening behaviour, shouting and uncontrolled anger triggers, abuse and humiliation in public or in private, blocking promotion possibilities	nit-picking at an individual's work, persistent criticism and/or sarcasm, refusal of reasonable work requests	exclusion from work information, setting of impossible targets and deadlines, taking credit for ideas and work, ignoring or isolation from work discussions and normal conversations

(Adapted from *No Offence?*, The Industrial Society, 1993)

Is it harassment?

Case Study

If You Could See What I See . . .

"I watched in fascination the behaviour of two of my work colleagues some time ago.

Everton, a marketing consultant, was discussing with Merrill, leader of our administration team, an aspect of project work. Everton, 6ft 2" and slender, is very conscious of his height and was standing over Merrill's desk (who was sitting at the time) leaning forward towards Merrill. As Everton got more involved in the discussion, he leaned further towards Merrill. Merrill slowly slid backwards in the chair, and when that did not create enough space, pushed the chair (which was on castors) backwards. I could see that Merrill was uncomfortable and Everton was confused (they were still discussing the project, but their facial expressions and body language told a different story). However, neither one of them had any real idea why this was happening, and what impact this behaviour could have on each other. Any second now, I thought, Merrill will be telling Everton to back off and keep his distance!

This was amazing. I walked over to them both and asked them if they realised what was happening.

Everton, feeling that he would intimidate Merrill because of his height, was attempting to compensate for his height by making himself smaller. Merrill, misinterpreting this as inappropriate closeness, attempted to create space by moving backwards.

It was then that I realised how easily certain behaviours could be misconstrued as harassment and how essential it is to be aware of the effect of our unaware behaviour. How could this be achieved? With great difficulty, it seemed. Does it mean that every working relationship would need to have a skilled observer of human behaviour to assess it – what is acceptable and what is unacceptable behaviour?"

(Christina, behavioural psychologist)

We've explored the behaviours that make up harassment. Some people may look closely at these behaviours and say: *"That can't be harassment – a touch on the shoulder? It's ridiculous!"* The reality is that certain types of behaviour that constitute harassment can be acceptable to others.

However, the key to understanding why these behaviours make up harassment is to acknowledge that we are all different: the saying "one man's meat is another man's poison" says it all. What you may find acceptable, others may not. It is also important to state that just because you can cope or handle unacceptable behaviours in others, it does not in any way excuse those behaviours – Chapter 4 looks at this issue closely.

Measuring harassment – a litmus test

One way of evaluating whether certain actions constitute harassment is to apply the following guidelines:

● Would you say or do this in front of your partner, children or parents?
● Would you say or do this in front of a colleague of the same sex?
● Would you like to see your behaviour reported in an article in a local newspaper?
● Would you like a member of your family to be on the receiving end of the same behaviour you had subjected someone else to?
● Does it need to be said or done at all?

Reflection

Setting standards of behaviour in the workplace is necessary to promote a positive working environment. Developing a sensitivity towards others and challenging unacceptable behaviours is not just about extending common courtesies to each other, it is about defining and creating the type of climate that exists in order to conduct the daily business of the organisation. In simple terms, setting high standards of behaviour makes good moral and business sense.

Harassment can go beyond our own personal experiences and imagination. The following case study highlights extreme sexual harassment behaviours, and explains why we are writing this book and why the whole area must be taken seriously.

Case Study

Gender Terrorism
In 1980, BJ Holcombe became the first woman oil production worker on Shell Oil Company's "men-only" island called East Bay, located off the Mississippi River delta in Louisiana, The Gulf of Mexico, USA.

For nearly nine years, BJ suffered treatment beyond the realms of harassment. She was threatened physically, verbally abused, humiliated publicly in front of other men, and was subjected to sexual innuendoes. She was the victim of an attempted rape, and men constantly "exposed" themselves in front of her. BJ was given demeaning tasks as part of her job, was passed over for promotion (it would take her much longer than any of the other men to achieve upgrades), tolerated unacceptable working conditions because of her gender, and was shunted from job to job when she became too much of a threat to the job stability of the men she worked with.

As the only woman amongst 175 men, BJ experienced isolation which was soul destroying. In this, she was determined to win against those who practised "gender terrorism" – systematic, threatening, intimidating behaviour with violent undertones, which is gender-based and, in BJ Holcombe's case, was used in an attempt to force her to leave the Shell Oil Company.

BJ recounts one of her experiences:

"Gender-based harassment involves discrimination in work assignments, promotions, work conditions, and other circumstances of the job. In all sorts of ways, my bosses and co-workers manipulated my work environment because they didn't like having me, a woman, at East Bay. My first day assignment was just one example of harassment. Although I didn't realise it at the time, I later learned that my original assignment was to Central Facilities, but it had been changed because the supervisor of that division refused to accept me as a worker. He announced to the Operations Foremen that 'he would trade me for the laziest, worst worker they had'. So while I might have ended up with warehouse work, instead I went to a work gang that worked mostly in the marshes – the hottest, hardest, lowest job at East Bay. Another problem was Shell Oil's policy about toilet facilities. It was indeed a problem for me, as any woman who has been on a boat with men can well imagine.

Except when they were at the living quarters, the men of East Bay defecated and urinated directly into the open water from the boats, barges, and platforms. The men who disliked having a woman co-worker often urinated near me, hoping to embarrass me. At some platforms, toilet seats even hung over the water from catwalks for the convenience of the lease operators, who spent much of their time on them. This assault on the water's purity was directly contrary to Coast Guard regulations, but the company itself promoted the practice by giving the men no alternative. Once we left the living quarters on the barrier island for our work day on the water and in the marshes, there was nowhere else to go.

Like everyone else, I was forced into polluting the Gulf, but unlike everyone else, I couldn't just turn my back, unzip my pants, and let myself go. Having to hold it was uncomfortable and unhealthy for me as well. I was often forced to do without relief for almost twelve hours. I wasn't about to do anything in front of men already too aware that I was different from them. On the days when the work barge was available, I was able to go down into the bilge for privacy. A bucket, crassly labelled 'BJ', was given to me to use. Every time I grabbed it and took it down into the barge's bilge, I felt the men's eyes on me and felt embarrassed.

The company should provide toilet facilities for us, I thought. After all, I was built different from the men, and so my basic human need to relieve myself had to be dealt with differently. Since the company had assigned me separate sleeping quarters, it recognised my need for privacy, at least while on the island. Why not put port-o-lets on the platforms, I asked my boss? I made my suggestion to my supervisor. His response was one I would become used to: 'Don't be a trouble-maker. If you don't like the way things are, lots of people are waiting to get your job. Pack up your clothes and go to the bank.' 'The bank' was a way of saying 'final paycheque'.

The threat that I would be fired certainly stopped me in my tracks. Yet, I felt frustrated at my supervisor's resistance. Surely, I should have a right to make suggestions and point out problems in the way the company operated. Where could I go with my suggestion? Should I protest these threats, and how? As I look back on these first few years at East Bay, I realise that I was incredibly naive. I simply did not understand how I might stand up for myself. I didn't know how to file a harassment complaint. And I had no one to ask.

Thus my simple need for toilet facilities began a moral crisis for me. I either had to fight the injustice directly, and so jeopardise my job, or stick with it in the hope of changing Shell's policies and my co-workers' practices. I chose to stick with it, and the legacy of that decision is guilt. I became an accomplice in the company's discrimination against women, as I see it now. When I first came to East Bay, more than anything I wanted to fit in. I thought that if I didn't make waves, the supervisors would see me 'as easy to work with' and 'able to get along with others'. That would pave the path to promotions. By pursuing the company's high pay without challenging the company's practices, I accepted the discriminatory system."

(Adapted from *Search for Justice*, by BJ Holcombe and Charmaine Wellington. Reproduced by kind permission of BJ Holcombe)

References

Bullying at Work: How to Confront and Overcome it, Andrea Adams (Virago Press, 1992).

Equal Opportunities Review: Discrimination Case Law Digest, IRS, Spring 1995.

Human Resource Management: Global Strategies for Managing a Diverse Workforce, Michael R Carrell, Norbert F Elbert, and Robert D Hatfield, 5th edition (Prentice-Hall, 1995).

Search for Justice: A Woman's Path to Renewed Self-esteem from the Fear, Shame and Anger of Sexual Harassment and Employment Discrimination, BJ Holcombe and Charmaine Wellington (Stillpoint Publishing, 1992).

One Race: A Study Pack for Churches, Churches Commission for Racial Justice, 1994.

No Offence? Sexual Harassment: How it Happens and How to Beat It (The Industrial Society, 1993).

Sexual Harassment in the Workplace, Ellen J Wagner (AMACOM, 1992).

Preventing and Remedying Sexual Harassment at Work: A Resource Manual, Michael Rubenstein (IRS, 1992).

The Equal Opportunities Guide, Phil Clements and Tony Spinks (Kogan Page, 1994).

Forms of harassment

Chapter 2 discusses harassment in its different forms and explodes the myths and assumptions about the subject: sexual and racial harassment, religious harassment, the harassment of people with disabilities and harassment on the grounds of people's sexual orientation.

Harassment may affect people in various ways, and can be more wide-reaching than is commonly known. Sexual harassment attracts the main media focus in the UK, with racial harassment coming a close second. However, there are many other forms of harassment and grounds for harassment, and these include:

● harassment of people with disabilities
● harassment of lesbians and gay men
● harassment on the grounds of religious belief.

Each form of harassment is examined, looking at why they exist in the workplace, and highlighting some of the issues that those who suffer from them face. There are, of course, overlaps between them, as each one represents behaviour which manifests from prejudice and fear. We have looked at each type depending on the social group that people may belong to in order to understand the nature of each form of harassment. However, a victim or target suffering from harassment may not comfortably "fit" into one particular group (indeed, some people cross over two or more) and therefore the emphasis must be on recognising the effects of harassment on that person as an individual, and not as a presumed member of a group.

Sexual harassment

It can be argued that sexual harassment has become the social employment issue of the 1990s. It is not a new phenomenon – it has been around for a very long time. But why does it still exist?

There are powerful cultural perceptions of how men and women should interact in various situations, and these have become translated into acceptable social norms. Difficulties arise, however, when these social norms are applied in the workplace and become manifested in the following ways:

● Women are still receiving strong subliminal messages about their social roles, which conflict with the theme of gender equality: for example, "women should be supportive of men". This role, enacted in the workplace, leads to a higher concentration of women in supportive occupations and these are often at lower levels in the organisation.

● In comparison, a lot of men are still perpetuating an old-fashioned social role of *"I am the dominant sex, therefore women need to be dominated"*. Some go as far as to rationalise this – with disastrous consequences. These messages need to be identified and changed radically to prevent harassment from occurring.

● There are more women in the labour force now, and the figure is still rising (estimated at 45.3% by the year 2001). This rise may account for the increase in the number of harassment complaints. The EOC reported a 58% increase in the number of complaints in 1993 and, again, women at lower levels within the organisation are more likely to be targeted for sexual harassment.

● Most men have not experienced working with groups of women, particularly at senior management level. How many times have you heard men say: *"Work for a female boss? Over my dead body!"* This type of mindset reinforces the sexual stereotyping of social and work roles, and makes it difficult for women to break through the male power systems that exist within most organisations. Men may – unconsciously or consciously – attempt to redress what they see as a power imbalance by using harassing behaviour.

● The differences in the use of language between men and women are myriad and lead to misunderstandings and misconceptions in the communication process. In her books *You Just Don't Understand Me* and *Talking from 9 to 5*, Professor Deborah Tannen refers to the "rapport" talk of women (conversational) and the "report" talk of men (formal statements). This difference in communication may lead to some men making the assumption that conversations with women are on a social

not business basis, and could lead to incidents of harassment.
● There is an undeniable preoccupation with sex in society. However, sex is the tool used in harassment to assert power over an individual – harassment is not about sex.

The myths and realities about sexual harassment

The media has been responsible for the hype and panic-stricken misconceptions of sexual harassment. It has been said that the tabloid press look specifically for sex discrimination cases that are being heard at tribunals, and report the "juicy" details of the case.

Men, in particular, feel great discomfort about the topic, and have begun to voice fears that sexual harassment prevents them from behaving "normally" and hinders any kind of social interaction between men and women. *"It's ridiculous, I can't even offer a genuine compliment, or take part in a meaningful conversation, without fear of being accused of harassment"* is a familiar complaint. These fears, although understandable, are unfounded, and have been spread because of a lack of knowledge and awareness about what sexual harassment really is.

Below are the most common myths about sexual harassment:

Sexual harassment is a crude attempt to initiate sexual relationships . . .
Sexual harassment is commonly an exhibition of power and has little to do with expressing "lustful" designs on female colleagues. Behaviour is directed as a display of hostility towards women workers.

It's only a problem for attractive women . . .
There are no typical recipients of sexual harassment. Divorced and separated women and those working in "non-traditional" areas and new entrants to the workplace are amongst the most likely women to be harassed. Harassment is closely associated with the perceived vulnerability of the recipient and not their physical appearance.

Those women who are harassed have provoked it themselves . . .
It is illogical to think that many women provoke something that is offensive to them. However, women can be responsible for their own appearance and dress sense. Women who wish to ensure they are treated as work colleagues and not as sex objects dress appropriately and with common sense.

It's part of the natural order of things that women have to endure . . .
Several organisations both in the UK and abroad have campaigned and

lobbied in order to reduce the incidence of sexual harassment. Harassment stopped being part of the "natural" order of things when women stopped putting up with such behaviour.

All men are harassers . . .

This is the reverse of the argument that sexual harassment is "natural". There is an increasing number of men who have enough sensitivity to recognise when their behaviour can be offensive, and the introduction of awareness training and harassment policies increase these numbers. There is evidence, however, to suggest that some men are habitual harassers, in the sense that they are likely either to harass more than one woman or the same woman more than once.

We wouldn't employ a man who would be a harasser . . .

Sexual harassment often has nothing to do with sex but manifests itself as an abuse of power. People are harassed by persons who have greater power as a result of their position, seniority, physical size, etc.

Men are never sexually harassed . . .

Sexual harassment is linked with power and in the majority of cases is directed at women. However, surveys have shown that harassment does present a problem for men, albeit of a lesser magnitude.

Taking steps to prevent it would be an unwarranted intrusion into employees' private lives . . .

Employers have a legal responsibility to provide a safe and healthy working environment. Employers are potentially legally liable for any sexual harassment in the workplace, whether or not the employer has knowledge or condones such activity. All harassment in the workplace makes use of the facilities and opportunities granted by the employment relationship, and sexual harassment is not a personal problem between employees. Where the harassment is by a manager, it exploits the authority granted by the employer.

Employers need only be concerned with harassment by superiors . . .

This is particularly serious, because it often contains elements of coercion, such as compliance with requests for sexual favours, which may become the criterion for granting work benefits. Sexual harassment may also involve relationships amongst those on the same grade. Conduct of a sexual nature or sex-based conduct has a harmful effect on a person's working environment.

(Adapted from *Sexual Harassment at Work: A Resource Manual*, by Michael Rubenstein. Reproduced by kind permission of Eclipse Group Ltd)

What about men?

The majority of perpetrators of sexual harassment are men. Although men do experience sexual harassment from women, it does not occur frequently. However, when it does, it takes on different dimensions, as the following case study discusses.

Case Study

Men Are Never Sexually Harassed?

Only a small percentage of top executives in the UK are women.

Companies such as Jenny Craig International, a weight-control chain, where 90% of its workforce are women, are even rarer here than in the US.

But there is a "white male backlash" sweeping the US. The case of eight male counsellors at the female-run Jenny Craig weight-loss centres has taken the US by storm.

The men complained that they were "fired, denied promotion, or given unfavourable assignments". Some were taunted about their "tight buns", excluded from office chit-chat, and asked to perform demeaning tasks not related to their jobs. They were anguished at feeling excluded from the workplace culture, as their colleagues chatted about periods, babies and fashion.

The Jenny Craig Eight sued their employers for sexual harassment and discrimination. "I feel like a token pair of biceps", one complainant told the judge in a Boston courtroom.

In only 5% of sexual harassment cases, men accuse women of misconduct, and fewer than 1% of all sexual harassment cases prove to be based on false accusation. The EOC states that sexual harassment of male workers by female superiors does happen, but on nowhere near the scale of women being harassed by men. Out of 800 sexual harassment inquiries to the EOC in 1994, only three came from men.

There are bound to be victims who have been too scared and embarrassed to come forward and may be encouraged by the current climate, but there won't be the flood of complaints people are expecting. In general, there is no evidence that women in power turn into men.

However, organisations who are serious about combating harassment in the workplace will pursue their procedures just as vigorously for a man as they would for a woman who has complained of sexual harassment. The following is an example of this . . .

In the first case of its type at British Rail, a woman train conductor has been sacked for sexually harassing a young male train driver.

Janette Hustwitt sent numerous love letters to Richard Gula over a period of five months. Some of the letters contained lines such as "Can I say you are gorgeous, a vision of beauty and so damned sexy. I'm single and very available for you. If you fancy some excitement I'll make your eyes water."

> *Ms Hustwitt, who received counselling for her obsession with Mr Gula, maintained that she had been wrongly sacked and that her mistake was to have fallen in love, although she admitted that some of her letters were written when she was drunk, and that they were explicit. Ms Hustwitt claimed that she was not given a copy of sexual harassment policies and is considering court action over her dismissal.*
>
> *Regional Railways North East said Ms Hustwitt had been sacked for serious breaches of the company's harassment policy over a number of months. "She was spoken to repeatedly by her managers and the policy was explained to her. It was quite apparent that she fully understood the policy and its associated procedures," they stated.*
>
> *Mr Gula said: "It wasn't very pleasant. I didn't find her at all attractive and I gave the letters straight to the Railway Board. Her attentions were certainly not desired by me. She has brought it all on herself. She has done it before and could do it again. I just want to put all this behind me and get on with my job."*
>
> *Earlier this year it was disclosed that Ms Hustwitt sent a risqué Christmas card and a red rose to another train driver, Steve Brady. She claimed they were sent as a joke and said: "He is flattering his own ego by thinking I fancy him. I sent him a red rose on the spur of the moment. We had a little fall-out the day before. I saw an advert saying 'Say it with flowers', so I bought him one at York station."*
>
> (Adapted from an article in The Times by Paul Wilkinson, 22 September 1994.
© Times Newspapers Ltd, 1994/5)

Men in the UK working in female-dominated environments seem to take the imbalance more in their stride than the Jenny Craig Eight. One way to deal with "close-to-the-bone" remarks is to treat them as fun – most men feel that women don't go over the top!

Reflection

Ellen Wagner, author of *Sexual Harassment in the Workplace*, answers all the fears and concerns of people who feel the focus on sexual harassment has gone over the top, and that they can no longer relate to each other in a friendly, jocular manner:

"As long as no reasonable person is offended, normal, pleasant, friendly interactions between the sexes does not constitute sexual harassment. Common courtesy, genuineness, common sense, and a habit of close observation of each other's behaviour and reactions to what is said and done can go a long way in achieving a friendly work environment. There is no reason why both sexes cannot feel comfortable and secure, and enjoy each other's company in an atmosphere free of sexual harassment."

Racial harassment

Very little research has been carried out to establish the extent of racial harassment at work, although much has been done to combat it in the community. However, it is evident that racial harassment in the workplace is on the increase – the CRE reported a 27% rise in the number of complaints of racial harassment in 1991–92, and believe that the figures may be much higher, as many people are afraid to make complaints.

A research study produced by the CRE revealed that less than half of large firms have formal procedures for dealing with racial harassment. The study states that *"many employers are unaware of the statutory Race Relations code of practice in employment under which racial harassment at work may be considered a discriminatory offence"*. This lack of knowledge is worrying. Although our current legislation makes most forms of racism unlawful, our social structures still perpetuate more subtle forms of racial harassment which spill into the workplace and mirror the ignorance that exists in society about the true nature of racism.

The roots of racial harassment – a brief history

Why harp on history? Surely we should let bygones be bygones and concentrate on the future. Although there is a lot of truth in this, one of the reasons why racial harassment is on the increase is precisely because there have been attempts to bury history and the experiences of the past, instead of building on them in order to draw vital lessons. Analysing the way history has shaped present thinking can help to broaden perspectives on racial harassment.

In the seventeenth century, the slave trade was created out of a need to invest in British industry and improve the economy by increasing exports. It is estimated that £12 million in profit was generated between 1630 and 1807 from the slave trade alone. Feelings of racial superiority increased, and led Europeans to colonise countries in Asia and Africa, creating political systems and ideologies based on colonialism and imperialism.

In the nineteenth century, it was necessary to create more subtle and divergent forms of racism in order to justify and maintain these political systems. For example, racist anthropologists of the time developed theories which "proved" that black people were closer to apes than to Europeans and were their intellectual inferiors. This meant that the only role for Europeans was to humanise, civilise and govern these people!

Some of these forms of racism are at the root of behaviours which govern racial harassment now. For example, the controversial argument of the intellectual inferiority of black people still exists today. Racist academics attempt to prove the theory by use of "scientific techniques and research". Some psychometric tests in recruitment, selection and career development effectively discriminate against ethnic minority groups (and women), because the norms used to validate the tests are largely based on the results of research, using those in management and professional roles (the majority of whom are white men) as participants.

The United Kingdom – A Multi-cultural Society
There is still a feeling amongst the majority population that people of different races are immigrants, and because of this they are treated as aliens or foreigners. Much of the debate about racism and racial harassment centres around immigration policies of the 1950s and 1960s, omitting the historical context that helped shaped our society and employment demographics of today.

For centuries, Britain has been home to people from many parts of the world:

● The Angles, Saxons and Normans came as invaders and conquerors in the tenth and eleventh centuries. Others came as traders to find work.
● There were also those who had no choice in settling in Britain – Africans were brought to Britain by force as slaves or servants. In 1764, there were 20,000 black people in London alone.
● Jewish and Irish people came to escape from war, famine or religious hatred in their own countries. In the late nineteenth century there were approximately 60,000 Jewish people living in Britain (half of whom were born in Britain). Irish emigration can be traced back as far as the late eighteenth/early nineteenth centuries.
● People from countries such as India, Pakistan, Bangladesh and the West Indies were invited here after the Second World War, because there were not enough people to fill the jobs and do all the work needed to rebuild the country.
● The list of ethnic groups who have a right to British nationality status in the 1990s is growing: Africans, Afro-Caribbeans, Americans, Australians, Bangladeshis, Chinese, Cypriots, Greeks, Indians, Iranians, Italians, Kurds, New Zealanders, Pakistanis, Poles, South Asians, Spanish, Taiwanese, Turks, Ukrainians . . .
● 5% of the population is of an ethnic minority, the largest group being Irish, and an estimated 20 other languages are spoken by at least 200,000 people.

History states that ethnic minorities have lived in the UK since the seventeenth century – the reality is that we were a multi-cultural society then and we are a multi-cultural society now. A diverse workforce free of harassment need not be a pipe dream but a reality, reflecting our society as a whole.

Challenging assumptions about racial harassment

There is an underlying fear surrounding racism, which explains the unwillingness to acknowledge that it exists – an acknowledgement that is necessary in order to combat it effectively in the workplace.

Racial harassment is sometimes viewed as an emotive issue which people are not comfortable with or willing to discuss for fear of being blamed for its existence. It is also a political issue and because of this, politics too often cloud the important social aspects, creating an air of "taboo".

Dealing with sexual harassment in the workplace is, in one sense, easier to cope with. This is because there is a wider level of awareness about gender issues, and most people have (or know of others who have had) first-hand experience of sex discrimination. In contrast, most people's experience of racial harassment comes second or third hand by the perpetuation of assumptions and myths. This blocks practical development around solutions, and maintains it as a "taboo" subject, giving assumptions and stereotypes more power than they deserve.

Some of these assumptions are challenged below:

Racism and racial harassment are not a problem for us because "we have no blacks working here"

Geography and demographics may play a role in perpetuating this particular assumption; however, "no blacks" does not mean no problem. In fact, the systems and procedures used in an organisation may effectively prevent the entry of different racial groups, and the corporate image of some organisations may (unintentionally) exclude ethnic minority groups. Systems and procedures need to be examined to ensure that they do not encourage racial discrimination.

The higher up the social ladder ethnic minorities climb, the less racism they face

Racism is not distinct from class or different across backgrounds, although it may manifest itself in different ways. Linked into this particular myth is the belief that ethnic minorities who move in the higher classes of society do not experience racism. The implication here is that racism only exists amongst the "working classes". Also, the more popular a public figure from an ethnic minority group, the more open they are to racial harassment, such as hate-mail and death threats. Racial harassment is perpetuated by an abuse of power, and most of the power base is still held by those who occupy the higher ranks of the class system or by those who hold the purse strings, leaving ethnic minority groups in those same circles at just as much risk of racial harassment as others.

Racial harassment is only manifested in physical attacks

Although racial attacks and physical abuse are on the increase, the subtler, less obvious forms of harassment are more common. Verbal abuse, racial jokes, insults and taunts, mimicking speech and mocking styles of dress happen on a frequent basis and are much more difficult to deal with in the workplace.

People who claim that they have been racially harassed have a "chip on their shoulder"

This particular myth serves as a denial of an individual's right to complain about unfair and/or ill-treatment, and perpetuates the stereotype of ethnic minorities as victims. Misinterpreting cultural messages and responses to racial harassment are at the root of why organisations do not deal with complaints of racial harassment effectively. A consequence of this is that most people who experience racial harassment at work will not complain because they do not believe their complaint will be taken seriously.

Only "black" people suffer racial harassment

The assumption is often made that racial harassment is about colour only, ie black and white issues. Because of this, many people have difficulty understanding the true nature of racial harassment, as incidents other than those relating to skin colour are not immediately identified as racial harassment. Harassment on the grounds of race affects nationality, ethnic or national origin and race, as well as skin colour.

Racial harassment is only perpetuated by extreme racist groups

The effect that extreme racist groups have on our society should not be underestimated. There is a resurrection of extremist parties in Europe – Austria, Belgium, France and Italy in particular.

However, most incidents of racial harassment involve everyday transactions between people: the Runnymede Trust estimates that there are 70,000 racial incidents a year, 200 a day and one every seven or eight minutes. They believe that racial harassment is "endemic to British society", and not just the domain of extreme racist groups.

Racial harassment will not occur in our organisation because we have a good equal opportunities policy

The best organisations, with excellent written equal opportunities strategies and policies, have found this assumption to be untrue. Equal opportunities policies do not in themselves eradicate racial harassment. The most common reasons why policies are rendered ineffective are: a lack of awareness of racial harassment amongst employees; a lack of appropriate skills needed to deal with issues of harassment; and very little or no acceptance of individual responsibility for making the policy work at all levels within the organisation. Chapters 5 and 6 examine this issue further.

Case Study

"The Higher Up the Social Ladder Ethnic Minorities Climb, the Less Racism They Face . . ."

Racial harassment does not stop according to the status or role that people take on in society. Relating her experience of harassment in her term of office as Mayor of Windsor, Baroness Shreela Flather describes herself as an "archetypal Tory lady, middle class, middle aged and not seen as a radical, not seen as a 'sister'" – a long way from the stereotype of a racially harassed person. She recalls her experiences:

"I have suffered some very subtle forms of discrimination and some not so subtle forms of discrimination. On one occasion in a train, going home to Maidenhead, a middle-aged man started being abusive and was shouting away in this train. Not one person in the train got up to say to that man 'shut up!'"

Racism stalks the corridors of power as well as trains. She has known repeated discrimination in her professional life:

"I applied for a job teaching English as a second language to Asian boys in a secondary modern school. Mind you it was a while ago, but at the interview the head-teacher told me there were two problems he had with me. I was not as he put it 'one of us' and I was a woman. I had to tell him that I couldn't do much about either of those, then he said, 'Of course you won't wear those flowing things to the school, will you?'"

Rise as high as she did in her public life, there was always something to bring her down with a bump:

"When I was Mayor, there was a group of people who resented me enormously, who didn't really see me, an Asian woman, as Mayor of Windsor, and they did everything possible to undermine me. I had a very difficult time. They wouldn't do the sort of things a mayor has a right to expect them to do. Once I was in my office and I said that everything had been moved around again, because I wanted it set up in a certain way, and this chap shouted at me. He said, 'You shouldn't even be in here at this time!' I said, 'Is there a restriction on me being here?' And no other mayor has been spoken to in this way. I had a chauffeur who was so rude and unpleasant to me that I had to give an ultimatum to the borough secretary to say that if he didn't go I wouldn't travel in the Mayoral car. So those sorts of things are pretty blatant."

Less obvious things – subtle things, all the more insidious for being unconscious . . .

"The subtle racism actually, I think, comes very often from the 'white liberals'. It is a very interesting experience. I think in life you discover that you have been assigned a role and a niche, and if you fall out of your crease, so to speak, jump out of your crease, then people don't like it. I am an Asian woman, I should be on the receiving end of people's kindness. And I shouldn't be wanting to do things myself. I have found white liberal women particularly undermining. And if there are any Asians reading this – watch out for those who claim to be your friends, for they are the ones who want control and power, and they see you as a source which will lead them to have that control and power, so that they can exercise this over you, and they can actually gain something. It's happened here. There are people who are so-called experts and the white liberal fraternity, and they are the ones who have been the least friendly to me!"

(Baroness Shreela Flather. Transcript adapted from *One Race*, a study pack. Reproduced with kind permission from the Churches Commission for Racial Justice)

Reflection

The challenge of getting rid of racial harassment in the workplace begins with an acknowledgement that it exists, and the extent to which it occurs. This can be achieved by raising employee awareness about the issue, and giving staff at all levels the skills to deal with it. The reality is that racial harassment is a cancer that is spreading over Europe at a fast rate – its prevention in the workplace is a big step in contributing to its elimination from society as a whole.

Religious harassment – a brief mention

Harassment on the grounds of religious beliefs tends to take the form of religious jokes, taunts and tricks played by work colleagues.

There is a very thin line between racial harassment and religious harassment, and it most affects those minority groups whose religion forms an integral part of their ethnicity and cultural practices. Acts of racial harassment can cross over the line and offend religious beliefs, as the following example illustrates.

Case Study

The Thin Line between Race and Religion

Mr A Hussain had put up with racial abuse for all of the three years he was with Westcroft Castings Ltd. Westcroft Castings, a small metal castings foundry, only employed 33 people at a time, however was still found liable for its actions, even though it is a small company.

The incidents that occurred were horrifying and unacceptable. Mr Hussain, a Muslim, suffered the humiliation of having a pig's head shoved in his face, with his work colleagues standing around laughing, as he came out of a shower one day. Muslims do not eat pork, because, similar to Jewish dietary laws, the pig is an animal which does not chew its cud and has a cloven hoof. The deliberate insult to his religious beliefs went far deeper than the surface racial abuse which he also suffered.

Complaining to his supervisor did not stop the harassment. Once again in the shower, Mr Hussain felt something warm on his leg. He turned around to find Mr Irvine urinating on his leg, again to everyone's amusement. Mr Irvine told him: "That's all you Pakis are worth: a piece of piss". His supervisor asked Mr Hussain what he had done to "stir this up", and took no action against Mr Irvine.

The tribunal did not accept that this was merely "jocular banter" – they ruled unanimously that he had been a victim of racial discrimination and found the supervisor's responses as "deplorably inadequate".

(Adapted from *Racial Harassment at Work: What Employers Can Do about it*, by the Commission for Racial Equality)

In a report in *The Telegraph*, a Jewish policeman won an undisclosed compensation settlement from the Metropolitan Police.

PC Paul Thomas told an industrial tribunal how his colleagues had waved pieces of bacon in front of him and taunted him with nicknames such as "The Milky Bar Yid". The effect on Mr Thomas of this harassment was dangerous, as he developed the eating disorder bulimia after suffering the racial abuse from fellow officers.

The tribunal upheld his claim of racial discrimination, and approved the compensation payment.

(Adapted from an article in *The Daily Telegraph* by Mark Storey, 6 June 1996.
© Mark Storey)

Although the Race Relations Act 1976 does not recognise religion as a form of discrimination, most religions are closely linked to ethnicity, and religion forms the basis of cultural practices.

Often, everyday language and actions which may not appear to be outwardly offensive can take on different meanings to many others who have strong religious beliefs, as the following illustrates.

Case Study

Oh Lord, Not Again . . .
"I've been a committed Christian for most of my life, and a great deal of my social life centres around my local church, where I am a member of the PCC (Parochial Church Council) and help out with the young members' music group.

I work in an advertising company as a graphic designer, in an open-plan office. There is a lot of banter and joking, which is borderline, and at times the team tease me (my nickname is the 'office bible basher'). I tend not to say much about it, but it is really difficult, especially when the 'Oh Lords' and 'Jesus Christs' start pouring out when the team is under pressure.

What's my way of overcoming it when their teasing gets really rough? This may sound pathetic, and in some ways passive, but I send up to God a short prayer for strength and guidance, and I pray for them. I believe there is no point in confronting the team, as they would never take it seriously – after all, as a Christian, I'm supposed to turn the other cheek, aren't I?"

(Peter A)

Sectarian harassment

At present, there is no legislation that gives protection from discrimination on the grounds of religion in the UK – except in Northern Ireland, where harassment on the grounds of religious beliefs and political opinion is known as sectarian harassment. In contrast, Northern Ireland currently has no anti-racist legislation, even though over 1% of its population is of ethnic minority origin.

The Northern Ireland Fair Employment Act 1990 was introduced in recognition of the fact that little had been done previously to improve the employment rights of the Catholic minority. Employers must put in place measures to prevent sectarian harassment and conduct regular reviews of their policies.

However, the rising number of financial settlements paid to employees alleging sectarian harassment indicates that the legislation is not a deterrent to every employer, as the following case study shows.

Case Study

Sectarian Harassment

Four Northern Ireland employers have agreed to pay out more than £133,000 to five people in settlement of alleged sectarian harassment cases, according to the Fair Employment Commission. The five victims all left their employment because of the alleged harassment. The Royal Mail Cash Company is to pay two men, a Protestant and a Catholic, £27,500 each, having accepted that they had been subjected to sectarian harassment.

The Catholic alleged he had been harassed by Protestant colleagues and that the company, though fully aware of the case, failed to take remedial action. The Protestant claimed he had been ostracised and subjected to continuing harassment because he associated with Catholic colleagues.

The Colin Glen Trust, in West Belfast, agreed to pay a Protestant man £36,000 following his allegation that his position within the organisation had been undermined and that he had been subjected to sectarian harassment.

In a third case a Protestant man who was employed as a labourer with Kennedy (Contractors) Ltd in Macosquin, Coleraine, Co. Derry, accepted £22,500 in settlement of his case involving sectarian harassment and unfair dismissal. He alleged he had been subjected to sectarian remarks by Catholic colleagues and that he had been called "Orange bastard" and "a jaffa". He reported the remarks but the company took no action.

In the fourth case a Catholic man who felt that he had to leave his job as a steel worker with Harland and Wolff Shipbuilding and Heavy Industries Ltd because of sectarian harassment accepted £30,000 in settlement of his case.

(Gerry Moriarty, *The Irish Times*, 12 March 1997.
Reproduced by kind permission of *The Irish Times*)

Northern Ireland is going through a rapid process of change. Although there is a peace settlement, and hope that the "troubles" become a thing of the past, employers cannot be complacent about the issue of sectarian division in the workplace. Putting in place preventative measures will play an integral part in rebuilding Northern Ireland.

Religious differences have created (and still do) wars and divisions amongst countries and cultures for centuries. Respecting others' religious beliefs in order to prevent harassment, bullying and violence is not just about good management and organisational practice – it sets the tone for acceptable behaviour and good relations in local communities and wider society as a whole.

Harassment of disabled people

The harassment of disabled people in the workplace does not get the same attention as sexual harassment or racial harassment. In fact, very little research has been carried out as to its extent.

Why is this the case? Awareness of disability issues has increased, largely because of the introduction of the Disability Discrimination Act 1995. However, there remains an apathy about the issues that workers with disabilities face and the barriers that still exist seem to be taking an unnecessary length of time to break down.

Awareness levels (even though they are increasing) are not high enough, and this in itself perpetuates the harassment that workers with disabilities may suffer. 14.2% of the adult population in the UK have some form of disability, and of these, 93.2% live in the community and 6.8% live in institutions, exploding the myth that the majority of disabled people are in mental homes or rely on the state to look after them. Unemployment figures for disabled people are high in comparison with the rest of the population. Only 31% of disabled people are in employment – and 16% have experienced discrimination at work.

The barriers that exist for disabled people arise from obstacles in the environment in which they live and work and the negative attitudes and behaviours people hold about them. We live in a society where being "different" is still difficult to cope with. In the workplace, there is a pressure for people to "look good" and contribute to the image of the organisation by creating a personal image of a smart professional – *"Dress to impress and be groomed for success"* is the key. In many "able-bodied" people's minds, disabled people do not fit this criteria comfortably. Their perception is that people with physical disabilities may put customers and clients off (causing shock and discomfort), and employers who fear this will not put disabled people in contact with the public.

Another commonly held, but rarely talked about, belief concerns the disabled person and their sexuality. Most "able-bodied" people view disabled people as asexual, unable to have any sexual relationships or understand sex, because physically and psychologically they are not able to experience it. This myopic view has serious implications for those disabled people who suffer sexual harassment in the workplace – they are less likely to be believed and have their complaints taken seriously. Disabled people can enjoy the same healthy sexual relationships as "able-bodied" people, and as a result can suffer the same detriment from unwanted, unwelcome sexual attention.

Prejudice in action

How do you react when you see a disabled person? The majority of people respond in the following ways:

- They stand and stare.
- They stop talking.
- They may point the person out to a friend or colleague.
- They may talk behind their hand to a friend while indicating the person who is disabled with a nod or stare.
- People will move away.
- Children will mock and laugh.
- Parents may even gather their children around them.

These prejudicial behaviours turn into physical and verbal harassment, the effects of which are devastating for disabled people. Interestingly, it seems that disabled people very rarely use the word "harassment" to put a label on these behaviours that they so often experience. Could this be because they are such an integral part of their lives that it is difficult to see them in any other light?

(Adapted from *The Equal Opportunities Guide*, by Phil Clements and Tony Spinks, Kogan Page Ltd, 2nd edition 1996. Reproduced with kind permission from Kogan Page)

Employers make little attempt to change the work environment so that more disabled people can be employed. The justifications of cost and that the type of work is not suited for people with disabilities are based on little fact and discriminate against people with disabilities indirectly. This also has the effect of restricting the number of people with disabilities in the workforce. Thus our personal experience of working with disabled people is very limited, giving rise to more prejudicial views and stereotypes about disabled people. As a result, when a disabled worker joins the workforce, harassment is more likely to occur because of the lack of awareness, understanding and basic etiquette.

How do disabled people feel about their experiences of employment? Renee Blank and Sandra Slipp conducted hundreds of interviews with disabled workers in many organisations for their book *Voices of Diversity*. Overleaf is a summary of their findings:

[1]***Workers with disabilities feel that they are defined by their disability and
not seen as whole individuals***
"I am blind, but that does not define the whole of me. And yet to
most people, that is the only thing that seems important. I have many
interests, yet when people talk to me, they seem stiff and ill at ease.
Why can't people talk to me about whatever it is that people talk
about at work?"

***Many disabled workers say that employers don't consider them for career
progression because they should think themselves fortunate even to have a job***
Because of the reality that it is difficult for disabled people to find
employment, many disabled people are unwilling to ask for promotions once they are employed. Employers take advantage of this concern and keep them at lower levels. "If we're not promoted, it's hard
to tell if it is because they think we should be grateful to have a job,
or because they doubt our abilities. I think it's a combination of both."

Disabled workers say they are patronised, pitied or treated like children
"I've been working for a local Benefits office for years now, and the
attitudes don't seem to be changing. I am often addressed as 'sweetie'
or 'my dear' in the high-pitched tone that is used when speaking with
a child. It seems as if we have to be treated as lesser people, and not
adults in our own right." People who use wheelchairs complain that
others pat them on the head. Some do it condescendingly, others seem
to think it's a form of humour. Either way, it is unacceptable for disabled people.

***Many workers with disabilities say they are called courageous and brave
unnecessarily***
A magazine writer who was born with spina bifida and who walks
using arm crutches gets annoyed when others commend her for "getting around so well". She said, "I want to be commended for my
work and my abilities and not for dealing with the disability which is
a part of me. Most people with disabilities don't want sympathy or
undue admiration. We want to be seen as equals in the workplace."

Some disabled workers say they are seen as very dependent
Because being independent is so important to people with disabilities,
these workers are horrified when people rush in to help when it is
not necessary. Virtually all disabled people prefer to ask for assistance
themselves or to be asked whether they need assistance. Therefore a

---

1 Adapted from *Voices of Diversity*. Copyright © 1994 Renee Blank. Reproduced with kind
permission from AMACOM, a division of American Management Association International,
New York, NY. All rights reserved. http:/www.amanet.org

person using a wheelchair should not be pushed without being asked and a person who is blind should not be assisted without first checking whether assistance is needed.

People who hardly know disabled workers very often ask personal questions about the disability

Personal questions are embarrassing and intrusive. A careers adviser who uses a wheelchair because of paralysis in her legs was asked, on the first day of her new job, how she went to the toilet. A man who is blind was bombarded with questions when he first started to work. "Were you born that way?" "Do you live alone?" "Do you go out with girls who see?" "Who does your shopping for you?" Some disabled workers do prefer that people ask questions directly to them, as long as it is done tactfully and sensitively. "Sometimes, it is obvious to me that people are dying to ask me something but they are too embarrassed. I would rather be asked a question and then decline to answer than not be asked at all. I find that people will either ask someone else or will make up an answer which will be totally inaccurate."

Many disabled workers say that others shun them in informal settings and don't include them in social activities

Many disabled workers feel that so much of being effective at work depends on informal contacts and co-operation, that when people shun them or are uncomfortable in their presence, this in itself can be a barrier to being successful at work. A worker recovering from cancer said, "I think sometimes we remind people of their own vulnerability. It's as if people are superstitious. If they associate with me, maybe this will happen to them too. Casual acquaintances at work who used to be quite friendly seem to stay away from me now."

Workers who have learning disabilities say that supervisors and managers are too impatient with them

A housekeeper with a learning disability in a large hotel chain said, "My supervisor wants me to work much faster. She doesn't understand that it takes me a little longer to do the work, but I can be as good as anyone else. I never miss a day's work like some of the other people, and I always get in on time." Connected with this is the problem that workers with speech difficulties have when trying to make themselves understood. An engineer with cerebral palsy said that working colleagues sometimes pretend they understand him when it is clear that they don't. "I know my speech is slurred and that it may be hard to understand. But if someone doesn't understand me, they should just tell me. I don't mind repeating it, if people at least make an effort to listen. And what is worse is when people insult me by saying 'never mind, it's not important'. Their impatience is quite hurtful."

(Adapted from Voices of Diversity by Renee Blank and Sandra Slipp, AMACOM, 1994. Reproduced with kind permission from AMACOM.)

It is clear from these views that the harassment of disabled people at work occurs because of ignorance, and this is reflected in the negative attitudes that are held about people with disabilities.

Disabled workers want recognition in the workforce for their ability to do their job. This recognition can manifest itself in the form of being provided with the appropriate equipment to help them do their jobs, as well as an increase in sensitivity and awareness amongst their colleagues. Being judged by their appearance and treated unfairly because of their presumed incapabilities is discriminatory and leads to harassment.

Case Study

Does He Take Sugar?

A typical scenario, used frequently to raise awareness of disability issues, is that of two friends, one who uses a wheelchair, ordering tea and coffee in a café. Individually, they both order their drinks. The person serving, ignoring the person in the wheelchair, asks his "able-bodied" friend, "Does he take sugar?" The following case study illustrates a similar scenario.

Paul Doncaster is a graphic designer working in a large advertising company. Three years ago, Paul was involved in a serious car accident, in which his spine was damaged severely, paralysing his lower body. Paul uses a wheelchair for mobility.

At a staff meeting, arrangements were being discussed for the launch of a new advertising campaign for a popular product. The product was going to be given a new image, and it was essential that the launch took place in the appropriate setting. Paul, who was instrumental in the design of the image, was sitting next to Karen, a colleague, when discussion about the venue for the launch started. Karen and the other team members start to talk across Paul, ignoring him completely. "It's the perfect setting, but there is a problem. I don't think Paul's wheelchair will go through the passage leading to the gallery area," Karen said. "Can't we lift him in? I'm sure the wheelchair is collapsible." "Maybe he can use crutches on that day, and sit near the front of the podium, before doing his introductions."

"Why don't they ask me what I think?" Paul said to himself. "This is not the first time Karen has done this. I feel as if I don't exist when people ignore me."

(Adapted from Voices of Diversity, by Renee Blank and Sandra Slipp, AMACOM, 1994. Reproduced with kind permission from AMACOM.)

Reflection

Employers often justify their ignorance by using "lack of information and a lack of disabled people" as an excuse for inaction. In the United States, in the late 1980s, MacDonald's finally got wise, investing millions of dollars in advertising and campaigning for disabled people to use their restaurants. It has worked (they also increased their disabled workforce as a result). Disabled people are an untapped, rich resource, not just as customers but as valued members of the workforce. There is no excuse – employers must not only break down the psychological barriers of prejudice but also the physical barriers that exist in order to accommodate workers with disabilities and eliminate the discrimination and harassment they face.

Sexual orientation

In sharp contrast to sexual and racial harassment, the harassment of gay men and lesbian women (heterosexist harassment) is the one topic that people will actively resist talking about, and find it difficult to address in the workplace. The reality is that gay, lesbian, bisexual and heterosexual people have been working together for years; the difference is that people are now more open about their sexuality and want to be accepted for it. This challenges the stigmas, fears, prejudices and assumptions that exist about gay men and lesbians and brings out the worst homophobic behaviour in others.

The discrimination that lesbians and gay men experience at work is problematic and far-reaching. A survey conducted in 1993 by the gay lobbying group Stonewall, called *Less Equal than Others*, highlighted that 48% of respondents had been harassed at work, and had experienced the following:

- 51% of lesbians and gay men suffered homophobic abuse.
- 79% suffered jokes or teasing.
- 41% were victims of aggressive questioning.
- 14% have been threatened.
- 5% experienced physical violence in the workplace.

Whilst society is beginning to accept and acknowledge the rights of lesbians and gay men, Stonewall's survey shows quite clearly that there is a lot of work to be done if the rights of lesbians and gay men are to be recognised in the workplace.

The perception that homosexuality is an "unnatural" type of sexual behaviour forms the basis of homophobia (the fear of homosexuality) and homophobic behaviour. On a personal level, the more strongly you disagree with a person's sexual values, the more likely you are to enact prejudicial behaviours. This is how homophobia develops, and eventually results in acts of harassment.

A greater understanding of why homophobia exists in the work-place – particularly in male-dominated environments – can be achieved by exploring some of the myths that lead to misconceptions about sexual orientation.

Exploding the myths about sexual orientation

The following myths give rise to acts of harassment and violence against gays, lesbians and bisexuals in the workplace:

Homosexuality is a disease

The view that gays and lesbians are suffering from an illness which prevents them from behaving "normally" is unfounded, and there is no scientific evidence which proves this to be the case. In some cultures, being gay or lesbian is a normal, acceptable, natural part of social life, proving that attitudes and beliefs can differ. Another homophobic justification is to call homosexuality a medical condition that leads to mental illness, which explains why referring to gays and lesbians as "homosexuals" can be offensive.

The Bible says that homosexuality is a sin . . .

This myth argues against the morality of homosexuality on a higher level. The fact is, however, that there are relatively few texts in the Bible that address directly the issue of homosexual behaviour. No other religious studies make any specific reference to, or directly handle, the issue of homosexuality as we know it now. They are, however, explicit in their condemnation of sexual exploitation, whether it be institutional or personal, against heterosexuals or homosexuals.

AIDS is a gay disease: gay men are responsible for spreading HIV/AIDS

Homophobia has taken on another guise now. As HIV and AIDS is wrongly perceived as being a "gay disease" only associated with gay men, the rise in incidents of harassment has escalated dramatically. However, the World Health Organisation reports that 79% (1997) of people with AIDS were infected through heterosexual sex. There can be no denying the effect that HIV and AIDS has had on the gay community. However, blaming gay men for spreading this disease only serves as a denial by heterosexuals to take responsibility for their behaviour.

Gays are just dressed-up women, and lesbians want to be men
This myth grows from the need to perpetuate the images of gay men
as effeminate and lesbians as butch, in order to give masculinity and
femininity a sense of normality. For example, heterosexist men justify
their feelings of being threatened (and having their masculinity threatened) by believing the theory that being gay means being feminine.
Likewise, lesbians are seen as masculine, because in order to have a
lesbian relationship one partner needs to act out the role of a man,
hence proving the theory that women cannot do without men.

Sex from a good man would cure most lesbians
Lesbians are not suffering from a disease or illness, therefore there is
nothing to cure. This myth perpetuates the view (once again) that
men are the dominant sex and women need men to confirm their
sexuality. It also reinforces the stereotype that being gay and lesbian
is just about sex; relationships are the same as those between men and
women. Whilst sex is an important part, trust, friendship and love are
integral to relationships too.

Gay men and lesbians are more likely to be harassers
No evidence exists that suggests gays and lesbians are more likely to
abuse power over others or use their sexuality to harass or elicit relationships with straight people. In fact, a gay man or a lesbian who is
"out" in the workplace will have a higher profile, and therefore will
be noticed more if they perpetuate unacceptable behaviours. The reality is that they are more open to harassment, than able to harass
others.

*Gays who are friendly towards you are trying to turn you into "one of
them"*
Normal everyday friendliness and casual touching take on a different
interpretation when carried out by gays and lesbians. Some gestures
are given a deeper meaning by heterosexuals than is necessary, and
these tend to escalate out of control. *"He patted me on my back – I
think he fancies me"* is an example of the type of paranoia that creates
discomfort and perpetuates discrimination. Harassment of this kind
needs to be dealt with quickly before it blows out of proportion.

Staying "in the closet" v "coming out"
It is clear from the nature of the myths described above, how deep
rooted is the prejudice towards gay men and lesbians. It is not surprising, therefore, that the decision to be open about one's sexuality in
the workplace – "coming out" – is a difficult and often dangerous one.

Safety is a major issue for gays and lesbians. Social disapproval and the lack of legal protection create an unsafe work environment. Every interaction in the workplace brings up the issue of how safe it is to come out.

The danger of a violent, anti-gay assault ("gay-bashing") is a reality that gay and lesbian workers have to face, and one that is not readily appreciated by heterosexual workers.

The following case study explores the realities of coming out in the workplace.

Case Study

Workplace – A Case of Gay v Pay?

Nick Coppack was driven out of a company where he held a senior position after he took his partner to his work's social event. "It was someone's leaving party. It wasn't on work premises or in work time. Yet I was told by a director not to bring my lover again," he says. After Mr Coppack insisted that he would bring his partner another time, and that being gay had no bearing on the way he did his job, life at work was made so unpleasant for him that he felt obliged to leave. Luckily, Mr Coppack was able to find employment among more enlightened souls. But for some, such homophobia can blight their working lives.

Kevin, a forklift truck driver, was beaten up by his warehouse supervisor, who was also the union shop steward. "I have not been able to work since. I have to take painkillers twice a day and I am registered as disabled."

More than half of the homosexual employees surveyed by Social Community and Planning Research (SCPR) in May 1995 said no one at work knew they were gay. Only a fifth said everyone knew.

The research – based on a randomised, representative sample – suggests gay people are right to be wary; the more open they are, the more discrimination they suffer. Employers can often discriminate with impunity. While it is unlawful in this country to treat someone less favourably because of their sex or race, it is not unlawful to do so on the grounds of their sexuality. Companies can refuse employment to gays, withhold promotion or, in some instances, even fire them.

The worker would only be able to claim unfair dismissal if they had been with the company for two years or more. But even then there is no guarantee of protection, as some tribunals have ruled that the prejudice of other workers can be a relevant factor in selection for redundancy.

A 1993 survey by the lobby group Stonewall found that 48% of respondents had suffered harassment. Behaviour ranged from "being prayed over" to, in the case of a former sailor in the US Navy, imprisonment. Verbal abuse, teasing and aggressive questioning were the most common forms, but 5% of respondents had suffered physical violence, while a further 14% had been threatened.

One way of trying to avoid discrimination is to stay in the closet, but SCPR argues that having to be secretive is discrimination in itself. But while it may be preferable to being beaten up and verbally abused, staying in the closet is not always an easy option.

Edinburgh-based financial adviser Neil Renton has found that even telling people where you drink can give you away. "It can get very, very tricky. People I used to work with would say 'What did you do last night?' 'I went out.' 'Where did you go?' 'Here and there . . .'." Mr Renton now works in a more easy-going business where he need not be so enigmatic. But even in the relatively liberal world of London publishing houses, coming out has to be done sensitively.

Mark is a journalist who has worked at a number of publishing houses and has never made a secret of his homosexuality. He describes coming out at each new job as a process rather than an event. "I tend to do it by osmosis, rather than walking in and saying, 'Hi! I'm gay'." Mark will gradually drop clues by talking about his "other half" and his social life. "It's like a military campaign", he says. He believes the key to coming out painlessly is first to establish friendships with workmates. "If you get on with people, they are unlikely to suddenly turn against you. And anyone who might have a negative reaction knows they are likely to risk the opprobrium of their colleagues."

Being open with clients may be even more difficult. Stonewall found that in 1993 nearly 70% of respondents hid their sexuality from clients or customers.

But there are circumstances in which being open can pay dividends. Sebastian, a professional adviser, was at a boozy lunch just before Christmas. The client kept saying how much he liked people who were different, so Sebastian decided to tell him he was gay. Rather than being shocked, the client responded with a revelation of his own: "As you've been open with me, I'll be open with you – I cross dress." A few days later, Sebastian received a fax saying "It was the best business lunch they could recall. That was wonderful."

(Fiona Bawdon, The Observer, 21 January 1996. Reproduced by kind permission of The Observer, © The Observer)

It is not surprising that a large majority of gay men and lesbians decide to "stay in the closet" and not reveal their sexuality at work – not least because sexuality has nothing to do with a person's ability to do their work, but also because of the forms of harassment and bullying gay men and lesbian women will inevitably have to put up with. Being open about one's sexuality should be a matter of choice, and one which can be made freely without the fear and threat of losing a job, destroying a career, verbal and physical abuse and violent attacks.

Case Study

Staying in the Closet – The Experience of Caroline

"I lead a bizarre and stupid double life – out to family, friends and neighbours and firmly in the closet at work. I am a gynaecologist and have only loved one woman, with whom I am in a long-term relationship (seven years). I know there is no contradiction between being a lesbian and being a gynaecologist – in fact my personal traumas have enriched my practice as a doctor. I spent several years of agony believing that maybe I shouldn't do both if society disapproved. I denied my sexuality. Then, I gave up obstetrics and gynaecology which I adore. Eventually I decided I could do both but as I achieve more professionally my fear of ending up on the front page of *The Sun* increases. I've recognised that I can't live in fear and so I'll brave it out if it ever happens. I'm happy to be discreet – only the deception depresses me. I have to shroud my social life in mystery, avoid awkward questions and often tell lies. I am not paranoid; I'm quite sure that a majority of my colleagues (90% male and largely with sexist views on women) would disapprove and a small minority would be extremely hostile. I have enough trouble being a 'sassy woman', let alone a 'dyke'."

(Adapted from an article by Stonewall, 1993. Reproduced by kind permission of Stonewall)

Reflection

The gay rights movement is catching up with other minority groups, and it is at a crucial stage in the development of the campaign for equality and recognition in the workplace. Although people are more open about sexual orientation, there is still a lot of work to be done to shift the prejudices and negative attitudes which exist towards gay men and lesbians. Acknowledging the rights of these workers means accepting more than sexual preferences; it means equal treatment in terms of career development, pay and reward, and ensuring that the partners of gays and lesbian workers receive the same pension payments and other benefits given to the long-term partners of straight workers.

Employers who are serious about creating a positive working environment cannot be left in any doubt as to what this actually means in practice for gay and lesbian workers. It means an environment which is safe and free from harassment and violence. Employers need to develop policies and practices which enable this to happen, and promote an openness which will encourage people to deal with their fears, and not view sexual orientation as a controversial topic that stays in the closet.

References

Bullying at Work: How to Confront and Overcome it, Andrea Adams (Virago Press, 1992).

Bullying at Work: How to Tackle it – A Guide for MSF Representatives and Members, MSF, August 1995.

Discrimination against Lesbians and Gay Men at Work. Information leaflet, Stonewall, 1993.

Search for Justice: A Woman's Path to Renewed Self-esteem from the Fear, Shame and Anger of Sexual Harassment and Employment Discrimination, BJ Holcombe and Charmaine Wellington (Stillpoint Publishing, 1992).

One Race: A Study Pack for Churches, Churches Commission for Racial Justice, 1994.

No Offence? Sexual Harassment: How it Happens and How to Beat it (The Industrial Society, 1993).

Voices of Diversity: Real People Talk about Problems and Solutions in a Workplace where Everyone Is Not Alike, Renee Blank and Sandra Slipp (AMACOM, 1994).

Racial Harassment at Work: What Employers Can Do about it, Commission for Racial Equality, 1995.

Sexual Harassment in the Workplace, Ellen J Wagner (AMACOM, 1992).

Preventing and Remedying Sexual Harassment at Work: A Resource Manual, Michael Rubenstein (IRS, 1992).

Talking from 9 to 5, Deborah Tannen (Virago Press, 1995).

The Equal Opportunities Guide, Phil Clements and Tony Spinks (Kogan Page, 1994).

You Just Don't Understand Me: Women and Men in Conversation, Deborah Tannen (Virago Press, 1992).

CHAPTER 3

Violence and bullying in the workplace

This chapter looks at the phenomenon of violence in the workplace, its effect on individuals and organisations, and ways in which to reduce its occurrence. It also examines the nature of bullying, as a form of unacceptable behaviour.

Violence on the increase

Violence in society – spilling into the workplace

Few people would argue with the proposition that we live in an increasingly violent society, and this is confirmed by Home Office statistics. It is therefore no surprise that this is reflected in the work environment, and employers, employees and trade unions have become increasingly concerned. Whilst the UK has yet to see the levels of violence experienced in the US, where shooting incidents account for 17% of all workplace fatalities, there is little cause for complacency. The increasing incidence of violence in the workplace means that many employees are at risk – and not only those who work in sectors such as the police force, transport and the health service, areas traditionally associated with high levels of violence.

In order to have a strategy which deals effectively with the problem of violence at work, it is important to adopt a definition that encompasses the vast spectrum of violent behaviour and which takes into account the wider organisational culture. Personal factors about the individuals concerned should also be considered, such as their age, race and gender, as these might increase their vulnerability.

Concerns about the health and safety of employees in the work-place should include *all* work-related violence from clients, customers or the general public. Even where staff are not physically harmed a daily diet of swearing, threats and verbal abuse can lead to depression, stress, low morale and absenteeism.

The extent of violence in the workplace

This increase in violence in the workplace has been confirmed by recent research studies undertaken in various occupational groups. The 1992 British Crime Survey found that the number of assaults at work had more than doubled between 1991 and 1998. Other studies have made a detailed examination of the patterns of violence experienced by particular groups of workers. In a survey by the shop workers' union USDAW (1986) nearly a third of the respondents revealed that they were verbally abused more than once a week, and a 1994 survey for the GP magazine *Pulse* found that over one-fifth of those responding had been assaulted in the previous year. USDAW have reported that the situation has worsened: in the first half of 1997 in the insurance sector, six insurance sales people in Leeds were stabbed during the course of their work.

For many people, the threat of violence at work is a very real fear. Strategies to deal with the problem have focused most attention on physical assaults on staff, but it is important to recognise that violence is not always physical. Tragic cases like that of John Penfold, the assistant manager of Woolworth's in Teddington who was stabbed to death in November 1994 following a robbery attempt, indicate that although the actual number of physical attacks is low, their severity has worsened.

Racial and sexual abuse are probably the most prevalent forms of "verbal violence", but due to social pressures are probably the least reported and recorded. Verbal abuse also includes patronising and belittling comments as well as swearing and insults, and sometimes physical abuse will consist of no more than shoving, pointing or rude gesturing. The Suzy Lamplugh Trust offers guidelines on the scope of violence, which they see as encompassing verbal abuse, sexual harassment, bullying and even silence if this is perceived as threatening by the individual.

The problem of under reporting

One major difficulty facing managers is the lack of information about the extent of the violence that exists in their organisation. Statistics detailing known levels of violence present an incomplete picture because of the problem of under reporting and under recording of incidents. A survey conducted by the Local Government Training Board in 1991 indicated that one in three incidents of physical attack and two out of three incidents of aggressive behaviour were not formally reported. Similarly a survey of publicans carried out by Cox, Hilas, Higgins and Boot in 1988 revealed that only one in seven of all violent incidents were reported by the managers who responded.

The bare facts – statistics on violence in the workplace

Because violence in the workplace is a topic that few organisations feel comfortable about discussing openly, it is still difficult to estimate the true size of the problem. Nevertheless, the few figures that exist indicate the tip of the iceberg, as many incidents go unreported.

In their chapter "Criminal assault at work" (taken from *Counselling: the BAC Counselling Reader*), Peter Reynolds and Tricia Allison found that figures tend to be industry-wide rather than related to specific organisations. The two examples they included were:

● The British Retail Consortium reported that in 1992/3 14,000 employees were subjected to physical violence, a further 106,000 to threats of violence and nearly 300,000 more suffered verbal abuse at work (Burrows and Speed, 1994).

● In a survey commissioned and published by the Banking, Insurance and Finance Union (1992), they discovered that in 1991 a total of 1,633 robberies took place in banks and building societies. Nearly all involved a weapon or threat of violence.

Reynolds and Allison surmise that abuse, violence and crime now affect a huge range of different organisations, from multi-nationals to corner shops, and as the effects on individual employees can be devastating, it is necessary to develop a more effective method of assessing the true extent of the problem.

(Reprinted by kind permission of Sage Publications Ltd from "Criminal assault at work", by Peter Reynolds and Tricia Allison – taken from *Counselling: the BAC Counselling Reader*, 1996)

Reasons given for under reporting reflect an acceptance by some employees that exposure to violent or threatening behaviour is part of the job. Those who have been the victim of a violent incident fear it may be taken as an indication of their lack of competence, and so will hesitate to ask for help. Other explanations for non–reporting reflect the inadequacy of management structures to deal with the problem. One reason commonly cited is a fear that management will fail to respond appropriately.

Case Study

Nursing Abuse . . .
Dolly was a retired black nursing sister who had 18 years' experience. She had often been subject to racial and sexual abuse by patients and even colleagues. "It was not unusual for patients to scream at me that I should take my black hands off them or to question if I'm sure I know what I'm doing. One patient threatened that if I dared to touch him he would get one of his brothers to waylay me in the car park and 'sort me out'.

I did feel terrible about all the abuse at first, but in all my years as a nurse I never reported any of these incidents to anybody. Who could I tell and what would they do? You just develop your own ways of dealing with it. Sometimes I would just leave them to stew, other times I would make sure the water was cold when giving them a bed bath!"

Working in fear – jobs that traditionally attract violence

Given the growing scale of the problem of violence in the workplace, far more employees than those who are traditionally thought to be at risk are in fact vulnerable. Staff who handle large amounts of cash or valuable property are always particularly at risk. But there is also real concern about other groups of workers. According to the Health and Safety Executive (HSE), other risk categories include:

- staff who provide care or advice, teaching or training
- staff who carry out inspection or enforcement duties
- staff who work with the mentally ill, or with people who abuse drink or drugs.

Banks, building societies and security firms have long been alert to the possibility of attacks on staff, and many of these workers benefit from extensive and often high–tech protection measures. But for the many other workers also at risk, especially those in the public sector, medical staff, transport workers and bar staff who all have to deal with potentially aggressive or volatile members of the public, the safeguards are often fewer.

The reasons why certain groups of workers are more vulnerable are many and varied, and they are not always easy to ascertain. Sometimes the causes of violence relate to general problems in society or in the specific local area, such as drug or alcohol abuse. In other cases the cause reflects a particular grievance, such as the campaign against the poll tax or community charge. Often the member of staff is simply having to take the flack for negative attitudes towards the organisation they work for.

Case Study

A Reason to Safeguard against Violence

Silvia was a senior manager in a local authority housing department. A disgruntled tenant who was unhappy with the outcome of his transfer application had been disruptive and abusive to her staff at a local housing office. This was one of a number of incidents in which female staff had been sexually harassed and accused of being biased against him because he wasn't a homeless single mother with nine kids.

Events came to a head when, after refusing a transfer offer, he was told that he would not be offered another alternative and he began shouting, swearing and throwing furniture around. Silvia was contacted and sanctioned the decision to call in the police to help deal with the situation, although she was not directly involved on the ground with the incident at all.

Somehow the tenant got hold of her name and phone number and started making a series of abusive phone calls. He threatened that unless his housing situation was resolved to his satisfaction she would suffer the consequences. Silvia ignored the threats and carried on work as usual.

In hindsight, though, she felt that the situation had exposed a policy vacuum. The original staff who had been involved with the client should have been given more support to prevent the situation from escalating. She, too, should have been able to talk to someone about her anxieties, rather than having to maintain this stiff upper lip. The incident led to a thorough review of policy in this area.

Legal provisions that protect employees against violence at work

Statutory duties

All employers have a legal duty under the Health and Safety at Work Act 1974 (HSWA) to ensure the safety of staff by providing a safe place and system of work for employees. S2 of the HSWA states that "it shall be the duty of every employer to ensure so far as is reasonably

practicable the health, safety and welfare at work of its employees."
This means that employers have a duty to identify the nature and
extent of the risk of violence to their staff at work, and ensure that
the employee remains safe from reasonably foreseeable risks. Violence
is defined by the HSE as: "*any incident in which an employee is abused,
threatened or assaulted by a member of the public in circumstances arising out
of his or her employment*".

The Management of Health and Safety at Work Regulations 1992
require employers to carry out a "suitable and efficient" assessment of
the risks to which employees are exposed whilst they are at work.
According to the HSE, this includes the risk of violence.

A risk assessment should identify the preventative and protective
measures an employer needs to take to comply with the statutory
obligations under the Act. If an employer does not carry out a proper
risk assessment, an employee cannot take any direct action under the
legislation, but it may amount indirectly to the employer being held
to be negligent.

The HSE produces advisory material for employers which makes it
clear that employers must keep risk assessments under review. Their
guidance to employers also recommends that they should investigate,
analyse, monitor and record all violent incidents.

The Act also empowers the HSE to issue improvement and prohibition notices in order to deal with situations of imminent and/or continuing risk, pending the outcome of prosecution. This power has
been rarely used, however. One of the few examples was the notice
issued in 1992 ordering Rotherham Borough Council to reduce the
risk of violence and make the working environment safe for its workers. This followed campaigning by NALGO (now part of UNISON)
after a rent collector, Doreen Taylor, was killed on her rounds.

Further statutory protection for employees is provided by the
Employment Rights Act 1996 s100, which was recently introduced
into the Act and as yet is untested in the tribunals and courts. It gives
any employee the right to leave the workplace if he/she reasonably
believes that there is a serious or imminent danger which he/she could
not be reasonably expected to avert. The employee can refuse to return
to the workplace until the danger is passed and in so doing should
not be subjected to any detriment.

It remains to be seen how these provisions will affect the situation,
but it is clear they can be applied to protect employees who are in
imminent danger of being attacked by members of the public or by
fellow employees.

Common law duties – the law of negligence

In addition to their statutory duty, employers also have a similar duty of care under the law of negligence and by virtue of an implied term in the contract of employment. This is a civil legal duty to take reasonable care for the health and safety of employees and is set out in the case of *Wilsons and Clyde Coal Ltd* v *English*. It lays down a threefold obligation on employers to provide:

- a safe place of work
- safe plant and equipment
- competent and safe staff.

Breach of any aspect of this duty will entitle an injured employee to bring a claim for damages. Any liability which may devolve onto management will depend on the failure of the employer to take reasonable care to avoid reasonably foreseeable risks. The standard the courts will apply is that of the "reasonably prudent" employer. This is not a static test. It will be affected by various factors, including current technical, scientific or statistical knowledge within the relevant industry.

Criminal sanctions and the criminal injuries compensation scheme

Where there has been a serious assault on a member of staff, this may amount to a criminal offence. Causing actual or grievous bodily harm is any offence covered by the Offences against the Persons Act 1861. Anyone who commits either of these offences can be arrested by the police and prosecuted. Such cases will need to be vigorously pursued, and victims should be given the necessary support through what can often be a gruelling prosecution process. Many attacks at work, however, are likely to fall into the category of "common assault" for which the police cannot make an arrest, but which are none the less traumatic for the victim: for example, being pinned up against a wall, shoved, pushed or dragged.

Criminal courts now have the power to make compensation orders requiring a convicted person to pay compensation for any injury, loss or damage resulting from an offence. There is also the Criminal Injuries Compensation Board (CICB), which makes ex-gratia payments of compensation to applicants who have sustained personal injury which is directly attributable to:

- a crime of violence
- the apprehension of an offender or prevention of an offence or attempts to do so

● an offence of trespass on the railway.

Awards will only be made where the police have been notified immediately, or the assailant has been prosecuted in the courts. Applications should be made in writing to the CICB within three years of the incident giving rise to the injury.

Developing effective strategies

Whilst there are many different problems, causes and potential solutions for workplace violence, there are also some measures that can be implemented to reduce the risk. These must focus on the specific needs of the organisation and of the individuals concerned, and often go beyond what is required by the strict confines of the law.

For some organisations, the lack of action stems from a lack of formal awareness and recognition that the problem of violence exists. It will sometimes take a tragic incident, such as the disappearance of Suzy Lamplugh or strike action or the withdrawal of co-operation from members of staff, to precipitate policy development.

Each incident of violence or abuse in each individual workplace is unique. However, a systematic approach will include adequate reporting systems, effective preventative and reactive measures and sensitive and sympathetic aftercare.

1. Recording and classifying violent incidents

The problems caused by the under reporting of violent incidents have been outlined in general terms earlier in this chapter. In order for any strategy for prevention to be effective, it is crucial to obtain information about any incidents of violence that occur, whether they involve physical contact or not. Therefore, once a problem with violence has been identified within an organisation, it is necessary to initiate a formal system of recording and classifying any violent incidents. This is important, because in many instances there will be an escalating pattern of violence, which may start with verbal abuse and proceed to physical attack. Unless the initial verbal abuse is recorded, an organisation could miss the opportunity to prevent any escalation.

Most employers will keep records of the more serious incidents, but record-keeping should encompass the broader spectrum of violence that has been referred to earlier, to include threats, rude gestures and verbal abuse. Also issues of access, confidentiality and easy retrieval need to be considered carefully, and reporting systems should be customised to meet the needs of the organisation. Wherever possible, it will be important to group similar incidents, characteristics of assailants or types of interaction. This will assist in developing preventative measures.

An incident report form will typically include the following information:

- Date and day on which incident took place.
- Details of the employee involved, including age, gender, job/department and grade.
- Details of perpetrator(s), including age, gender, description.
- An account of the incident.
- Details of any witnesses.
- Description of location of incident.

2. Preventative measures

Design

Inadequate attention to the design of a company's premises can increase the risk of violence and make any assaults which do occur more dangerous. The redesign of premises can deter robberies, reduce contact with the public, where appropriate, and ensure that staff remain in control.

Important factors to consider include:

- Open, airy spaces where staff have clear lines of sight.
- Adequate exits from interview rooms.
- Fitting of panic buttons, safety barriers and protective screens.
- Avoiding aggressive colours, installing brighter lighting and clear signposting.
- Adequate parking spaces for staff.

Training

Training in the dynamics and management of conflict is one of the most effective ways to reduce the risk of violence to staff. Any training should be both comprehensive and widely available to all levels of staff who are adjudged to be at risk.

Whilst training should be tailor-made to the needs of the organisation, the following elements should also be considered:

- Scheduling the training once staff have been in post for a short while and are aware of the types of situations that can arise, rather than only focusing around the induction process.

● Training that covers techniques for stepping away from conflict and non-aggressive responses.
● Training can enable staff to realise that the unhappy client or customer is attacking the organisation and not making a personal assault on them.
● Some employers place reliance on self-defence training, especially for women. However, this is not always appropriate and great care should be taken before pursuing this route.

Adopting safer working practices

Working practices and systems should be reappraised to help staff who face the risk of violence. This will often have wider resource implications for an organisation, as it will involve scrutiny of staffing levels and the maintenance of high standards of service.

The particular organisational culture and the needs of individual members of staff will have to be taken into account. This will involve the following considerations:

● Avoiding the possibility of vulnerable staff working alone or working late hours.
● Ensuring that vulnerable staff are kept in contact with colleagues through adequate reporting systems.
● Increasing the number of accompanied visits, use of escorts, provision of mobile phones.

The risk of casual assaults is often reduced if standards of service are high and, for example, waiting times for clients and members of the public are kept to a minimum.

3. Reactive measures

A systematic approach to the problem of violence should also include development of reactive strategies which will deal with each individual problem as it arises.

This will often involve management intervention as well as the implementation of techniques learned during staff training. In addition, the systematic monitoring and recording of incidents of assaults and abuse is crucial to help identify problem areas and devise new tactics to protect employees.

4. Aftercare measures

Even with a comprehensive range of preventative strategies, violence may still occur in the workplace. It is important therefore also to implement effective aftercare measures to minimise the long-term effects of violence. These may include some or all of the following:

- Review of relevant policies, procedures.
- Physical layout etc. as well as monitoring procedures.
- Provision of counselling either internally or by outside professionals/specialists.
- Compensation for injury and damage to property.
- Adequate time off work to recuperate which is not counted against total sick leave.
- Assisting staff to take legal action and help with CICB claims.

A strategy for comprehensive action

The model overleaf, developed by Peter Reynolds (1994), is useful in helping organisations develop comprehensive strategies when helping staff deal with aggression and abuse at work, as well as violence and crime.

The dangers of not tackling the issue of violence

Quite apart from an employer's responsibilities to staff, it makes financial sense to ensure that the workplace is as free as possible from the risk of violence.

A good employer will manage the risks and effects of crime, and all businesses should look at the facts and figures of crime prevention. Violence in the workplace costs the employer – through time off work, absenteeism, insurance charges, loss of morale and greater staff turnover. The cost of violence should not just be seen in terms of how such stock has been lost or physical damage done; there is a far greater cost in terms of the threat to the welfare of employees.

If the organisation does not respond in a sympathetic way, the employee may feel that the organisation is responsible. It is important for those who have been attacked to know that they are in a responsive and caring environment, where the employer acknowledges the effects of the crime and offers support.

A well-intentioned response, however, is not necessarily the right one. Sending somebody home to an empty house after an attack can exacerbate the trauma. Sensitivity and immediate support are needed once an incident has occurred and in helping the person back to work. Chapter 4 looks at support for those suffering from Post-traumatic Stress Disorder (PTSD) as a result of abusive behaviour.

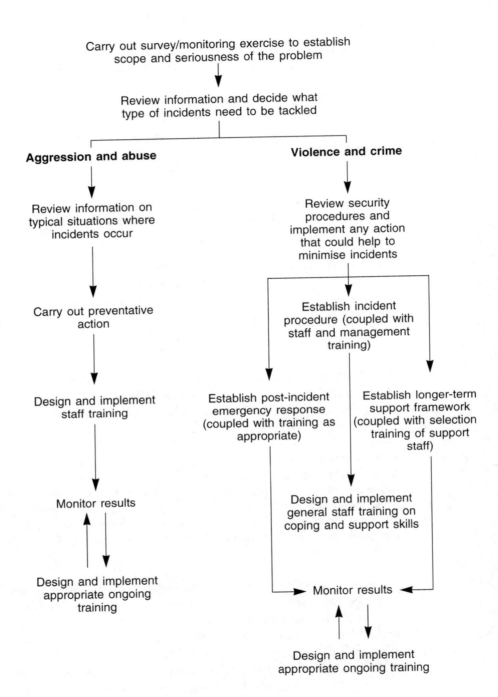

Figure 2. A strategy for comprehensive action
(Taken from "Criminal assault at work" in *Counselling: the BAC Counselling Reader*, by Peter Reynolds and Tricia Allison. Reproduced by kind permission of Sage Publications Ltd, 1996. © Sage Publications Ltd, Peter Reynolds).

The image of the organisation can be damaged if the problem of violence is not tackled, and this will ultimately affect profits. For example, if a retail shopping outlet or shopping precinct has a reputation for violent attacks, then customers will avoid it.

Case Study

Strathclyde Regional Council (SRC) – Recognising the Problem
In 1985 the social work department of the SRC conducted a large-scale sounding to investigate the extent to which its care staff (other than social workers) were exposed to violence.

Prior to the exercise the council had failed to officially recognise that staff were exposed to violence as part of their everyday working lives. This was particularly true for those staff who, though not professional social workers, were involved in the day-to-day running of the caring services, including having direct intimate contact with clients.

Early in 1985 there was a violent incident in one of the department's children's homes, when a member of the caring staff was attacked by an older child. The incident led to an immediate strike spearheaded by NALGO (now UNISON).

The union claimed that this was just one of a number of violent incidents involving its members, and that action should be taken to develop appropriate policies as a matter of high priority. The strike only ended when a joint working group of management and union members was set up to consider what policies and procedures were necessary to deal with violent incidents.

The aims of the exercise were, first, to discover the range of violent incidents that occurred and, second, how violence was dealt with at a local level and in which types of establishment the violence occurred.

A wide variety of replies were received from 173 establishments detailing 70 recorded incidents. The overall impression was of a caring, concerned workforce who, because of the nature of their clients, had an expectation, and in some cases even an acceptance, of a level of violence in their work. Most of the staff had no training in the handling of violence or aggressive feelings.

The exercise highlighted the need for ongoing data about specific incidents of violence if an effective policy response was to be achieved. Policies were also developed for following up incidents and providing appropriate training for all staff who had a caring role.

(Adapted from an account of Strathclyde's social work department *Violence to Staff: Policies and Procedures in Preventing Violence to Staff*, by Barry Poyner and Caroline Warne. The Tavistock Institute of Human Relations. Reproduced with kind permission from the Tavistock Institute of Human Relations)

Advice to employers – examples of good practice

Advice is available to employers from a number of large unions and from the HSE. For example, the HSE has published guidelines for the prevention of violence to staff in the retail sector, which will also prove useful to employers in other areas.

The HSE recommends that employers set up a clear policy, adopting a strategic approach to the issue which is actively supported by senior management and communicated to all staff. The next stage is to establish management systems which will eliminate risks to staff. These should be continuously monitored and reviewed for their effectiveness.

Key elements include:

● Establishing the scale of the problem, by talking to staff, managers and victims and analysing evidence and information.
● Implementing a reporting system, classifying data on incidents and devising a clear, confidential reporting procedure.
● Developing and implementing suitable preventative measures and good practice, targeting prevention at the areas which present the greatest risk.
● Training all staff; briefing them on the organisation's policy and procedures; delivering advice, information and skills on prevention and safe working practices; involving staff in sharing experiences and thoughts on the issue.
● Monitoring and review, ensuring that the measures introduced are successful in controlling and managing the risks, and revising them if they are inadequate.
● Communicating to and involving staff throughout the process.
● Providing staff with adequate support, help and guidance.

Union policies

Although unions have generally declined in terms of their representation in the workplace, employees should not be complacent about their role, as most of the best practice has been developed from the unions' proactive policy and action in this area. The following are examples of this.

MSF

The Manufacturing Science and Finance union (MSF) identifies several groups of its members as being at particular risk from violence. These include NHS staff such as psychiatric nurses and health visitors, insurance agents and construction workers.

The MSF believes that a successful strategy for the prevention of violence at work can only be achieved if employees are fully involved in its development. It suggests that a risk assessment should identify the likely hazards and preventative and protective measures needed to control the risks arising from those hazards. To assist employers in the development of strategies the MSF employs special safety representatives. In common with other unions it also provides model policies, survey questionnaires and an incident report form for use by union branches and employers.

National Union of Teachers

The NUT has been developing measures to reduce violence against teachers by pupils, parents and members of the public since the Elton Report in 1989. Recent cases involving compensation to injured teachers and threats of strike action following refusal to teach violent and disruptive pupils have highlighted the problem of violence in schools. The tragic death of headmaster Philip Lawrence prompted the commissioning of a report to look into the issue of security in schools. The union advises teachers to involve parents in discipline and get them to recognise their own responsibility for their children's behaviour. It also backs the provision of video cameras where appropriate to protect against violence, vandalism and arson in some schools, whilst also recognising that a school should not be turned into a fortress.

Royal College of Nursing

The Royal College of Nursing believes that community nurses who often work alone in unfamiliar areas are particularly at risk. It recommends that employers should provide training to enable nurses to recognise and deal with potentially violent situations. Its advice to nurses includes the following:

● They should record and highlight anything about the patient's or client's environment which might lead to violence.
● They should consider carefully the appropriate method of transport to be used to visit the patient.
● They should discover as much as possible about the local community, the population and known dangerous areas.

Reflection

There is much that employers can do to reduce the problem of violence at work. Preventative measures, good record-keeping, appropriate training and aftercare measures will go some considerable way to providing protection for employees. Employees should also, where appropriate, make use of the guidance and advice that is available from the HSE, specialist organisations like the Suzy Lamplugh Trust, the police and trade unions.

Danger ahead – bullying in progress . . .

Bullying, unlike any other form of harassment, is one of the few issues in the workplace that is difficult for people to understand, not least because of past images of the school playground, but also because of its shadowy nature. Bullying has been in existence since workplaces were first established. However, as the move towards creating and maintaining healthy working climates has become a corporate priority, bullying and its effects have leaked through organisations like cracks in a wall.

Statistics show how serious the problem of bullying really is in the workplace. A survey commissioned by the BBC and carried out by the University of Stafford in 1994 revealed that 78% of respondents had witnessed bullying, whilst 51% had actually experienced it themselves. The Institute of Personnel and Development (IPD) survey on bullying in 1996 showed that one in eight people had been bullied at work in the previous five years. Research carried out by the public sector union UNISON amongst its members in 1997 revealed that in 84% of cases bullies had bullied before, and while management knew about this, in three out of four cases they took no action.

Complaining about bullying brings its own sets of difficulties. Without the knowledge and awareness necessary to understand the subtle, covert forms of bullying, complaints are often not taken seriously. As a result, many people suffer bullying in silence, afraid that complaining will lead to further abuse and, at worst, the loss of their jobs and damage to their career prospects. It is astonishing how much stress, fear and worry employees will endure in order to keep their jobs, and also to meet the responsibility of financially supporting themselves and their families.

So what is bullying? As with other forms of harassment there is no set definition. However, a working definition might look like this:

"persistent, offensive, abusive, intimidating, malicious or insulting behaviour, which amounts to an abuse of power and makes the recipient feel upset, threatened, humiliated or vulnerable. Bullying undermines a target's self-confidence and may cause them to suffer stress."

Andrea Adams, author of *Bullying at Work* and one of the first people to identify workplace bullying as a serious issue, goes on to describe bullying that takes place in the work environment as *"persistent, demeaning and downgrading of human beings, through vicious words and cruel unseen acts which gradually undermine their confidence and self-esteem"*.

Bullying makes individuals feel inadequate and disempowered. It is a gradual wearing-down process, an abusive pattern of behaviour that employs both physical and psychological methods to undermine and incapacitate targets. Bullying belittles people who are ordinarily very competent and makes them feel totally inadequate. It engenders stress, illnesses and, at the other extreme, violent reactions which have led to attacks on bullies and the suicide of victims.

In the US, the experience of bullying is often referred to as "employee abuse", or "workplace terrorism" or "workplace trauma". However, its effects go beyond the words of any definition, and the failure to identify it can have devastating effects on the personal performance of individuals, as well as on the overall effectiveness of the organisation. (Chapter 8 looks at these consequences more closely.)

Bullying normally starts, or is triggered off after a change in line manager in a team. Soon, criticisms will be made about the performance of one or more individuals, where previously performance was good or, at least, not an issue. It also appears when professionals or experts are moved into management positions without the relevant management skills, or when the pressure to perform well creates insecurity and uncertainty, and low team morale leads to a breakdown in relationships.

Because workplace bullying is often misunderstood, badly misinterpreted and unrecognised as a problem in the workplace, it is necessary to have written definitions to appreciate the nature of bullying.

The true nature of bullying

Bullying is often disguised and hidden behind excuses and pseudonyms in an attempt to defend behaviours which have perceived pay-offs. The pseudonyms also hide some employers' inability to confront the issue – often bullying behaviours are not recognised as such and are considered "the norm" within organisational cultures. Here are some typical examples:

- abrasiveness
- an attitude problem
- a personality clash
- autocratic style of management

- macho management
- working in an idiosyncratic way
- unreasonable behaviour
- poor interpersonal skills.

Behaviour which is very covert and difficult to pin down needs to be labelled as bullying, as it helps targets of bullying make sense of their experience and recognise what is happening to them.

Case Study

Understanding Bullying and Using the Label

In her book *Bullying at Work*, Andrea Adams relates a number of cases of targets who have been bullied, and looks closely at the behaviour experienced by the victims and the tactics used by those who bully.

Helen, who worked for a well-known British company, describes her initial experience when she first used the word "bully" to her boss.

"My immediate boss was constantly making arrogant and abusive complaints about other employees in my presence, but because I enjoyed my job so much, I simply sat and listened. He used foul language to me too, but I took a conscious decision to avoid confrontation, to calm him down as best I could for the sake of the other staff, and hope that I'd come out of it relatively unscathed. One day when we were alone together we had a clash of opinion, and because I was sick of absorbing all his complaints, I felt I had to stick up for myself. He was really going for me over a petty office policy of his that was proving difficult to enforce. When I said to him 'Martin, please don't bully me about it' he just exploded. He jumped up in the air and behaved like a lunatic, shouting, 'Don't you dare use that word with me'.

His raised voice attracted everyone's attention . . . and I knew what would be going through their minds because I had watched others be humiliated and verbally torn to shreds.

Up until then, I was forever excusing his behaviour to the secretaries, convinced that he must have had some sadness in his life, or a lousy childhood. Now, he frightened me. 'I said I was going to have you out and now you're going' he threatened, 'and I'm never going to speak to you again from this day.' After that he only ever addressed me through my secretary. If he needed to tell me something, he would relay it directly to her, even though I was sitting right beside her in our office."

Helen's experience worsened, and eventually she was made redundant.

(Reproduced with kind permission from *Bullying at Work: How to Confront and Overcome It*, by Andrea Adams, Virago Press. © Virago Press, 1992)

The origins of bullying – from the school yard to the workplace

The connection between bullying in schools and bullying in the workplace cannot be ignored. Bullying is a problem for many children and can have long-lasting effects both on the child who is the target and the child who is the bully.

Recently, there have been many well-documented cases of children who have committed suicide or sought revenge by killing the bully as a result of the torment suffered by experiencing bullying. Although these cases are extreme, what has become clear is that it is no longer acceptable to overlook the magnitude of the problem, and make the excuse that bullying has always gone on. The safety and welfare of children is a major concern, and organisations such as Kidscape, which was founded with the specific aim of helping children to recognise and cope with potential dangers, have developed practical and successful programmes to fight bullying in schools.

Organisations need to learn from those schools which, following the implementation of good policies and practices on bullying, have achieved remarkable reductions in bullying behaviours. Also, much can be learned from childhood experiences of bullying.

Michele Elliott, author of *Keeping Safe*, conducted a two-year study which included asking children about being bullied. Thirty-eight per cent of the children who participated in the study had been bullied, and although 30% of parents were worried about their children being bullied, only 4% tried to do something about it. Michele gives the advice that not only do children need to be taught the best way of dealing with bullying but bullies also need specific help to change their behaviour.

Children who are affected or who are victims of bullying and abuse will use the bullying tactics they have learned from peers and adults. The following case study shows how childhood experiences of bullying and abuse can create an adult bully.

Case Study	**Learning How to Bully**

After David, aged 35, was unexpectedly promoted to the position of head chef in a West Country hotel, his bullying was at its worst. As the product of a violent childhood and the experiences of previous bosses who terrorised their kitchen staff, David could not accept anything less than perfection in his professional role:

"Once I was in charge of my own kitchen, if I saw an apprentice getting cocky, I'd decide to take him down a peg or two by criticising everything he did, all the time finding fault and looking for improvement. I would scream, and bawl and swear at them, and tear them to pieces in front of the others. If I didn't like their presentation I'd pick up their work and chuck it on the floor. I didn't trust other people to get it right, and because I felt under such tremendous personal pressure, I would never take days off, so then I got tired. One morning, as I arrived at the hotel, an apprentice charged out of the door and shouted at me. Inside, tables had been overturned, plates smashed, there were eggs and flour all over the kitchen walls. He'd just flipped, but I knew there had been days when I'd set out to make his life a misery. He had the potential to be a good chef, but he got on my nerves because he didn't have the right attitude towards self-discipline so that I constantly criticised everything he did. I can remember thinking: Why don't they get it into their heads that there's a job to be done? They shouldn't be able to laugh a lot. Although I wished I could be like that, if I saw someone who was free from hang-ups being happy it really got up my nose. I'd think: You've got it easy, you haven't suffered like I have yet, you don't know what life is about. I was feeling strong in one way, because even after all I'd been through, I had survived.

It certainly never occurred to me that I bullied anyone, although I did notice that one chef was so knocked flat after I'd had a go at him that I couldn't get any work out of him for the rest of the day. I'd see him shaking, but I didn't realise it would destroy him. Another chef, who was very talented, was also rather a weak person, so even when I piled on the work he'd just take it and say, 'Yes, chef'. That's all he ever said – 'Yes, chef'. I put him under pressure because I knew he was reliable. I saw him as a wimp, I suppose, but one day he turned round and punched me, and that made me think. I wondered what I had done to make him do that. Had I been making his life a misery? But it didn't make any difference. I kept piling on the stuff, and eventually he left. But you have to take the mickey out of people. Teasing them and sending them up is a matter of survival, because other people do it to you. It's part of the cut and thrust of going to work. If I can make a remark that puts someone down, it makes me feel powerful.

As an only child I remember my dad wanting to completely dominate me and my mother. His father was the same. He terrorised my grandmother, and ruled all five kids with fear, yet in the local town people thought he was a nice bloke. It was the same with my dad. All my school friends thought he was great, and everyone in the surrounding villages who knew him would say, 'What a lovely man'. At the school where he worked they thought the world of him, and certainly outside the home he was a very popular person. In the home there was a complete lack of love. He was constantly shouting at me, and if I wanted to force any encouragement out of him, whatever I did had to be excellent. Then, if I was lucky, I might get the odd mumble. He acted as if he wasn't interested, although I suspect he probably was. We had a big garden, and when Dad asked me to go and help him, there was no father-and-son-having-a-good-time sort of relationship. If I didn't pull up a weed, or if I accidentally trod on a plant, he would whack me across the head every time.

I remember one incident, when I was about ten, which was particularly distressing. I was watching TV when he sent me to my room because I hadn't written any birthday thank-you letters to my aunts and uncles. So I went upstairs, put a record on, and set about doing them at once. Within a few minutes he came storming in, fuming that I couldn't possibly do two things at once, took off the record and smashed it on the floor. Then he started chasing me round the bed, shouting, 'You little bugger, you little sod, you do as you're told.' He went berserk, and I can remember thinking: I was doing what he asked, why doesn't he leave me alone? When I was older, he'd complain if I switched on the TV and say, 'Who do you think pays the licence?' At other times I'd say, 'Dad, can I put the TV on?' and he'd say, 'You don't have to ask me, son, this is your home', so you just couldn't win. He was a trade-union shop steward at one time, and it was almost as if he thrived on arguments so that he could prove his intellectual powers. When I was 16, after going to church every Sunday throughout my childhood, he told me one day that my parents weren't going to force me to go any more if I'd rather not, that I was old enough to make my own choices. The moment I said, 'Okay, I don't want to come to church', he just picked me up, pinned me against the wall and started banging my head. Then, with his face pushed right up against mine, he went into the most vile temper I've ever seen and said, 'Right, then you're going to join the army, I'm putting you in the army.' I left home before he had a chance. I once challenged him, and called him an out-and-out bully for always ripping me to pieces, but he just argued. My mother is a very sweet, calm, wise woman who never loses her temper, but I'm only just talking to her about these things now. Neither of them can figure out why I eventually had a nervous breakdown.

When I was working at the West Country hotel, a new manager constantly criticised me and did everything to put me down and try to undermine my knowledge. It made me feel like giving him a good thumping. I can see now that my own bullying behaviour has affected every area of my life, including friendships. Recently, a woman colleague who had been quite friendly suddenly turned haughty and refused to speak to me. I actually felt her hatred and I thought: What have I done here? When I eventually asked her, she told me I was patronising and condescending and treated her as if she didn't have a brain in her head; that I was always barging into her territory, always telling her what to do, always trying to take control. I apologised and thanked her for telling me, but I don't think that at the time it really

> sank in. Using sarcasm instead of your fists is just as damaging,
> especially if deep down you are feeling inferior."
>
> David has since turned to his belief in God to help him change, and
> now that he can recognise his own behaviour, he finds he is able to
> avoid working out his own fear and resentment on others.
>
> (Adapted from *Bullying at Work: How to Confront and Overcome it*, by Andrea Adams,
> Virago Press. © Virago Press, 1992)

Further studies have shown that chronic bullies at an early age are much
more likely as adults to be violent, involved in crimes and have difficulty
with relationships, not only with partners and children but also in the
workplace. Although changing the behaviour of chronic bullies is difficult,
it becomes all the more necessary to try to modify their behaviour as
children, to prevent them from going through life using bullying as a
technique to succeed and gain power.

Common characteristics of bullies

There are a number of reasons why people use bullying behaviour.
Listed below are some of the characteristics that lead people to bully,
although it is not exhaustive:

● Constantly criticised and humiliated as a child and in adult life.
● Unable to express emotion easily or not allowed to show feelings.
● Experienced relationships based on aggression.
● Have very little or no interpersonal skills which will enable them
to create loving, positive relationships.
● No sense of "belonging", often felt isolated and not part of the group.
● Lived in an environment where mistakes were not allowed, success
is important and fault and blame the norm.
● Do not feel valued or have no sense of accomplishment.
● Often neglected or experienced emotional, sexual and/or physical
abuse.
● Feels constant pressure (internally as well as externally), which can
develop into violent behaviour.

Bullying behaviour as a form of aggression

Some psychologists have studied the behaviour of bullies at a psychological level, examining some of the reasons why people bully. They
note that bullying behaviour sometimes reflects a conscious or unconscious need to control and intimidate others, and that this is characterised by open or indirect aggression.

Aggression has four different dimensions: Hostility, Anger, Verbal and Physical. These factors give clues as to how a bully uses aggression to attack their targets. Table 3, based on Buss and Perry's Aggression Inventory (1992), shows the relationship between thoughts, feelings and behaviour.

Table 3. *The relationship between thoughts, feelings and behaviour*

Dimension	Element	Examples
Hostility	Cognitive or thought patterns	"When people are especially nice to me, I wonder what they want" or "I am sometimes eaten up with jealousy"
Anger	Emotional or affective response	"I sometimes feel ready to explode" or "I fly off the handle for no good reason"
Verbal aggression	Behavioural response	"I tell my friends openly when I disagree with them" or "When people annoy me I tell them what I think of them"
Physical aggression	Behavioural response	"If I have to resort to violence to protect my rights, I will" or "Given enough provocation or put me under pressure, I may hit another person"

Is there a bully in all of us?

Given that we all have these thoughts and feel these emotions, does this mean there could be a bully in all of us? What is necessary is to be able to maintain a balance between reasonable, self-disciplined behaviour and undisciplined, harmful bullying.

The capacity to contain our behaviour and respond reasonably to situations, rather than allowing our thoughts and feelings to make us behave unacceptably, differentiates bullies from those who behave assertively.

Chapter 4 explores the psychological profile of bullies, bullying behaviour and the relationship between bullies and victims more fully.

Bossy or bully?

Some people are often described as being "bossy" or "domineering".

Although this type of behaviour is also aggressive, when individuals are labelled as "bossy" they usually accept this, and can accept the consequences of their behaviour by dealing with the conflict they have created.

Sometimes being "bossy" is linked to a particular management style, and providing the bossiness does not affect the rights and well-being of individuals, it can be seen as a legitimate (albeit not effective) use of power. In most cases, a bullying boss does not have the level of interpersonal skills necessary to use workable compromise. Bossiness is also short-lived: most people feel able to challenge this type of behaviour, and can comfortably deal with its effects. However, bossiness can turn into bullying when an abrasive style is used in a personal, vindictive manner.

Recognising bullying behaviours

Bullying can take the form of persistent negative attacks on an individual's personal and professional performance. These attacks are unpredictable, irrational and often unfairly meted out. There are some obvious bullying behaviours, yet most of the time the behaviours are covert and hidden, subtle and insidious, gradually wearing the person down over a period of time.

Below are some of the most common signs, adapted from the BBC for Business training pack *Bullying at Work*:

Obvious signs of bullying

● The use of terror tactics, open aggression, threats, abuse and obscenities towards targets. Shouting and uncontrolled anger are often triggered by trivial situations.
● Subjecting targets to constant humiliation or ridicule, belittling their efforts, often in front of others. Persistent criticism or sarcasm.
● Personal insults and name-calling, as well as spreading malicious rumours which are unfounded.
● Freezing out, ignoring, excluding and deliberately talking to a third party to isolate another.
● Never listening to others' points of view, always cutting across people in conversation.
● Persecution through threats and fear, and physical attacks.

Less obvious signs of bullying

● Subjecting targets to excessive supervision, monitoring everything they do and being especially critical about minor things with malicious intent. This can happen with or without the employee's knowledge.

● Constantly taking the credit for the other person's work, but never the blame when things go wrong.

● Constantly overruling an individual's authority without prior warning or proper discussion; using lengthy memos to make wild and inaccurate accusations.

● Removing whole areas of work responsibility from a person, reducing their job to routine tasks which are well below their skills and capabilities. Refusal to delegate because of a belief that work will not be done to the required standard.

● Setting the person impossible targets and objectives, or constantly changing the work remit without telling the person, and then criticising or reprimanding them for not meeting the demands.

● Deliberately withholding information which the person requires in order to do their job effectively. This includes interfering with post and other communications.

● Refusing reasonable requests for leave or training, blocking promotions, tampering with personal report marks or appraisal ratings.

(Reproduced with kind permission from BBC for Business)

Bullying can be an isolating experience – what might appear to be normal behaviour from the outside can be terrifying to the bullied. If you were to examine the above lists carefully, most people would be able to name someone who constantly or repeatedly used some of those behaviours, yet would probably not have labelled them as bullying, because, in isolation, the behaviours seem quite normal for the individual concerned. Taking complaints seriously and not judging the validity of someone else's experience from a personal viewpoint is essential when identifying behaviours which are considered to be bullying.

Bullying and organisational culture

If all of these behaviours are evident in the workplace, and the problem has existed for a long time, why then are employers reluctant to admit it is a problem, and furthermore are hesitant to confront it?

[Organisations are reluctant to put a label on bullying – doing so means that they may have to face deep cultural issues ingrained within the organisation, or deal with individuals who, for example, have poor interpersonal skills, yet perform highly] An organisation which believes in and encourages "pressure management" will be unwilling to admit that this style of management amounts to bullying, particularly when targets are achieved and bottom-line results improved.]

In its guide for tackling bullying, the MSF states that:

"Bullying may be part of the culture of an organisation. It is often condoned and even encouraged. In some organisations there may be a deliberate policy of employing or promoting bullies to certain positions, as an effective way of getting tasks done."

Organisational factors play an important part in whether or not bullying takes place at work. The sorts of workplaces where bullying might exist, or is more likely to occur, are those where there is/ are:

● an extremely competitive environment which promotes a culture of putting personal needs first
● fear of redundancy
● envy amongst colleagues, manifested by putting colleagues down
● an authoritarian style of management and supervision
● poorly planned organisational changes and constant uncertainty
● little participation and involvement amongst staff
● lack of training and development opportunities and de-skilling in areas, losing expertise
● no respect for others and their point of view
● no respect for differences in the workplace
● poor work relationships generally
● no clear codes of acceptable conduct and behaviour
● excessive workloads and unreasonable demands on people
● impossible targets or regular shifting of deadlines
● no procedures for resolving problems.

Often, the behaviours that bullies use against their targets stem from the anger that they may have with the organisation – it may not be appropriate to express dissatisfaction publicly because of the culture that exists within the organisation, or if there is no apparent positional power. Bullies will vent their anger and frustration on others, when it is really aimed at the organisation.

Chapter 5 explores the issue of the effects of bullying on the organisational culture and climate further.

The myths and realities of workplace aggression and bullying

Peter Randall, in his book *Adult Bullying*, recorded some of the misconceptions people held about bullying and workplace aggression during his work with Employee Assistance Programmes (EAPs). The differing views held by people about bullying clearly show the need to raise levels of awareness about the nature of bullying and how it affects people.

It is easy to spot bullies because they fit a particular profile.

Although there may be one or two features in common, there is no standard profile of a bully. Instead, it is necessary to focus on the behaviour of bullies and what drives them, rather than on their personal characteristics.

The threat of losing a job is the main reason why employees become aggressive in the workplace.

There are a variety of reasons why individuals use workplace aggression and bullying as a form of behaviour. Most of these have nothing to do with the employer or the workplace environment. They may result from domestic and family problems, drug or alcohol abuse, financial difficulties and low levels of self-worth (Chapter 4 looks at this more carefully).

Personnel departments should know that bullies can be spotted and they shouldn't be hired in the first place.

Evidence suggests that the workplace is a particular environment in which many bullies may feel secure enough to demonstrate aggressive behaviour. They may not be aggressive at home, or in public places where their behaviour would lead to repercussions. Even those who commit murder in the workplace are liable to lead relatively peaceful lives until a few months before their violent act.

Bullies don't prosper very well in terms of promotion and become more aggressive because they are frustrated.

There is some truth to this, and indeed, the larger the organisation, and the greater the competition for promotion, the less likely it is that aggressive individuals will rise beyond middle-management positions. The reverse is true, however, of organisations that encourage bullying and aggressive behaviour, where the bully may also be the one who is seen by senior management to get the job done well. As a result they are favoured for promotion.

Bullies seek out particular people to bully usually because they want some kind of revenge.

It is true that bullying employees do pick out particular victims. However, the reason for this is generally to be found within the characteristics of the victim who is selected. Revenge is not often the primary motive. There may be a desire for revenge against some people but their position or their personal characteristics prevent the revenge from taking form. Other individuals, however, are vulnerable to the aggression of the bully and therefore selected for intimidation. Again, Chapter 4 explores the relationship between the victim and the bully in more detail.

It is understood that bullying can be a very serious problem for victims, but because it doesn't happen very often and there are so few victims it is not really a problem for the workplace.

This is a very common misconception. Evidence suggests that throughout the industrialised world, one out of four employees is the victim of harassment, threats or physical attacks.

(Adapted from *Adult Bullying: Perpetrators and Victims,* by Peter Randall. Reproduced with kind permission from Routledge Publishing)

Bullying and the law

Unfortunately, there is at present no specific legislation that recognises bullying as a form of discrimination or that prohibits it. Various attempts have been made to introduce Dignity at Work bills in Parliament which include the issue of bullying. Although they have not as yet been successful, it is predicted that the new millennium will see in the UK some form of legislative framework, and that employers will have to meet the requirements within it. It is possible, however, as a result of bullying, to claim constructive dismissal, particularly if the working environment is intolerable and means that the targets of bullying cannot work. Some unions have also attempted to use health and safety legislation to get redress for members who suffer bullying. Chapter 7 looks at this issue more closely.

Bullying as a means to an end

Often bullying behaviours are used in various ways to undermine individuals or certain target groups. The incidence of bullying in these areas is frequent, yet very rarely discussed. The next section reveals the bullying tactics used to discriminate on the grounds of age and against ex-offenders, and examines the phenomenon of group or "gang" bullying.

Bullying and age discrimination

Age discrimination is very much on the employment agenda at the moment. Britain is one of the few countries that still perpetuates age discrimination, and has no legislation to combat it. A consortium of employers, The Employers' Forum on Age, have developed a strategy for combating age discrimination in the workplace. However, the bullying that exists for both younger and older workers because of their age will take a long time to disappear.

Younger workers often experience bullying in apprenticeship roles, as they are treated as children rather than professionals because of their lack of work experience. They are sometimes expected to go through initiation ceremonies and also to earn credibility with their peers before being accepted as part of the team. They are also subjected to constant supervision and monitoring, as it is assumed that they are not competent enough to carry out their roles independently.

Traditionally, older workers would be targeted by employers for redundancy or pushed out of the workplace once they reached mid-forties, to be replaced by younger workers who are viewed as a cheaper source of labour. Demographic predictions and changes in the workplace prove that this practice will do more damage to the skills base and shorten the pool of resources, so that by the year 2000 there will be 1.5 million fewer workers between the ages of sixteen and twenty-four in the UK labour market.

The stereotypes of older workers losing the ability to learn new skills and being "set in their ways" give rise to bullying tactics that are designed to push them out of jobs by making them appear slow or incompetent. Questions might also be raised about the quality of their health, thereby forcing older workers to retire early on medical grounds, as the following case study shows.

Case Study

Old and Unfit for Work

Simon, a long-term career employee of a chemical-processing company, was fifty-one at the time he became a victim of bullying. He had worked well for the company and had a superior work record. He got on well with senior management and with shop-floor personnel. He had accrued good bonuses and an enhanced pension.

The company went through a period of downsizing and reorganisation. Simon's line manager was replaced by a man in his early forties who lost no time in letting him know that he was too old for the job and should look elsewhere.

Simon's administrative assistant was given to someone else and he was moved into a smaller and uncomfortable office two floors down from the level where he did most of his work. Next he received a series of poor performance reviews from the younger manager, who unobtrusively let people know that Simon was "past it". The manager also started to follow Simon into corridors and stairwells, where he would deliberately bump into him, push him and talk about wanting to "kick his wrinkly old arse out of the company". After ten months of continuous harassment, Simon left the company on medical grounds. He now works as a storeman in an electronics factory.

(Taken from *Adult Bullying: Perpetrators and Victims*, by Peter Randall. Reproduced with kind permission from Routledge Publishing)

Bullying and ex-offenders

Although there is much evidence to suggest that ex-offenders are dis-criminated against because of recruitment practices, little research has been carried out on the treatment of ex-offenders in employment. The National Association for the Care and Resettlement of Offenders (NACRO) have many anecdotal examples of individuals who, after disclosure of their previous offences, have suffered harassment and bul-lying as a result. The following case study is an example.

Case Study

Ex-offender Offended

"It had taken me over two years to find a job. In 1989, I was given a long prison sentence for handling drugs at university. I had enough time to reflect on my misdemeanours in the cell, and finished my studies whilst in prison. Finding a job was soul destroying: I had to declare my conviction, and out of all the applications I submitted, I was only interviewed three times – once at second interview stage. I was overjoyed when I finally got a job as an invoicing clerk – way below my capabilities (my degree is in economics and politics), but it was the break that I needed.

My first day in the office was great. I went home with positive feelings about my future career prospects. Things went very well for about four months, and as my probationary period was successful and I was kept on permanently, I moved to another department.

My welcome to this department could not have been more different to my first day in the organisation. The head of department greeted me with 'I know about people like you. And because I know about people like you, I know the best way to deal with you. Please remember that.' As he calmly walked out of the office, I noticed my reactions. I was shaking, my palms sweating. My new supervisor, Judy, came into the office and showed me to my desk. 'Don't worry, he's always tough on new people – ignore him and you will gain his respect.'

After two months of ignoring him – which was difficult enough when he became abusive – I began to feel depressed about the situation I was in. I was at a stress level that was almost equivalent to the days during my trial, and I had caught a cold (obviously because my resistance was so low) that kept me away from the office for the best part of a week. When I returned, there were two pieces of paper on my desk. One was a memo from the head of department, demanding that I complete a report by 12.00pm on the Friday *before* the Monday I came back, and a leaflet outlining the company's alcohol and drugs policy, and where we could go if we recognised that we had a 'problem'. The word 'problem' was underlined in red ink.

I was devastated, and didn't know how to handle it. I asked Judy about the report, who reassured me that it had been completed by someone else. However, she was not surprised about the memo on my desk: 'That's one of his tactics, Tony, he probably left it there to make you sweat a little and panic.'

Although I knew that others were suffering from this man's behaviour, it was difficult for me to see the reality of my predicament. All of my worst fears about myself were coming true. I needed this job, but as an ex-offender it was obvious to me that I had not fully paid my debt and any ill-treatment I received, I deserved. I couldn't confide in anyone for a long time (I believed that if I did, people would stop trusting me, and treat me as an outcast).

I went off sick for two weeks, thoroughly depressed and demoralised, and when faced with the prospect of returning to work, I called the personnel unit to ask for a transfer. When the personnel officer asked me why I wanted to move, I cried. I had not fully realised the pressure I was under, and talking it through with the personnel officer galvanised me (and them) into action.

I did not get my transfer – however, eventually, we did get a new head of department. I also began to get a sense of value in myself, and felt able to work on an equal footing as everyone else, because of my past, and not despite it."

(Tony, a rehabilitated member of the workforce)

Group bullying

When an individual is the target of bullying from a group of bullies, the experience can be much more stressful, as the behaviour is meted out by more than one individual in varying ways.

The "pack" mentality describes the psychology of the group, and is the norm for bullies who form the group. There is normally a ring-leader, who is the main perpetrator. Although others in the group may have similar backgrounds, thoughts and feelings to each other, it is far easier for them to follow the leader of the "pack" as a survival tactic rather than stand independently. The lead bully is normally the person who has the most difficult relationship with the target, and often manipulates others to behave negatively towards the victim. Colluding with the ringleader automatically gains acceptance and acknowledgement within the "pack", and group bullying situations are very difficult to break down for this reason.

Case Study

Bullying by Manipulation

"There was one woman in the office who disliked me intensely. Claire was well known in the organisation as ambitious and political; creating close relationships with senior managers in order to gain favour (she had been involved in a relationship with a senior director that others felt was unethical), getting involved in high profile projects and products that would guarantee her publicity, and volunteering for the work that she believed would further her ambitions. Claire also had a reputation for using very underhand tactics, putting her name to other people's work, using others to complete tasks that she herself was unable to complete.

In a short space of time of me joining the organisation, I became the target of Claire's manipulative behaviour. Whilst I was working in the chief executive's office, she had tried to befriend me in order to gain information about what was happening in the organisation. When I refused to play ball, she got angry and started to turn other working colleagues against me. Claire spread rumours about me such as saying that I was a lesbian (because no one had ever seen me with or heard me talk about 'my man'), that I only got my job because of who I knew, and that I always looked as if I had a chip on my shoulder. As a result, the other women in her 'club' ostracised me and would only talk to me when it was really necessary. It felt as if every action I did was questioned or queried by Claire and members of her group. I was not invited to social events, and when one of the group (Amanda) met me for a business lunch, Claire reportedly sent her a long memo explaining the dangers of working with me on client projects, and that I was not competent enough to work at a high level. Amanda admitted to me later that Claire also warned her off making friends with me. I knew Amanda felt sorry for me, but it was clear that she wasn't going to risk upsetting Claire. In fact, for a short while, Amanda's bullying tactics were far worse and more direct than Claire's. Amanda once created a fictitious client visit in my diary, nearly a hundred miles from the office. Luckily, I had to ring the client because I didn't know where his office was, and was informed that the client had no idea why I was arranging to visit them.

For a number of years, I wasted a lot of energy in side-stepping Claire, her group and their behaviour against me. New members of staff were also brought into the bullying circle. Once, an administrator who was fairly new to the team, told me when I asked her to type a piece of work for me that she was not allowed to complete any of my work, however urgent I felt it was, until the other team members' work was finished. What upset me was that it did not take her long to follow the patterns of behaviour of existing staff – she had been told that one of the rules of acceptance into the group was not to associate with me, and had embraced it wholeheartedly. The final straw came when Claire manipulated my assistant into giving her a copy of a piece of my research which she needed in order to complete a project that she had accountability for, but which, clearly, she did not have the expertise or awareness to carry out effectively. It was then that I realised the extent of Claire's bullying, on me and on others. When I complained about Claire, her manager tried to justify her behaviour. 'Everyone knows what Claire is like, Yasmin. I will talk to her, but you have got to make an effort to get on with her. People will like you more if you did.'

The manager's reply made me so angry. After the meeting, I spoke to Amanda privately. Amanda admitted that she had often wanted to break free from Claire's influence, but was always concerned that they would turn against her, and that I might join them – she felt that I would have good reason too. She was very apologetic, but still hesitant about acting against Claire.

After a period of time, however, Amanda supported me in challenging Claire whenever she attacked me. Two other members of the group (out of eight) joined us and now Claire is less powerful, although she still is very influential. I do think I should leave the organisation – there is still too much ill-feeling for me to turn things around completely, but not before I can be instrumental in ensuring that Claire gets her comeuppance."

(Yasmin, equalities consultant)

As the behaviour of the "pack" is similar to that of children in the playground, the techniques for breaking up the group reflect those used in schools with child gangs:

- Interview each group member separately.
- Establish and isolate the group leader.
- If necessary, discipline all the members of the group, with harsher measures for the group leader.
- Gain commitment to change behaviour individually.
- Reinforce the message that bullying is unacceptable on an individual basis as well as in the group.
- Get each member of the group to repeat their promises to change behaviour in the larger group; and
- Reinforce the consequences if the bullying behaviour is repeated.

Strategies for tackling bullying

Organisations must develop policies and strategies for eliminating workplace bullying. The measures that need to be adopted include:

- Full risk assessment to meet health and safety requirements.
- Policy development with the involvement of unions and staff associations.
- An impartial complaints procedure, with informal and formal action.
- Counselling support and behaviour modification support.
- A full training and development plan.

Chapters 4, 7 and 8 deal with these strategies in depth.

Reflection

In a BBC Radio 4 production in 1990 called *An Abuse of Power*, Andrea Adams said *"In order to solve a problem you have to be able to recognise it, and to be able to recognise it you have to be able to give it a name."*

There are a number of organisations and individuals who are dedicated to ensuring that the public is aware of bullying, can recognise what it is, and the impact that bullying has not only in the workplace but in society as a whole. It would be unrealistic to expect that bullying as a phenomenon can be eradicated entirely (indeed the nature of human beings would indicate that there will always be those who use bullying behaviours, for whatever reason). As a result, the creation and maintenance of a working climate that makes it unacceptable must be viewed as a top organisational priority, along with the need to encourage those who bully to see the benefits of modifying their behaviour, and those who are targets to gain additional skills to challenge the bullying. Acceptance that bullying in the workplace exists is the first major step in finding the solutions to resolving the problems it perpetuates.

References

Violence against Staff (Incomes Data Services Ltd., No 54, 1994).

Preventing Violence to Staff, Barry Poyner and Caroline Warne (Tavistock Institute of Human Relations for the HSE, 1989).

Prevention of Violence to Staff in Banks and Building Societies (HSE, The Stationery Office, 1994).

"Surviving the school of hard knocks", Widget Finn, *The Times*.

Violence against Employees: A Legal Perspective, Health and Safety Information Bulletin 218, Roger Walden, 1993.

Counselling: the BAC Counselling Reader, Peter Reynolds and Tricia Allison, edited by Stephen Palmer, Shelia Dainow and Pat Milner (Sage Publications, 1996).

Bullying at Work: How to Confront and Overcome it, Andrea Adams (Virago Press, 1992).

Bullying at Work: How to Tackle it — A Guide for MSF Representatives and Members, MSF, August 1995.

Keeping Safe: A Practical Guide to Talking with Children, Michele Elliott (Hodder/Headline Coronet Books, 1992).

Bullying at Work: Combating Offensive Behaviour in the Workplace, Facilitator's Guide, Andrea Adams (BBC Enterprises Ltd, 1994).

Adult Bullying: Perpetrators and Victims, Peter Randall (Routledge, 1997).

Voices of Diversity: Real People Talk about Problems and Solutions in a Workplace where Everyone Is Not Alike, Renee Blank and Sandra Slipp (AMACOM, 1994).

You Don't Have to Take It!: A Women's Guide to Confronting Emotional Abuse at Work, Ginny Nicarthy, Naomi Gottlieb and Sandra Coffman (Seal Press, 1993).

Social Skills in Interpersonal Communication, Owen Hargie, Christine Saunders and David Dickson (Routledge, 1994).

The Ethical Organisation: Ethical Theory and Corporate Behaviour, Alan Kitson and Robert Campbell (Macmillan Business, 1996).

The mindset and behaviours of victims, targets and perpetrators

Chapter 4 is addressed to individuals. Why do some people appear to be prime targets for harassment, bullying and violence, and others often display behaviour which is unacceptable? Exploring the psychological aspects in the behaviour of both the target and the perpetrator may broaden our thinking on why harassment exists.

This chapter gives practical advice, not only to people who may be the victims or targets of abusive behaviour at work but also to those who may be perceived as perpetrators.

Are you a victim or a target?

There are different schools of thought as to whether people are victims or targets of harassment. A victim implies helplessness; targets are people who are singled out or who have a perceived weakness, making them more vulnerable than others.

A victim (in the context of harassment and bullying) can be described as someone who does not use their internal power or identifiable resources to prevent abuse. Victims quite often find it difficult to take personal responsibility for their behaviour, and sometimes (through lack of skills) don't know how to deal with such personally difficult situations as harassment.

Targets often have the resources to deal with abusive behaviour, but find it difficult to exercise them because of the external pressures placed on them. It is possible, however, for targets to be *victimised* by perpetrators who abuse their position of power and relationship with power.

The answers to the following questions can give an indication of how the individuals view themselves and their particular situations:

- What is happening to me?
- Why is this happening?
- How can I handle it?

The individual on the receiving end of unacceptable behaviour needs to ascertain whether they are being harassed or bullied because of membership of a target group, whether they are displaying the behaviour of a victim, or whether it is a combination of the two.
Consider the following two case studies.

Case Study

Example: Victim
Elise is a personal assistant to a consultant surgeon called Liz. Elise has worked in this capacity at the hospital for many years and has worked with several consultants prior to Liz's arrival. She gets on well with people and is known for being a good, diligent worker. Liz is a bully and bullies both men and women. Her behaviour has allegedly led to one colleague in a previous hospital suffering a heart attack, and soon Elise is on the receiving end of some very nasty behaviour: shouting when small mistakes are made; rudeness for no apparent reason and sarcastic comments about the quality and efficiency of her work. Elise is appalled and shaken. No one has ever had cause to complain about her work, and she prides herself on her ability to deal with people tactfully and in a friendly manner. She goes on a variety of women's confidence-building courses where

Example: Target
Conrad has recently started work as an assistant conference organiser working in a small team of people. He is the only black man in the team, and this is his first job. Although he enjoys his work and finds the team members friendly, helpful and very sociable, problems emerge with Jim, their boss. He makes covertly racist jokes and singles Conrad out consistently as the butt of his humour. After a while, this behaviour escalates and becomes more aggressive. Conrad finds that Jim frequently criticises his work and finds fault, even though Conrad's work is consistently good and he is performing as a valued member of the team. Due to his age (he is 18), his lack of experience at work, and the fact that he is the only black person in the section, he feels unable to confront Jim directly and ask him to stop. However, he does talk to his

she speaks at length about her problems and gains a great deal of support. However, back in the workplace, the bullying continues and Elise's misery is compounded by her inability to confront the situation.

colleagues and gains plenty of reassurance. He is thinking about taking this issue up with the union and is keeping a diary of events.

In this situation, the answer to the question "what is happening to me?" is clear. Elise is being bullied. The causes of the bullying lie in the behaviour and personality of her boss – not with Elise. How could she handle it? Here, Elise does little apart from seek some external support and validation of her innocence in this situation. However, in terms of handling the situation directly, she does nothing. Elise is not using internal power or any form of internal or external resource to deal with her situation; she accepts the unacceptable behaviour she receives every day. She is thus targeted due to her status within the organisation as a PA (a common target group) and she is a perfect victim.

In this situation, Conrad is clearly being racially harassed and bullied by Jim. Conrad feels constrained from confronting Jim for the reasons outlined above – he is, after all, in a very vulnerable position. He clearly has some inner resources to deal with the predicament and is engaged in building support for himself from colleagues and is trying to resolve the situation.

As we can see from these two examples, the work context and power networks can be an important restraint to action, but this did not prevent Conrad from doing what he could and resist being victimised any further. He does take some form of action and has not ruled out going further. However, Elise seems incapable of taking action at work – even if it only involves talking to a good friend. This only serves to exacerbate her isolation and reinforces Liz's power over her.

Common target groups

The following groups of people are often targeted for harassment, bullying and violence:

- women
- ethnic minority men and women
- administrative staff
- gay men and lesbian women
- people with disabilities.

Administrative staff

The Industrial Society produced two surveys featuring sexual harassment, and the working conditions of administrative and secretarial staff. In *No Offence?*, 27% of people experiencing sexual harassment were office/clerical workers, and 89% of those experiencing sexual harassment were women.

The *Typecast* survey found that only 15% of the secretarial staff surveyed said they had been sexually harassed at work by a colleague. Because of the differences in the two figures, ad hoc research produced anecdotal evidence which indicated that non-verbal and verbal forms of harassment (innuendoes and lewd comments, whistling and winking) were seen by the majority of secretaries as "something I have to deal with as part of my job", and were not considered to be forms of harassment at all. Many administrative staff considered sexual harassment to be actual physical contact and not other forms of sexist behaviour.

It would appear that secretaries and administrative staff were so used to dealing with this, that it did not occur to them that such behaviour was unacceptable. One comment received was *"I almost expect to have to put up with it really. I think lots of people don't take secretaries very seriously and so they think it's OK to do it."* However, awareness about harassment has now risen to the extent that secretaries and administrative staff no longer accept these behaviours as part of their roles.

(Sources: *Typecast* and *No Offence?*, The Industrial Society, 1993)

Because of the difficulties these groups of people face within work, coupled with their generally low status within their organisations, they are more vulnerable to abuses of power such as bullying and harassment. In addition to this, there is also the issue of double or even multiple discriminations, as this example of black women's experience shows.

| Case Study | **A Black Woman's Experience . . .** |

"Because I argued with them a lot, the management never liked me. There were a lot of black assistants at the shop, but they didn't stay long. That was their way of fighting back. With me, now, I had to stick it out a bit longer. At the time, I was six months pregnant and they were still picking on me. I was carrying some boxes, which were really heavy one time, and I asked this girl to help me but she said she was busy; so I didn't pick them up again. The manager came and told me I had to. I told him they were too heavy for me, and he accused me of not doing my job properly. I was sent to the personnel officer and given a final warning and sacked on the spot. Of course it was unfair. It was racial and sexual discrimination. I took them to the tribunal and won my case for unfair dismissal. I got about £1,000 and they settled out of court because they had a bad name for the way they treated their black employees . . . After I left, things began to change. Some of my friends even got through to management. I like to think it was down to me."

(Adapted from *The Heart of the Race: Black Women's Lives in Britain*, by Beverley Bryan, Stella Dadzie and Suzanne Scafe. Reproduced with kind permission from Virago Press)

The Women Against Sexual Harassment advice group found that ethnic minority women are over-represented amongst clients to whom they give advice and support, confirming the difficulties that black women face. Double discrimination means an increased level of potential abuse at work, where discrimination can take place on both gender and race grounds.

History has its impact. In the days when slavery was a thriving industry, black women were once viewed as "objects for the use (and abuse) of men", and were considered to be readily available. The stereotype of ethnic minority women being "exotic sexual objects" derives from this, and it is very difficult to break the myths associated with ethnic minority women and sex. As a result, black women are still more open to abusive behaviour in the workplace.

Double discrimination can also occur to those groups of people identified as targets, and where this occurs, organisations need to be aware of their vulnerability.

The psychology of the victim/target and perpetrator

Transactional Analysis is a useful theory to adopt when attempting to understand the behaviours of both the victim/target and perpetrator. Developed by Dr Eric Berne, an American psychiatrist, in 1972, and further developed by Thomas Harris (*I'm OK, You're OK*),

Transactional Analysis concentrates on the existential or "life" positions from which people operate, and how they interact with others.

The concept of being "OK" describes the level of competence an individual has, and whether they are in control of their lives. Being "OK" means that they have value as a person and their views and opinions are taken seriously. The opposite of this is being seen as "Not OK", having little or no control in their lives, and very little value as an individual. Their views and opinions are very rarely considered by others and are often ignored.

The "OK Corral" diagram (Figure 3) was created by Franklin Ernst (1971) and describes the four main behavioural combinations which have been analysed in relation to victim, target and perpetrator responses to harassment and bullying.

Figure 3.
The OK Corral

1 I'm OK You're not OK	4 I'm OK You're OK
2 I'm not OK You're not OK	3 I'm not OK You're OK

Let's examine each as it relates to harassment and bullying.

Box 1

1 I'm OK You're not OK	4 I'm OK You're OK
2 I'm not OK You're not OK	3 I'm not OK You're OK

If *I'm OK and You're not OK*, then I have value as a person and my ideas and views also have value. However, I do not recognise the value that you have as an individual. In fact, I think you have little or no value. Because of this, I feel I am justified in behaving towards you in an aggressive manner.

I keep my rights as an individual, but do not allow you to assert yours. I may also take your rights and use them to my advantage. In this interaction, I am likely to bully and harass you in order to keep my rights and use yours, and also to reinforce your lack of value as an individual.

Box 2

1 I'm OK You're not OK	4 I'm OK You're OK
2 I'm not OK You're not OK	3 I'm not OK You're OK

When *I'm not OK and You're not OK*, both individuals are behaving non-assertively. In this situation no one is in control. This describes the true state of both the victim and perpetrator's behaviour, where both sides are operating from a low value basis, and little or no feelings of self-worth.

Box 3

1 I'm OK You're not OK	4 I'm OK You're OK
2 I'm not OK You're not OK	3 I'm not OK You're OK

When *I'm not OK, but perceive that You're OK*, everyone else but me appears to be in control, and to have value as a person. In this situation, the logical action is for me to blame myself and do nothing to confront this behaviour.

I give up my rights as an individual and allow others to assert their rights, and sometimes allow them to take mine. This is very much the mindset of a victim, and those projecting this behaviour are likely to become long-term sufferers of harassment and, in particular, bullying.

Box 4

1 I'm OK You're not OK	4 I'm OK You're OK
2 I'm not OK You're not OK	3 I'm not OK You're OK

When *I'm OK and You're OK*, both parties have value and are in control. There may be disagreements, but this does not mean that either party dismisses the values or ideas of the other. In this situation, the motto is not "to get rid of" but "to get on with". People in this position are fully aware of how their behaviour affects others, and can communicate on a balanced level – not aggressing their rights – maintaining and acknowledging the rights of others, and using workable compromise.

How does being "not OK" show itself in harassers and bullies? When studying the behaviour of bullies at a psychological level, findings indicate that the origins of bullying lie in the bully's own childhood, where they may have had a history of exposure to negative behaviour. They may have been constantly criticised inappropriately, humiliated, shouted at, ignored, terrorised and subjected to abusive punishment by powerful or dominant people in their lives.

Bullies remain in the "not OK" ego state by adopting the behaviours meted out to them by their aggressors. This often means that most bullies have little control over their behaviour, learning few interpersonal skills, and therefore not having much choice about the way they interact with others. Bullying behaviour often represents a way of getting rid of intolerably painful feelings which persecute the bully from within. The way to understand the bully's own psychological experience is by assessing the feelings they generate in their targets.

Interactions between the bully and the target can also be seen in terms of people playing "games", a concept devised by Eric Berne as a way of describing a series of behavioural transactions (or interactions) with a perceived pay-off.

In their book *TA Today: A New Introduction to Transactional Analysis*, Ian Stewart and Vann Joines describe how Stephen Karpman devised a simple yet powerful diagram for analysing these games, known as the Drama Triangle (see Figure 4). Karpman suggests that people who play games assume one of three basic roles: *Persecutor, Rescuer* or *Victim*.

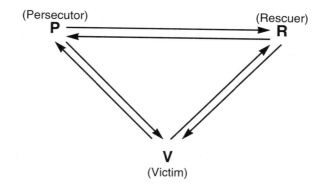

(Reproduced by kind permission of Lifespace Publishing from *TA Today: a New Introduction to Transactional Analysis*, by Ian Stewart and Vann Joines, 1996)

A *Persecutor* is someone who puts other people down. The Persecutor views others as being one-down and not OK. Persecutors tend to make unrealistic rules and enforce them in cruel ways, picking on "little people" rather than those who can stand up to them.

A *Rescuer* also views others as being not OK and one-down. However, the Rescuer responds by offering help from a one-up position. The Rescuer believes: "I have to help all these others because they're not good enough to help themselves." Rescuers offer unreal helpfulness to keep others dependent on them. In fact, they don't really help others and may actually dislike helping, working to maintain the victim role so they can continue to play Rescuer.

A *Victim* is one-down and not OK. Sometimes a Victim will seek a Persecutor to put them down and bully them. The Victim may also search for a Rescuer, who will offer help and confirm the Victim's belief that "I can't cope on my own". Victims provoke others to put them down, use them or hurt them. They send helpless messages, conveniently forget and often act confused.

Each one of the Drama Triangle roles entails a *discount*, which involves ignoring information relevant to solving the problem. The Persecutor discounts others' value and dignity. Extreme Persecutors may discount other people's right to health and the right to live. The Rescuer discounts others' abilities to think for themselves and act on their own initiative. Victims discount themselves and seek a Persecutor to confirm the view that they are unworthy. The Victim seeking a Rescuer will believe that they need the Rescuer's help in order to think, act or make decisions.

The Drama Triangle reveals how a bully's behaviour is linked to that of a victim. The bully in the role of Persecutor or Rescuer shows no regard for the right of the victim to exist as a valid person, whilst the victim in the role of the Victim gives up their personal power and allows others to exist for them. The relationship the bully has with the victim is also characterised by similar experiences: a history of childhood vulnerability, a lack of value and self-worth, immature interpersonal skills, and their inability to cope with their feelings.

Staying OK, and maintaining OK positions in others, will go a long way to eradicating the problem of harassment, bullying and violence. We will now explore the effects of not being OK, how you can be OK, and how staying OK can be achieved.

Not being OK

Experiencing harassment

Even if we are a confident individual who behaves assertively most of the time, it does not mean that we will never experience harassing, bullying or violent behaviour. Even if we behave fairly consistently from a position of Being OK, the effects of harassment and bullying behaviour can still be devastating – we can go from Being OK to Not Being OK very quickly. It is important when such experiences occur to recognise what is happening and to develop strategies for supporting ourselves and dealing with the situations.

For anyone, harassment, bullying and violent behaviour is painful and disempowering. The experience can be so negative that it affects the person's ability to recognise what is happening to them. Below are four levels of recognition which may determine how an individual copes with harassment and other unacceptable behaviours:

First level	Recognition of behaviours as harassment, has inner resources and coping mechanisms to handle it.
Second level	Non-recognition of behaviours as harassment. However, once identified as such, has inner resources to deal with the situation. May need help to recognise behaviours in the future.
Third level	Non-recognition of behaviours as harassment, does not have inner resources to handle the situation.
Fourth level	Recognition of behaviours as harassment, yet does not have inner resources to handle the situation.

Not recognising that you are being harassed can add to the pain, reinforcing a sense of powerlessness. Recognition is the first step to empowerment, and can help raise personal levels of confidence and give a sense of control when dealing with the situation.

The levels also reflect the boundaries an individual is faced with when making a complaint of harassment within the organisation. If the organisational climate makes it difficult for the target to complain about harassment without fear of reprisal, a person can move from level one to level four because there are no resources available to handle the situation.

The effects of harassment on the individual

The physical and emotional stress that individuals suffer is beyond measurement; however, the negative impact of harassment can leave behind devastating and harmful effects.

Emotional reactions to being harassed include surprise, anger, shock and disbelief, and can create feelings of anxiety, embarrassment, depression, guilt and pain. It is not unusual for an individual at the receiving end to be totally confused about what is happening to them and to experience a mix of these emotions. If these emotions go unnoticed or are not dealt with promptly, physical stress builds up, and this can have serious consequences for an individual's health. Some of the physical symptoms of stress include.

- palpitations
- breathlessness
- headaches
- skin trouble
- digestive problems
- frequent colds
- high blood pressure
- muscle cramps
- feeling too hot or too cold
- irregular sleeping patterns.

The following case study illustrates why the effects of harassment should not be underestimated.

Case Study

Suffering in Silence

"I worked for 16 years as a technician in an electronics firm. I suffered badly from bullying and racial harassment for most of those years, but it got worse as I became older and was ready to retire – all I really wanted to do was hang on, get my pension, and go back home to Italy.

The jokes that I got saying I eat garlic and lasagne all the time, I could take – but when they started to degrade my wife (saying how fat and miserable she must be after having at least eleven children – we have three) I hit back. And their [the other workers in his team] behaviour worsened. I knew there was no point going to the supervisor, he was fed up and couldn't do anything with them – and he had tried.

I didn't realise the stress I was suffering – almost every morning for the last year I began to break into cold sweats and even started vomiting. I had kept it in for so long, believing I was coping, and one day, just as I was clearing my bench to go home, I had the most painful stomach cramps I ever experienced. I don't know what happened next. I gained consciousness in the local hospital with my son at my side. 'Papa, why didn't you talk to me? You have an ulcer! This is serious! What has been troubling you? What's worrying you? Surely it can't be so bad as to nearly kill you?'

The distress of my son shocked me. I had not realised the effect this had had on my family – my wife knew about what was happening, but I wouldn't listen to her advice. She wanted me to give it all up and retire early.

I talked to my son, for the first time, and slept properly that evening. My family was the best support system I had, and after a lot of discussion, I negotiated a very good deal and left the firm – with my pension intact and a golden handshake. I think they were afraid that I would make trouble by filing a formal complaint. I wanted to go quietly, I didn't have enough energy left to fight and I didn't care about what happened to those sick people I worked with.

They had to be sick to behave in that way."

(Gilles, now retired!)

Becoming OK

When on the receiving end of harassment, bullying or violence, it can sometimes seem as though the world has fallen apart and feelings of powerlessness, anger and fear can dominate. This section will concentrate on developing ways of dealing with harassment by using your inner power in an assertive and appropriate fashion. Becoming OK requires the following strategies:

- Understand the process of power and your relationship with it.
- Don't become a victim – take personal responsibility.
- Become "stress fit" and create a strong support network.
- Behave assertively and get in touch with your feelings.

Understanding the process of power

The first step to dealing with harassment is to understand the process of power and your relationship with it. What is power? Power can be defined as:

the ability to get things done, and influence . . .
a means of doing . . . ability of body or mind

There can be no doubt that there is a relationship between power and harassment. Harassment is often defined as an abuse of power – especially if the harasser or bully is in a position of authority. However, we can say that bullying and harassment are abuses of power in so much as they abuse a "means of doing" or an "ability of body and mind", and in that sense, the harasser/bully is abusing both him/herself as well as the victim/target. Also, through controllable or uncontrollable influences, they are abusing their own mental and physical attributes.

In trying to Become OK and to Stay OK, we need to look beyond such definitions and consider how power relates to us in an individual way, enabling us to build our own self-worth and recognise our own personal power.

Internal (personal) power

Internal power is the source of power from within the individual. It is important to note that this resource cannot be taken away by others – it is often just not utilised effectively by the individual who is feeling disempowered. We all have personal power; however, like our physical body, our muscles and our bones, it needs constant gentle exercise and the right nutrients!

Internal power can be lowered by: unhealthy stress, particularly illness, tiredness and depression – the kinds of stress experienced by people who are being harassed. It can also be lowered by negative thoughts and self-talk: *"It'll never stop, he'll never go away and just leave me alone – I'm going to have to quit my job because I'm just unable to face this."* Refusal or inability to use power also results in lowering our internal power: this power must be exercised and cared for, just as we care for our physical well-being.

Sometimes we fail to use our internal power because the risk of taking responsibility for our actions and feelings is too frightening; maybe our power is a threat to others and it might conflict with our personal values of peace, love and goodwill. Our refusal to use our power might be based on very ethical and cultural principles, but exerting our power – especially when we are threatened – is absolutely acceptable and need not be unethical or conflict with our cultural values if we exercise it appropriately.

Internal power can be raised by: learning to manage stress and becoming "stress fit". A certain amount of stress is necessary for our well-being. We need to differentiate between healthy stress and unhealthy stress, and act quickly to combat unhealthy stress when the need arises. This can be done by creating the right support networks for ourselves at work and at home. We can use positive thinking and affirmations to boost our levels of self-worth, happiness and contentment. We can create options and choices for ourselves and get rid of the negative self-talk we often engage in when we face difficulties. Above all, we need to face our fears, confront our negative feelings and use assertive behaviour to deal with them – when and if we so choose.

Internal power has four main dimensions, which can be displayed negatively as powerless and overpowering, and positively as powerful and empowering (see Table 4).

Table 4. *Dimensions of personal power*

Powerless	Powerful	Empowering	Overpowering
Out of control	In control	Delegates and shares control	Dominates
Uninformed	Informed	Informing	Withholds information
Helpless	Self-reliant	Helpful	Takes over or offers no help at all
Insecure	Confident and secure	Complements and reinforces others' strengths	Arrogant
Inadequate	Capable	Trusts others' capabilities	Pushy, conceited
Fearful	Risk-taker	Offers others challenging opportunities and supports their efforts	Reckless, self-absorbed

(Source unknown)

The effective use of your own power will depend upon how you feel about one issue of power and its use. What are the sources of your own power? How do you use the power you have? Your answers to the following activity might help you define your relationship with power and powerlessness.

Identify the situations in which you feel:

Powerful Uncomfortable	Powerful Comfortable
Powerless Comfortable	Powerless Uncomfortable

Are there any patterns? For example:

● Are there certain people with whom you often feel powerless and uncomfortable?
● Do the situations differ at work or in the home, or are they the same?

What can you do to change the situations in which you feel "powerless and uncomfortable" and "powerful and uncomfortable"? For example:

I feel powerful/uncomfortable when I am in a position of authority for the first time. I can recall how I came to be in this situation and reflect that I am here through hard work and merit. I am rightfully in this position and I will not abuse the power I hold.

I feel powerless and uncomfortable when I witness men fighting in the street. I can change this situation by calling for the police, or removing myself from the situation.

Having completed this activity and digested the information above, consider:

● How do you feel about power and its use?
● What is the source of your own power?
● How do you use the power you have?
● How can you deal with situations where you feel powerless?

Taking personal responsibility

Blaming ourselves (self-blame) or blaming others is in itself a disempowering act. It discourages us from moving forward and taking responsibility for our behaviour.

Taking responsibility involves confronting our fear. In her book *Feel the Fear . . . and Do it Anyway*, Susan Jeffers identifies three levels of fear. Level one fear includes those things that "happen", like ageing, retirement, children leaving home, dying, illness, etc. Other level one fears require action, like changing career, making friends, driving, ending or beginning a relationship. These are described as surface fears; however, they affect every area of our lives.

Level two fears include rejection, success, failure, being vulnerable. They are to do with inner states of mind rather than exterior situations. They reflect your sense of worth and ability to handle the world. This explains why generalised fear takes place. If you are afraid of being rejected, this fear will affect every area of your life – friends, intimate relationships, etc. As a result, you protect yourself, thus greatly limiting your options. You begin to shut down and close out the world.

Level three fear is simply summarised by the phrase "I can't handle it". Jeffers believes that at the bottom of every one of our fears is simply the fear that you can't handle whatever life might bring you. "The truth is: if you knew you could handle anything that came your way, what would you possibly have to fear? The answer is – nothing." All we have to do is to diminish our fear by developing more trust in our ability to handle whatever comes our way. Some fear is necessary and keeps us alert, but the fear that holds us back is inappropriate and destructive. Perhaps it can be blamed on conditioning, however we do not have to accept it. As Jeffers says, "never let these three little words out of your mind – possibly the most important three words you'll ever hear: I'll handle it."

She has also developed five truths about fear. These are:

1. The fear will never go away as long as I continue to grow.
2. The only way to get rid of the fear of doing something is to go out . . . and do it.
3. The only way to feel better about myself is to go out and do it.
4. Not only am I going to experience fear whenever I'm on unfamiliar territory, but so is everyone else.
5. Pushing through fear is less frightening than living with the underlying fear that comes from a feeling of helplessness.

(Reproduced with kind permission from *Feel the Fear . . . and Do it Anyway,* by Susan Jeffers, Rider Publishing, 1994)

If everybody feels fear when approaching something new in life, yet so many are out there "doing it" despite this, then we must conclude that fear is not the problem. The real issue is therefore about how we hold the fear. For some, the fear is totally irrelevant, for others it is totally paralysing. The former hold their fear from a position of power (choice, positive energy and action), whereas the latter hold it from a position of pain (helplessness and depression).

Figure 5.
A pain-to-power
vocabulary

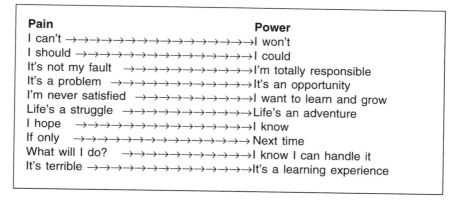

Pain	Power
I can't →→→→→→→→→→→→→→→→→	I won't
I should →→→→→→→→→→→→→→→→	I could
It's not my fault →→→→→→→→→→→	I'm totally responsible
It's a problem →→→→→→→→→→→→	It's an opportunity
I'm never satisfied →→→→→→→→→	I want to learn and grow
Life's a struggle →→→→→→→→→→	Life's an adventure
I hope →→→→→→→→→→→→→→→	I know
If only →→→→→→→→→→→→→→→	Next time
What will I do? →→→→→→→→→→→	I know I can handle it
It's terrible →→→→→→→→→→→→→	It's a learning experience

(Reproduced with kind permission from *Feel the Fear . . . and Do it Anyway* by Susan Jeffers, Rider Publishing, 1994).

The secret lies in moving from a position of pain to one of power – a healthy self-love (see Figure 5). What we need to do is to feel the fear we have when we approach a given situation, acknowledge that it is there, but move from paralysis to power and do it anyway. The more we keep going ahead by going through, the more confident we become. We go from a situation where we say "What will I do?" to one where we say "I know I can handle it". Consider these ways of reclaiming your power:

1. Avoid casting blame on an external force for your bad feelings about life. Nothing outside yourself can control your thinking or your actions.
2. Avoid blaming yourself for not being in control. You are doing the best you can and you are on the way to reclaiming your power.
3. Be aware of when and where you are playing the victim role. Learn the clues that tell you that you are not being responsible for what you are being, having, doing or feeling.
4. Familiarise yourself with your biggest enemy – your chatterbox. Replace this chatterbox with a loving, internal friend.
5. Figure out the pay-offs that keep you "stuck". Paradoxically, once you find them, you will probably be able quickly to become "unstuck".
6. Determine what you want in life and act on it. Stop waiting for someone to give it to you. You'll be waiting a long time.
7. Be aware of the many choices you have – in both actions and feelings – in any situation that comes your way. Choose the path that contributes to your growth and makes you feel at peace with yourself and others.

(Reproduced with kind permission from *Feel the Fear . . . and Do it Anyway*, by Susan Jeffers, Rider Publishing, 1994)

Understanding the links between thoughts, feelings and actions

Negative thoughts and feelings produce negative, non-assertive passive behaviour. This means that when we feel bad about ourselves, have low feelings of self-worth, we are less likely to stand up for ourselves when bullied and harassed.

In addition, as already stated, even when we are feeling OK, the impact of bullying and harassment can be a big blow to our self-worth. It is therefore essential to repair our confidence and levels of esteem.

The following diagrams (Figures 6–8), adapted from a model by Anni Townend, *Developing Assertiveness*, show the link between thinking, feeling and actions which are influenced by the situation you may be in.

Figure 6 shows how a situation is linked to thoughts and feelings (our mental processes), which in turn produce body sensations and influences our behaviour (our physical processes).

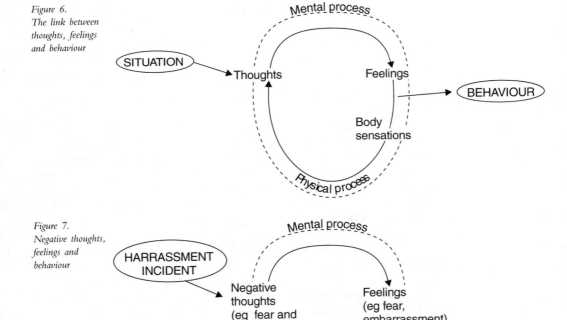

Figure 6.
The link between
thoughts, feelings
and behaviour

Figure 7.
Negative thoughts,
feelings and
behaviour

If we are in a negative situation, such as the experience of harass-ment, negative thoughts and feelings will produce uncomfortable body sensations, and we will behave non-assertively, as Figure 7 shows.

Positive thinking is essential to the process of empowerment. Whilst experiencing harassment is one of the most difficult and negative sit-uations we can face, Figure 8 shows that positive, confident thinking will produce assertive behaviour, and make the situation easier to deal with.

Figure 8.
Positive thoughts,
feelings and
behaviour

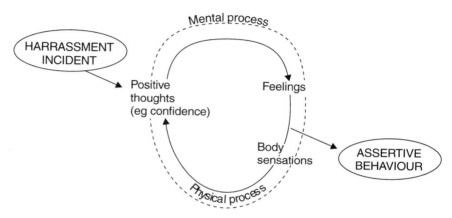

Affirmations

Affirmations are one of the most important elements of raising our levels of self-worth. To affirm means to "make firm". An affirmation is a strong, positive statement that something is already so. It is a way of "making firm" that which you are imagining.

Most of us are aware of the fact that we have a nearly continuous "inner dialogue" going on in our minds. The mind is busy "talking" to itself, keeping up an endless commentary about life, the world, our feelings, our problems, other people, etc.

The practice of making affirmations allows us to begin replacing some of our stale, worn-out or negative mind chatter with more pos-itive ideas and concepts. It is a powerful technique, one which can in a short time completely transform our attitudes and expectations about life, and thereby totally change what we create for ourselves.

An affirmation can be any positive statement. It can be very gen-eral or very specific. Here are some examples:

> *"I am a warm, intelligent woman, sharing my love for myself*
> *and others with serenity and grace."*

"When nothing is sure, everything is possible."

"Only as I am aware of the present will I have the opportunity to be fully alive."

The aim of positive thinking is to improve your self-worth. Other strategies for doing this concentrate on the use of language. Develop a strategy to improve your self-worth by changing sentences beginning with:

should . . .   into could
must   . . .   into might
have   . . .   into choose to
ought . . .   into prefer to

Why do this? To give ourselves choices, control and to lessen the power of guilt! We use words like "should", "must", "have to", "ought to" as a stick to beat ourselves with, and deny ourselves choices of action.

We can create choices, involve others and not feel guilty for doing so. These words also leave us in control: we are doing what we want to, working with others and respecting their rights, whilst respecting our right to ask and make choices too.

These choices can also extend to choosing to take action on harassment and bullying when it occurs. If we take action on these issues out of choice rather than from a "should" or "must" position, we are in control, instead of allowing some external pressures or internal negative self-talk to take over.

Becoming stress fit

One of the ways in which our internal power is lowered is by experiencing unhealthy stress. Harassment and bullying are extremely stressful occurrences and the stress feelings persist even when the perpetrator has been successfully dealt with, the behaviour no longer exists and the harasser has departed the workplace. However, stress itself is something which comes from the inside, and although we can often point to people and events as being connected to our reactions, they are not the only causes. To live with stress effectively, we must either change the circumstances or change ourselves. This is not easy and many of us might find it simpler to blame someone or something else which is beyond our control. The reality is, however, that in the long term, this approach will not work.

Peter Tyrer in his book *How to Cope with Stress* defines stress as *"the reaction of the mind and body to change"*. This is a very broad definition; however, the key issue for him is whether we adapt to the change when we notice it has taken place.

In a similar definition Caroline Toll and Eve Warren, in their book *The Stress Work Book*, describe stress as *"A response to the perceived relationship between the demands on us and our ability to cope"*. If we fail to cope or take action, the stress becomes distress and leads to mental and physical unease.

Some changes are so unpleasant that initial stress moves on quickly to distress – this is often seen in cases of harassment, bullying and violence (the symptoms of such distress have already been described in this chapter). So, what must we do to get "stress fit" in such a situation?

Action steps

Toll and Warren describe the process of becoming stress fit as "Training for Stress-Fitness", and the letters of the word TRAIN are a useful aid to remembering the steps we need to take in order to maintain healthy levels of stress:

T   is for talking
R   is for relaxing
A   is for activities
I   is for interests
N   is for nourishing

Let's talk about it

An important stress-buster is talking. Never bottle up your problems and worries; talk about them and build up support for yourself. Talk to people you trust, such as your immediate friends and family – they care for you and will want to assist. Talk to people you trust at work and with those who could help you deal with the harassment or bullying objectively, such as your boss or supervisor (assuming he/she is not the harasser!), a close colleague, confidential adviser, union representative or personnel or HR officer.

You could also talk to your local Citizen's Advice Bureau or your doctor, who could refer to you a counsellor if you want to talk to someone on a more professional basis.

Relaxation

Aspects of stress such as palpitations, headaches, digestive problems and difficulties in concentrating show that our mind and body are out of balance and inharmonious. We need to restore that balance. Dealing with the situation causing us distress will help in the long and short term, but we might need to get ourselves into a better frame of mind to tackle it. Relaxation methods have an important role to play here. The stress symptoms are the body's means of preparing for fight or flight. We need to channel that energy and simultaneously gain some inner stability or peace.

Body awareness plays an essential part in learning how to relax – once we learn to identify our areas of tension and stress, it becomes easier to adopt the right techniques to help you to relax. Breathing is a vital key to this process, and there are a variety of methods and theories designed to help us breathe effectively.

Activities – keeping fit

This is an important mechanism in the fight against unhealthy stress. Keeping fit helps us to manage the stress we are experiencing currently, and gives us additional resources to deal with future stressful situations. Physical exercise helps us maintain the mind and body balance and to alleviate frustration and anxiety by channelling the "fight or flight" energy into action. The palpitations and panic attacks we may have are due to an excess production of adrenaline as part of the "fight or flight" syndrome.

The type of activity you undertake will depend upon your lifestyle and preferences: anything from swimming and dancing to T'ai Chi and Yoga will help deal with the excess adrenaline and ease the panic attacks or palpitations. Exercise which increases the heartbeat and makes you a little breathless (not uncomfortable or in pain) is helpful. If you are in a stressful situation at work, try to refocus and relax your mind by taking a swift walk at an appropriate time (e.g. at a lunch break). Exercise also produces endorphins in the brain which are linked to feelings of pleasure – it does us good and boosts our self-worth, and is a vital component in combating unhealthy stress.

Interests

Having a life outside of our main area of stress helps to maintain the mind and body balance needed to cope with unhealthy stress. Active interests help us to keep a perspective on the pressures that we may face through harassment and bullying experiences, and give us additional physical release and emotional support. Interests can be pursued alone or in groups, as long as they are ones that we choose to under-

take, and which stimulate us on an emotional, spiritual or social level.
Types of activities include:

- listening to, or actively participating in, music
- reading books, magazines and papers
- doing something creative, such as writing or painting, or taking up a craft or hobby
- watching favourite television shows
- joining a religious group and practising your beliefs
- taking part in voluntary and/or community work.

Nourishing

Most people, when learning to use computers for the first time, are taught to remember "GIGO – Garbage In Garbage Out"! If you put rubbish into a computer, it will only give out rubbish. The same applies to our bodies: we must learn to nurture ourselves physically and emotionally, and not take in anything that will damage our health and general well-being.

On a physical level, cutting down on addictions such as smoking, alcohol, drugs and food by finding a diet that is balanced to suit our lifestyle helps. Emotionally, treating ourselves to "safe" pleasures and activities on a regular basis (such as massage, aromatherapy, buying inexpensive gifts or the occasional luxury, etc) keeps us motivated and our minds stimulated.

These methods will help us cope with stress – they will not make the stress go away. However, the ability to use assertive behaviour helps us to stay in charge of ourselves. Remember:

"We may not be able to control the circumstances we are in – however, we can control our response to those circumstances."

Using assertiveness and developing interpersonal skills

Equality is the value which underpins assertiveness, and it plays a significant role when learning new behaviours which empower individuals. Acquiring and using assertiveness skills ensures clear, direct communication skills which are underpinned by mutuality and the acknowledgement of rights.

Harassment and bullying represent a clear transgression of the rights of an individual by the harasser or bully. So, how does assertiveness assist in reasserting our rights?

Your Rights in Respect of Harassment
● I have the right to be treated with respect and dignity at work.
● I have the right to be appreciated because of my differences.
● I have the right to be seen as an individual, and not to be stereotyped.
● I have the right to say no, and have my choice respected.
● I have the right to maintain my personal values in a professional manner.
● I have the right to carry out my work effectively in a positive working environment.
● I have the right to complain of harassment without fear of reprisal.
● I have the right to have my complaint taken seriously.
● I have the right to challenge any discriminatory behaviours.

First, you have to believe that you have personal rights and that others are entitled to them as well. Second, you need to be able to "stand up" for them in a way which does not merely mirror the behaviour of the transgressor. Here is where the use of clear communication skills comes into play. The main skills of assertive behaviour are outlined in *A Woman in Your Own Right* by Anne Dickson. This book is the standard for assertiveness training and development in the UK, and the skills are just as useful for men as women. They are: deciding what it is you want or feel, saying so specifically and directly, sticking to your statement – repeating it again and again if you have to – and assertively deflecting any response which might undermine you from your assertive stance. Study the following example of a non-assertive (passive) and assertive approach to a particular situation.

Jane is a training officer within a large company. Her team has a new boss called Tony and he has just asked Jane out for a drink after work. Jane has the view that office and social life should be kept separate unless there are very good reasons, and therefore views a casual drink with a boss as being off-bounds.

Non-assertive response:

Jane: *"Well, it's very nice of you, and I hope you don't think I'm being rude, but I can't make it tonight."*

Tony: *"What about tomorrow night, then? I've got nothing arranged."*

Jane: *"Er, I think I've got something on."*

Tony: *"When are you free? I don't mind fitting in with you."*

Jane: *"Um, well, let me have a look in my diary – I haven't got it on me at the moment – and I'll let you know."*

Assertive response:

Jane: *"Thank you for the offer, but no, I don't want to go for a drink."*

Tony: *"What's the problem? It's only a drink."*

Jane: *"I appreciate your view, however I don't want to go out."*

Tony: *"What have I done to offend you? Why can't we go out for a quiet drink and get to know each other a bit better away from work?"*

Jane: *"I know that you would like to get to know me better, however I like to keep my work and social life apart. It's a general rule of mine and I'd like you to accept that please, Tony."*

Notice, in the assertive response, how Jane kept on using the simple phrase "I don't want to go out" and deflected Tony's attempts at persuasion by using aspects of his own language, acknowledging his point of view and assertively repeating her own. This technique of repetition is known as "the broken record", as it is reminiscent of a record which has got stuck in a particular groove and repeats the same bars of music over and over again. It is a skill small children often demonstrate when they want an answer to their question or want you to do something for them. Although very effective, it needs to be used with caution and balance – overdoing the technique can also appear aggressive, possibly provoking an angry harasser into behaving violently.

The other appropriate communication skills that Jane could have used in this situation include:

- listening
- clarifying her position and Tony's
- checking out any assumptions made
- using open and closed questions
- using "I" statements
- differentiating between what you think and feel, know and imagine
- using positive self-talk
- talking the same language
- using appropriate non-verbal behaviour.

Behaving assertively depends on the extent to which you use good, appropriate communication skills. One of the best ways to develop these skills is to find an assertiveness course or workshop which allows you to practise them in a safe learning environment. The more you can use assertiveness, the less chance there will be of experiencing harassment and bullying on a long-term basis.

Taking action

Should I complain?

One of the features of research undertaken into bullying and harassment, in particular sexual harassment, shows that only a small proportion of cases are ever reported and, therefore, acted upon. In The Industrial Society survey *No Offence?*, which concentrates on the experience of sexual harassment, although 45% of respondents experienced harassment, only 5% used their organisation's grievance process to complain about the incident.

Why don't people complain?

Some of the reasons why there are so few complaints of harassment include:

● fear of loss of job
● that the stress involved will be too much to bear – especially if the case goes to an employment tribunal
● that colleagues will brand complainants as trouble-makers
● that even if a complaint were to be made, the organisation would do nothing about it.

These fears are very real, and, sadly, are often borne out by organisational practice. The following case study highlights some of the costs of complaining.

Case Study

The Cost of Complaining

Sexual Discrimination Claims by Susan Clark and Annabel Heseltine
Samantha Phillips joined the many women who have made sexual discrimination claims against employers. But when the case is won, is the struggle really over?

The spotlight was occupied by Samantha Phillips, who had been at the centre of the "bimbo" broker case. The 28-year-old City worker had claimed that she was sacked for rejecting the sexual advances of a boss who had snubbed her at an office conference with the words, "Back down, bimbo".

In fact, the tribunal threw out Phillips's sexual harassment claims and pronounced that her business attitude had been "foolish", but did conclude that her former employer, the insurance firm Willis Corroon, had an "unconscious" attitude of sexual discrimination against women. The ruling that she had been unfairly sacked or "catapulted out of the door", as the tribunal chairman put it, left her with a payout of £18,000.

After the hearing, Phillips met the waiting cameras with a confident smile and the words: "I'm so relieved and delighted. I'm very satisfied with the way things have turned out." But her next sentence hinted at the ambivalence of the outcome of many such tribunals: "You never feel vindicated entirely." Phillips now runs a monthly newsletter for Lloyd's brokers, but, for many women, after the victory champagne has been drunk and the photographers have gone, a very different story starts to unfold.

Although tribunals can order a re-instatement, such orders are rare; more frequently, the complainant is compensated for loss of earnings in a one-off settlement and must look for other employment. If she does manage to hang on to her job, there is every chance that she will return to an office where she has now been branded a troublemaker, and find herself facing such a degree of insidious, covert victimisation from resentful colleagues both male and female that it is impossible to stay on. She may decide, to hell with it, she'll get another job. But when prospective employers see the words "industrial tribunal" on her application form as the reason for leaving her last position, she'll be lucky to get a letter acknowledging her application, let alone an interview.

In 1993, the number of complaints by women over sexual harassment at work which were investigated by the Equal Opportunities Commission (EOC) soared by 58% to a record high of 793. The Commission, which backed more than 100 cases actually brought to tribunal between 1990 and 1993, attributes this rise to the fact that women have become increasingly aware that they can challenge such behaviour and take legal action. What is also becoming increasingly clear, though, is that while may of these women do win their legal battle, their victory often marks the start of a much tougher personal struggle to be accepted in the workplace afterwards.

Alyson Rose, [then] spokeswoman for the EOC, warns "Although there is no official research on what happens to women who have brought a sexual harassment case, we know the majority end up leaving their jobs, which is very unfair on those who have been building a career path."

Louise, a bus driver from the Midlands, did keep her job after her employers, fearful of adverse publicity, settled her union-backed sexual harassment claim out of court.

Her problems had started when she was promoted over male colleagues, who responded with a year-long campaign of harassment which included using obscene language in her presence, and commenting on her sexuality and what she may have done to get the promotion.

Since the claim was settled and the ringleaders taken to task with letters of warning, Louise says that half her colleagues still refuse to talk to her and that she faces an undercurrent of hatred each and every working day. "There hasn't been any overt victimisation like before, they wouldn't dare step out of line like that again, but I am careful to keep myself to myself. I hate my job now, but I have to stay because it pays the mortgage. The symptoms that women who have been sexually harassed have to live with are the same as those suffered by rape victims. I find it hard to trust anybody now, and that is a scar I will carry for the rest of my life."

Paulette Keating, [then] co-ordinator for Women Against Sexual Harassment (WASH), says: "Women never find it easy to resume normal working relations in the same workplace, even when they have won their case.

The office is usually divided in its sympathies and there is often a lot of bad feeling. Management may harbour resentment over being forced to dismiss a senior executive whose work they valued, which can mean further victimisation for the woman."

A North London woman who was sexually harassed by her boss and dismissed from her £180 per week job at a courier company was awarded a total compensation of £24,000. The tribunal heard how the company director had exposed himself to the woman, pushed her against a wall and indecently assaulted her. He was eventually convicted of two charges of indecent assault and jailed for 18 months after the woman was wired by the police. The woman, who said she was delighted with the ruling, was also quick to add: "I would never work in an all-male environment again."

Diana Worman, [then] a policy adviser with the Institute of Personnel Management specialising in equal opportunities, believes women who rightly fight for their principles pay an unfair price. "It takes great courage and guts to bring an action for sexual harassment when you have no way of knowing if you are going to be penalised for it, whether you win or lose. And if you tell the truth about why you left your old job, you risk being branded a troublemaker by prospective employers who don't want any hassle, even if they think your case was justified."

Anyone faced with the dilemma of whether to enter the fray can take heart from the one sentiment widely expressed by women who have taken their courage in their hands, and their cases to the courts, namely, a sense of pride in the fact that they stood up for themselves against something they believed to be morally and legally wrong.

"The nightmare I went through because of the men who harassed me was worse than divorce," says Louise, "but I would take the same steps again because it is vital to fight against sexual harassment."

(From an article written by Susan Clark and Annabel Heseltine, *Sunday Times*, 14 August 1994. Reproduced with kind permission of *The Times*. © Times Newspapers Limited, 1994/5)

Clearly, taking on a case of harassment is not easy and it gets more personally difficult as the case progresses up the judicial system. However, before all hope is lost, we need to consider the following before giving in and doing nothing:

- If I do or say nothing, will the harassment go away?
- Is the trauma of bringing a case or challenging the harasser greater than the current trauma suffered as a target/victim of harassment or bullying?
- Is the situation tolerable – can I stand it? If so, for how long?
- Is my mental and physical health already suffering?
- What are the knock-on effects of this situation on those I love and/or live with?

Bringing a case or challenging the harasser or bully is certainly not an easy task, but what are the consequences for you if you decide to do or say nothing? Only you can make that judgement.

Challenging the harasser and making a complaint

What will happen to me if I make a complaint?
There are a variety of remedies which can be sought when dealing with cases of harassment within the organisation:

1. Challenging the harasser or bully yourself – asking him/her to stop.
2. Discussing the situation with your boss or someone else in the organisation.
3. Resorting to the grievance or harassment procedures at work.
4. Resorting to the law and legal remedies if all else fails.

Ideally, few cases should ever go to tribunal – it would be preferable for the organisation to deal with the situation appropriately internally. However, organisations do not always act appropriately or legally. Books like this will inevitably focus on the cases that are mishandled, because a learning process needs to take place within British industry to ensure that these cases, and others like them, do not occur again. Sadly, we do not focus so rigorously on the examples of organisations who have excellent policies, procedures and healthy workplace cultures. The good news is that they do exist!

Sometimes the thought of taking formal action seems an enormous step to take, and those who are suffering harassment feel that their case is too unimportant to burden anyone with. But what are the consequences of not making a complaint or at least asking the harasser to stop?

The consequences of not making a complaint

Some of the consequences of inaction could include the following:

● Others are harassed and bullied – the harasser may harass others as well as you.
● Stress symptoms may turn into more serious illnesses.
● The harassment you are experiencing may escalate and lead to physical violence.

A complaint by you could lead to others complaining – sometimes people who harass have a history of such activity, but no one ever makes a complaint. Whether the complaint is informal or formal, making it is very difficult. It may seem that there is so much to lose, and yet the consequences of not complaining are so far-reaching. Sometimes it is helpful to start by taking small actions and seeing what the outcomes are. There have been incidents where targets of harassment have responded by taking very simple forms of action which have nipped the behaviour in the bud, as in the following case study.

Case Study

The Greatest Tool of the Oppressor is the Mind of the Oppressed
Sarah worked in a hospital as a nurse. The only blot on her landscape came from Adrian, one of the orderlies. He insisted on making sexual innuendoes about her appearance in the presence of male patients and liked to touch her should she happen to come near him. After several weeks of this, Sarah had had enough. She went to see her union representative and asked what she could do. They talked through the situation and the union rep gave Sarah a leaflet on the union's policy on sexual harassment. Sarah decided that she would leave the leaflet on Adrian's desk in a prominent position. The harassment stopped.

Sometimes, a simple "no" or statement such as "please don't touch me like that, it's inappropriate" can have the power to bring people to their senses. However, making such a challenge does necessitate courage, an assertive approach and firm handling. Before going ahead with a formal complaint, think about the following:

● Are my friends and family supportive?
● Organisational support – where would I go, where would it come from?
● If the harasser or bully is a manager, will the complaint be taken seriously?

- Is harassment endemic in the culture?
- Do I feel uncomfortable or threatened at work?
- Do I have outside support if things go wrong?
- Do I have the stamina to go it alone if necessary?
- Is it affecting my home life, my personality and my relationships with others?

Confronting the harasser yourself will help in the process of empowerment: it will boost your confidence and self-worth, and assist in alleviating some of the stress. However, as already stated, this is a difficult process. The following steps are excellent guidelines (adapted from *A Woman in Your Own Right*) and will help you to handle the confrontation assertively:

Handling a confrontation

- **Tell someone that you have decided to confront the individual about their behaviour** – Particularly important if you are going to do this alone. Confrontation, however assertively it is handled, always has an element of risk, and the individual being confronted may use aggression as a form of response.
- **Choose the time and place carefully** – Remember, this is a formal meeting which has been arranged to achieve an end result.
An isolated office after working hours is not the right environment for this type of meeting. An informal chat in a wine bar or a pub gives conflicting messages about the serious nature of this confrontation.
- **If necessary have a friend or colleague with you** – Never feel that you have to confront someone alone. Choose someone who will be willing to act as a witness on your behalf if the situation does not improve.
- **Describe specifically the behaviour to which you are objecting** – "You make me feel nervous" is not as specific or as descriptive as "You stand too near when you are talking to me, and this makes me feel nervous."
- **Don't label the person, just the behaviour** – It is perfectly legitimate to criticise the process a person uses, but not them. Separating people from the problem allows you to focus on the issue at hand, which is to change behaviour that you find unacceptable.
- **Identify exactly what you would like changed, and in which ways you would like their behaviour to be different** – For example, "I would feel more comfortable if you sat at the desk with me to explain your work, rather than standing over my desk and bending forward." Concentrating on changes in specific behaviour prevents labelling people and reinforces positive messages of improvements in working relationships.
- **State clearly what you will do next if their behaviour continues** – If it means making a formal complaint to senior management or taking out a grievance against the individual, refer to your organisation's procedure on

dealing with complaints of harassment. If your organisation does not have a complaints procedure, make your complaint externally (to a Citizen's Advice Bureau, legal adviser, or, if appropriate, the police).

● **Don't make empty statements, mean what you are saying** – This is vital. If you state that you will make a formal complaint, and do not carry out the action when the person continues to harass you, this will be seen as an open invitation for them to continue the harassment, and abuse their use of power by using aggression.

● **At the end of the meeting, restate clearly what has been discussed and agreed** – This helps to clarify your position, and gives the individual being confronted about their behaviour an opportunity to agree or disagree with any of the actions. If necessary negotiate assertively to gain a commitment to actions which will change behaviour.

● **Write up this meeting in detail, for future reference if necessary** – The actions from this meeting may become important evidence if the situation worsens and it gets to tribunal stage. In addition, keep a diary of events and write down everything – however insignificant it may seem at the time. Also, offer to give the individual confronted a copy of the meeting's actions.

● **Take the matter further if there is no change in the behaviour identified** – Use your organisation's formal complaints or disciplinary and grievance procedures to resolve the issue if the harasser's behaviour continues.

Informal written complaints

Keeping a diary of events can help you keep focused about the harassing behaviour – it can be an essential source of evidence and could prove invaluable if ever you submit your complaint to a tribunal. Keep a note of the incident(s), detail changes of behaviour in the perpetrator(s), include time and dates of incidents and also any potential witnesses to the incidents.

If you are going to write to the harasser(s) informally about their behaviour, the following letter, adapted from a publication by WASH (Women Against Sexual Harassment), is an excellent guideline:

Dear . . .

I am writing to complain about what you did/said to me on (*date*) when you (*describe behaviour*).

or

Over the previous months you have (*describe behaviour specifically*). I want you to stop this behaviour now/I want you to stop harassing me.

or

I find this behaviour offensive and unacceptable. I am keeping a copy of this letter and I shall take further action if you do not stop immediately.

optional

I would like to talk to you (with a colleague present) about ways in which we can ensure this behaviour is not repeated.

Yours sincerely

(Adapted from *Guide to Legal Action*, Women Against Sexual Harassment)

Strategies for managing your boss

The relationship between managers and subordinates is a delicate one. If it works well, everyone in the organisation stands to benefit. If it falls apart, the damage can be difficult to repair.

Most of us have to work with bosses – few can escape them. Even if you are self-employed, clients soon take on the mantle of a boss who needs to be managed with special care. It is essential to remember to treat your boss with the dignity and respect that you would treat other colleagues, even when the relationship is breaking down. It can be tempting to behave unassertively when fighting difficult situations with your manager. However, this will probably work against you, especially as they may have more positional power than you. Behaviour breeds behaviour, and the more professionally you behave, the harder it will be for your boss to behave negatively towards you.

Create an effective working relationship with your manager by making it clear that you wish to work effectively with her/him. Keep emphasising this, especially when things are not going well.

Evaluate your relationship with your boss from time to time. The following questionnaire may be helpful.

Relationship with your boss

In the following questionnaire, indicate a point on the five-point scale (Low [1] to High [5]) which best describes the state of that aspect of your relationship with your boss. A high score indicates a strong supportive relationship, a low score indicates the reverse.

1. How much confidence and trust do you feel your superior has in you?   1 2 3 4 5
2. To what extent does your boss convey to you a feeling of confidence that you can do your job successfully?   1 2 3 4 5
3. Does your boss expect the "impossible" and fully believe you can and will do it?   1 2 3 4 5
4. To what extent is your superior interested in helping you to achieve and maintain a good income?   1 2 3 4 5
5. To what extent does your superior try to understand your problems and do something about them?   1 2 3 4 5
6. How much is your superior really interested in helping you with your personal and family problems?   1 2 3 4 5
7. How much help do you get from your superior in doing your work?   1 2 3 4 5
8. How much is your boss interested in training you?   1 2 3 4 5
9. How much does she/he help you solve your problems constructively – not tell you the answer but help you think through your problems?   1 2 3 4 5
10. To what extent does she/he see that you get the supplies, budget, equipment, etc, you need to do your job well?   1 2 3 4 5
11. To what extent does your superior try to keep you informed about matters related to your job?   1 2 3 4 5
12. To what extent is your boss interested in helping you get the training which will assist you in being promoted?   1 2 3 4 5
13. How fully does your superior share information with you about the company, its financial condition, earnings, etc, or does she/he keep such information to themselves?   1 2 3 4 5
14. Does your superior ask your opinion when a problem comes up which involves your work? Does he/she value your ideas and seek to use them?   1 2 3 4 5
15. Is your superior friendly and easy to approach?   1 2 3 4 5
16. To what extent is your superior generous in the credit and recognition given to others for their accomplishments and contributions rather than seeking to claim all credit for themselves?   1 2 3 4 5

Examine any items that received a very low score and ask yourself:

● What discourages my boss from being supportive in this area?
● What changes in my behaviour would encourage more support from my boss?
● What feedback can I constructively give to my boss in order to facilitate positive changes?

Make it your goal to understand your manager's style, and help her/him to understand yours. If you and your manager are communicating effectively, the likelihood of harassment or bullying occurring is slim.

If you are being harassed by your immediate boss, the situation is often more stressful. Most organisational policies tell you how to proceed in this case. Usually the first point of contact in such situations is another manager at the same level in the organisation. Alternatively, it could be your manager's manager. If you are thinking about making a complaint against your boss, your company's harassment policy should indicate the appropriate route.

In the absence of an appropriate policy, contact either a trade union/staff association representative, or the HR/personnel function. Either of them will be well placed to intervene, or to simply give advice. In smaller organisations where there is no formal HR/personnel function, and no union or staff association representation, go to your local Citizen's Advice Bureau or law centre for support.

In terms of the interpersonal relationship, there will undoubtedly be difficulties. If a formal complaint is made, your employer, having a duty to provide you with a safe working environment, should, as a minimum, move your boss for the duration of the investigation. In the event of your allegations being proven, your employer, again as a minimum, may move your boss permanently to an area in which there will be no opportunity for him/her subsequently to harass or victimise you. Whatever happens, do not allow yourself to be alone with him/her and take a friend/representative with you to every meeting. Good employment practice would ensure that the alleged harasser and victim/target are never in the same room together until the issue is dealt with satisfactorily, or the case goes before a disciplinary hearing.

Seeking professional assistance

Gaining the support of friends and family is invaluable during the process of challenging harassment. However, there are times when professional assistance is needed, an external supporter who is not involved with the process in any way and is there purely for you. If this is the case, then it might be appropriate to consult a counsellor or psychotherapist in order to deal with some of the serious emotional issues harassment, bullying and incidents of violence can bring up. Some organisations operate, and are part of an Employee Assistance Programme (EAP), which offers counselling free of charge to their employees.

Another source of professional assistance can be found via the trade unions – if you are a member of one. Organisations that recognise trade unions will allow you to bring in a trade union officer to represent you at any part of this process. Even where there is no recognition agreement in your organisation, and you are a union member, a trade union will still be able to provide you with significant personal support and free legal and procedural advice.

We have already mentioned the effects that harassment can have in terms of stress and illness. In very serious cases of abuse and violence, individuals may be traumatised by their experience and suffer Post-traumatic Stress Disorder (PTSD).

PTSD is a serious medical condition which is brought on by the effects of a traumatic incident. PTSD may emerge days, weeks or months after the trauma, and can have devastating psychological effects on a victim. It can also affect witnesses or observers of abusive and violent behaviour. Some of the signs of PTSD include:

● bouts of clinical depression and anxiety
● re-experiencing the traumatic incident that caused the initial stress
● repeated dreams and nightmares
● suffering sleep disturbances not previously experienced before
● avoiding situations likely to lead to remembering the event
● feelings of detachment and/or disorientation
● mild to extreme behaviour patterns not normally associated with the victim.

It is vital that anyone displaying a combination of these signs seeks immediate medical attention for proper diagnosis and clinical treatment.

Witnessing harassment

To speak out against an incident of harassment as a witness takes an enormous amount of courage. Maya Angelou, writer and poet, once said when interviewed on the subject of challenging discrimination, "It is easy to say I abhor bigotry and prejudice, but in the office, when someone tells the near-to-the-bone joke that you object to, it takes courage to face the abuse and the name calling, the shunning and the silences when you stand up for what you believe in."

The ability to challenge discrimination is the true test of courage. But it is sometimes a process which is fraught with problems. Those who challenge harassment and bullying might well be afraid of reprisals; of being shunned by colleagues, and resented as a trouble-maker. Others might fear the loss of work prospects within the organisation or a fracturing of team spirit and long-held friendships. Those things can be hard to bear – even for the most courageous. Hence the need for organisations and individuals to support those who bring cases and act as witnesses or give corroborating evidence. On a practical note, it is important to remember that the legislation underpinning harassment does give protection to those who witness incidents of discrimination from victimisation.

There is also the personal conflict of whether what you reveal as a witness will have an impact on the future of the individuals involved in the incident. It may almost feel as if your involvement is contributing to the detriment or pain of the complainant and alleged harasser, particularly if you may have seen something, but were not sure exactly what. In cases like this, remember that you have a role to play in providing truthful information that will help to resolve the conflict, and the responsibility (however great it may feel) of what happens to the individuals concerned does not directly rest with you as a witness.

Have you been accused of harassment and bullying?

It is not uncommon when people are accused of harassment to see horror and dismay written all over their faces. "I didn't know they felt like that" or "No harm was meant, I didn't think they would take it seriously" are some of the remarks often heard when their behaviour is challenged.

When such a situation arises for you, ask yourself: "What aspect of my behaviour has been interpreted as unacceptable?" Rarely do people bring malicious complaints of harassment and usually the person who has been subjected to bullying and harassing behaviour simply wants it to stop, and seeks an apology, or at least recognition from the harasser or bully that their behaviour has overstepped the boundaries of acceptability.

In addition to questioning what aspects of your behaviour might be unacceptable, examine how the relationship between you and your accuser has broken down – because it clearly has – as this may give pointers to understanding why your behaviour may be interpreted as unacceptable, and might enable you to improve the relationship.

However, there are always the few who are well aware of the impact of their behaviour on others, yet continue to abuse working relationships and their personal or positional power.

Figure 9.
Brainstorming
session with
confidential
advisers from the
Consumer
Association

Why harass?

The figure below charts some of the main reasons why people harass others:

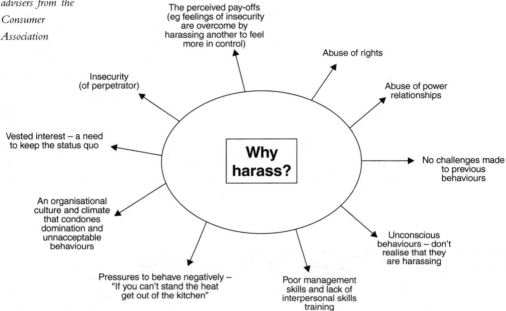

Abuse of power relationships

Harassment is perceived as involving a profound abuse of power: power of one individual over another due to status, gender, race, physical strength, ability, sexuality, etc. For example, in the case of sexual harassment, men abuse their societal status and power over women – be they junior, senior or on the same rung of the organisational hierarchy. This work status is not where true power lies; the main definition of power has its source within society itself and the higher value it places on the masculine over the feminine. When men harass and bully women, this act is a manifestation of an abuse of that power. Should the men who harass be in a more senior position than the women they harass, that represents a double abuse of power.

No challenges made to previous behaviours

As stated earlier on in this chapter, it is sometimes the case that harassers and bullies have a history of such behaviour and that this is common knowledge to many within the organisation. For whatever reason – absence of policy, organisational culture, the individual's status, etc – nothing has been done to challenge this behaviour and consequently these individuals have been allowed to carry on unchecked and unrecorded. This can set up a permission within the organisation/ department for others to abuse. If someone else has exhibited these behaviours and remained unchecked, a message is being sent out to others that the organisation will condone such actions, by being lenient or closing their eyes when it is being exhibited. It is therefore essential that an environment of safety be created within the workplace so that such challenges can be made and taken seriously.

Unconscious behaviours – don't realise that they are harassing

Some people do not realise the impact of their behaviour, and that their behaviour constitutes harassment. These people should be made aware of the impact of their actions, that it is unacceptable and could have serious consequences if the behaviour persists. What is unconscious must be made conscious, and relevant personnel need to challenge the unconscious mindset this person holds. This will lead them to a better understanding of why they think and behave in the way they do, and assist them in learning new and more appropriate behaviours. This is a difficult procedure, as the facilitator will need to keep up the process of challenge and help the harasser use the fear and anxiety they will be feeling to progress through their period of change.

Poor management skills and lack of interpersonal skills training

Management style is a controversial issue when discussing bullying and harassment. If managers are unaware of their personal style when dealing with members of their team, or send out conflicting messages, accusations of discrimination increase.

A management style which believes in exerting pressure to gain results will often lead to bullying and harassment, and will cause stress and worries about job security. Often this management style has its roots in the organisation's task-oriented culture, and therefore the organisation needs to look at the impact of such a culture and encourage its management to develop a high concern for people as well as for the task.

Most importantly, managers must formulate good interpersonal relationships with all those they work with, and organisations in their recruitment and selection procedures need to be vigilant in this area. The cost of appointing managers who lack people management skills is considerable and cannot be measured simply in loss of productivity. The calibre of an organisation's managers sends out a profound message about how the organisation views itself and its staff. Training can be given to managers who have deficient skills in this area. Increasingly, however, organisations are coming to the view that whilst there are certain aspects of work which can be taught, good inter-personal skills is not necessarily one of those areas.

Pressures to behave negatively

In an organisation which is very results-orientated, it is tempting to use the motto "If you can't stand the heat, get out of the kitchen". However, it is just such an ethos that leads to bullying and harass-ment, because concern for results takes precedence over the well-being of the individuals in the organisation. In Chapter 5 this book docu-ments the kinds of workplaces which are more likely to succumb to the pressures to behave negatively, and they ought to heed the results of research which show that companies which consistently perform well are usually those which combine high task concerns with a high concern for the well-being of the workforce. To become such an organisation will mean that attention must be paid to the company's culture, which necessitates an appropriate modelling of required behav-iour from those at the top of the organisation to facilitate change throughout.

Organisational culture and climate

The impact of organisational culture cannot be stated too highly, and Chapter 5 has been devoted entirely to this issue. Culture sets the boundaries as to what is and what is not acceptable behaviour. Changing an organisation's culture and climate is not easy and takes time, but specific actions will give a company clear indications about its levels of health or toxicity. Remember that people will learn and perform better in healthy cultures than they will in abusive ones.

Vested interest – a need to keep the status quo

Many people resist change and harassers will resist attempts to change the status quo, particularly if it might result in a change in their envi-ronment which will facilitate openness. Those who work in a task-oriented organisation might also resist change if they feel that it will work to their detriment financially or personally.

If organisations are serious about combating harassment and bully-ing they need to identify what the vested interests are and whether they are healthy. Obviously organisations are concerned with the bottom line, but the bottom line can be adversely affected in the short and long term by climates of fear, stress-related illnesses and the loss of skilled employees.

Change is a constant in our lives, and organisations must be able to use it positively. As work environments alter, they need to ensure that a high quality working environment only improves – it must not decline.

Insecurity of the perpetrator

Some people harass because of their personal insecurities and negative self-images. Sometimes perpetrators are unaware of the consequences of their behaviour and possess poor interpersonal skills.

The perceived pay-offs

People who harass as a result of insecurity do so because their feelings of uncertainty and negativity are overcome by harassing another person and gaining a position of power over them. There are pay-offs to harassment and these will vary according to the personality of the perpetrator and sometimes according to the environment in which they take place. Pay-offs can include feelings of power, the granting of sexual favours, an increased status in the eyes of colleagues, etc. These pay-offs, however, are often based on fear, and the harasser will have to live with the prospect of being either found out or made to justify their actions.

Abuse of individual rights

Harassment is ultimately an abuse of power, and where managers are the perpetrators, they are abusing their rights and authority over their staff. All individuals have rights and we have rights in law which stipulate that we should work in a safe environment, without fear for our safety.

Self-awareness – assessing your behaviour

In order to appreciate what aspects of your behaviour may be perceived as unacceptable, it is necessary to have a heightened level of awareness about your own behaviour and what drives it.

First of all, assess your behaviour. Ask yourself:

● Do I use verbal language which is insensitive? How does it come across?
● Am I aware of the effect of my body language? For example, do I stand too close to people?
● Have I let my personal prejudices show through unintentionally?
● Do I express personal views that hurt or discriminate against others?
● Do I reveal my anger or dissatisfaction in ways that offend or frighten others?

Next, assess your feelings. Ask yourself:

● How do I feel about myself as a person at the moment?
● Am I happy or unhappy at work?
● Are things going well for me outside the work environment (for

example, relationships, finances, family)?
● Am I suffering from unhealthy stress?
● Am I managing my stress levels properly?
● How is my health (for example, any illnesses or addictions)?
● Do I feel secure and in control, or insecure and out of control about life generally?

Then, ask yourself:

● How honest have I been with myself when exploring these issues?
● How open, willing and able am I to accept other people's perception of me?

Self-awareness – opening yourself to others

The next stage of raising awareness about your behaviour is seeking feedback from others on how they see you. Encouraging openness in your relationships at work is dependent upon how much trust and honesty exists amongst colleagues. This will be difficult if you have already been told that aspects of your behaviour are unacceptable. However, gaining the courage to seek feedback from your colleagues will help you resolve and learn from the conflict you have engendered.

By taking risks and increasing our level of openness with others we reduce the amount of unconscious behaviour which can cause misunderstandings and accusations of harassment.

If you feel comfortable, share the information from your self-assessment with someone you trust (for example, a close colleague, family member or a counsellor) who will give you honest feedback about your behaviour.

Ultimately, our personal beliefs, feelings and values drive our behaviour. Therefore, if we hold particularly strong views and prejudices, these can be projected negatively on other people who have differing views and values. For example, some men hold the prejudicial view that women should not be working in traditionally male environments. This may be projected by sexually harassing those women who work in these environments, in order to "get rid" of them (Chapter 5 cites an example of this in the fire service).

Similarly, if we are feeling insecure and no longer in control of our feelings, we can project them negatively towards others, and as a defence mechanism see them as being at fault or to blame.

We all hold prejudices and possess values which conflict with others. However, learning our own limitations and improving our level of interpersonal skills is necessary in order to enhance our ability to behave professionally with others. There are no rights and wrongs when interacting with people – what we have to learn to do is not act on bias, but be aware of the effect it has on others and behave appropriately according to the circumstances.

Guilty until proven innocent?

Quite a few harassment procedures have the unfortunate effect of making the accused appear guilty before all the evidence has been collected. It is important that alleged harassers are made aware of their rights whilst the complaint is under investigation, and that they are also entitled to representation (see Chapter 9). Although very few cases of harassment are actually false, sometimes malicious cases are brought – as the following case study demonstrates. When such an instance occurs, all the alleged harasser can do is to seek representation and trust in the impartiality and thoroughness of the process – even if that process might treat him/her as guilty, moving them or even suspending them on full pay.

In instances where malicious allegations of harassment have been brought, it has generally been the case that the accuser has been dismissed as a result of making those allegations.

Case Study

Malicious Intent

"Vernon, a senior architect for a large construction company based in the Midlands, walked into my office looking nervous and uncomfortable. 'I can't believe what is happening to me – I need to talk this through.'

Vernon and I started in the organisation within a couple of days of each other eight years ago, and had developed a supportive working relationship that was necessary in order to combat some of the racism we faced as two of the ten ethnic minority men who worked in the corporate and planning division of the company. As we were the most senior in the organisation, we also depended on each other for support, not only in development issues but also in managing the organisational politics, in which Vernon was now dangerously entangled.

I listened in horror as Vernon related what seemed to be a living nightmare.

Vernon had recently hired a female trainee architect on a short-term contract for a new project. Julia was having difficulties in settling down in the organisation, and Vernon, feeling responsible as her manager, spent a lot of time inducting and coaching her in the first two months of her starting.

Things seemed to be going well, until one of the more experienced members of the team left. Julia applied for the role. However, Vernon felt she still did not have the experience and promoted someone else in the department.

Angry about the decision and Vernon's feedback, Julia's work and her relationship with the team deteriorated. The other members of the team were dissatisfied with the situation, and they felt resentful about having to complete work that Julia did not have the motivation to finish, or deal with her mood swings. Vernon received complaint after complaint, and started to feel uncomfortable about handling the situation.

'I didn't know how to deal with it,' Vernon told me. 'Julia had cut me off totally, and I heard that she had been telling others that I was ineffective with my team and couldn't control them, and that I was allowing them to bully her. I wanted to help her through it, but she would not open up to me and talk.'

Vernon arranged a meeting with Julia, which she didn't turn up to. He then sent her a letter asking her to meet with him again to discuss ways in which they could work on improving her relations with the team. On the day that Julia received the letter, the team was under particular stress because of difficulties with the plans for a particular project. The team did not leave until 7.00pm that evening. Vernon was getting ready to leave, when Julia stormed into his office.

'You're doing this on purpose, aren't you? You didn't get what you wanted from me, and now you are getting the others to turn on me! You pick on my work now, and you never did this before. Is this what you people do when you can't get what you want from us women?' Just as quickly as she stormed in, Julia stormed out of the office. Two members of the team watched in amazement. 'What was that about Vernon?' asked Rob.

'I wasn't shocked, more confused and bewildered about what she was saying. I didn't understand where she was coming from,' Vernon told me later. It was this naivety that got him into the trouble he was now in.

Later, Vernon got a call from our HR office, asking him to attend a meeting. 'Julia has accused you of harassment. She says you are encouraging your team to bully her, because when she first came here, you asked her out and she refused. Julia believes this is the reason why you did not promote her. What do you have to say Vernon?'

What could he say?

'All I could see was a nasty investigation, false accusations flying around, the loss of my job, any promotion prospects, my career in ruins. I couldn't say anything. I thought I had treated her fairly, and now this? Julia was using my colour against me because I wouldn't promote her. Sexual harassment? It was ridiculous.

I knew I had the support of my team, but I didn't think the organisation would support me. They had taken a risk employing me,

> and now I had let them down. As a black man in my position I should know better. You have to keep yourself squeaky clean, and now it would seem as if I had not done so. I have unwittingly reinforced their assumptions and stereotypes. This is my fault, I should have seen the signs. I should have known better,' he kept saying to me.
>
> I listened to all of this, and felt his despair. He needed support, and I felt that I could give it. Maybe things were not as bad as he thought. But I couldn't help thinking: was he being pessimistic, or realistic?"
>
> (Ansell, Vernon's colleague)

In this case study, a good organisational investigation would spot Julia's inability to complete her job satisfactorily as being the root cause of the problem. Starting from the allegation of harassment, no assumptions about guilt or innocence should be made, and, on the basis of the case study as presented, the investigators should find enough inconsistencies to vindicate Vernon. In this situation, it would be confusing at best, and disastrous at worst, to make the assumption that Vernon is guilty and label him a harasser.

Reflection

Those who experience harassment must never be placed in a situation where they are blamed for the harassment and are isolated from the necessary organisational support. As harassment and bullying have their roots in the abuse of power, individuals experiencing harassment must examine how they can reclaim their internal power, and make every attempt (with the appropriate level of support) to stop the harassment from occurring.

People who harass and bully must be given the opportunity to learn that their behaviour is unacceptable and be supported in their efforts to find ways of developing behaviours that encourage good working relationships. However, if there is no commitment to change the abusive behaviour, then the individual cannot expect to remain in any organisation which takes the responsibility of combating harassment, bullying and violence in the workplace seriously.

References

No Offence? Sexual Harassment: How it Happens and How to Beat it (The Industrial Society, 1993).

Typecast (The Industrial Society, 1993).

Sexual Harassment in the Workplace, Ellen J Wagner (AMACOM, 1992).

I'm OK, You're OK, Thomas A Harris (Arrow Books, 1995).

TA Today: A New Introduction to Transactional Analysis, Ian Stewart and Vann Joines (Lifespace Publishing, 1996).

Social Skills in Interpersonal Communication, Owen Hargie, Christine Saunders and David Dickson (Routledge, 1994).

A Woman in Your Own Right, Anne Dickson (Quartet Books, 1982).

Bullying at Work: How to Confront and Overcome it, Andrea Adams (Virago Press, 1992).

Feel the Fear . . . and Do it Anyway, Susan Jeffers (Rider Publishing, 1994).

The Stress Work Book, Caroline Toll and Eve Warren (Nicholas Brearley Publishing, 1992).

Victimology: The Victim and the Criminal Justice Process, Sandra Walklate (Unwin Hyman, 1988).

Counselling: The BAC Counselling Reader, Peter Reynolds and Tricia Allison, edited by Stephen Palmer, Sheila Dainow and Pat Milner (Sage, 1996).

The Heart of the Race: Black Women's Lives in Britain, Beverley Bryan, Stella Dadzie and Suzanne Scafe (Virago Press, 1986).

Developing Assertiveness, Anni Townend (Routledge, 1991).

How to Cope with Stress, Peter Tyrer (Sheldon Publishing, 1980).

CHAPTER 5

Organisational culture and climate

This chapter explores the impact of power on organisational culture and climate, and sets out strategies for developing diversity in an organisation with the object of creating a positive working environment. It also examines those professions and organisations in which harassment and bullying is more likely to be prevalent, and discusses the effects of organisational culture on the behaviour of individuals in the context of harassment and bullying.

What is organisational culture?

The concepts of organisational culture and climate are difficult ones to define precisely. A popular and simple way of defining organisational culture might be "the way things are done around here". Another, more detailed, description might be that culture concerns the underlying assumptions about the way work is performed, what is acceptable and unacceptable, and what behaviours and actions are to be encouraged or discouraged.

Geert Hofstede, author of *Cultures and Organisations*, has done extensive research into this area, and much of his work helps us to understand why harassment and bullying thrive in most organisations. Hofstede once described it as *"a soft holistic concept . . . the psychological assets of an organisation, which can be used to predict what will happen to its financial assets in five years time"*. If ever there was a statement that makes the elimination of discrimination in the workplace good business sense, this is it.

Culture is not inherited by individuals, nor is it about individual behaviour, as is so widely misinterpreted. It is specific to groups and is a set of values and meanings which is learned over time. Culture is one of the three levels of human mental programming which sits between our character and personality and instinctive human nature (see Figure 10).

Figure 10.
Three levels of
human mental
programming

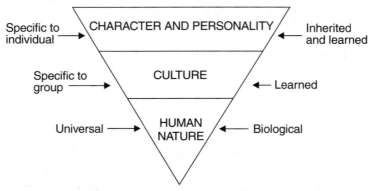

(Adapted from *Cultures and Organisations: Software of the Mind – Intercultural Co-operation and its Importance for Survival*, by Geert Hofstede, HarperCollins, 1994. Reproduced with kind permission of Geert Hofstede)

Figure 11 shows how cultural differences reveal themselves in different ways, from the surface-level symbols within organisations, to the deeper-level values which form the basis of an organisation's existence.

Figure 11.
The depth of
cultural differences

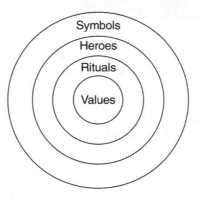

(Adapted from *Cultures and Organisations*, by Geert Hofstede, HarperCollins, 1994)

In addition, each individual brings with them a set of psychological differences which corresponds to the different layers of "cultural programming" they carry (see Figure 12).

Figure 12.
Cultural
programming

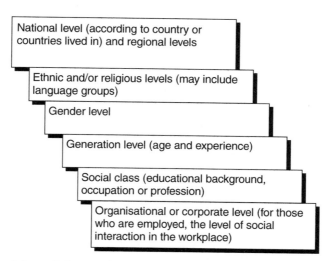

National level (according to country or countries lived in) and regional levels

Ethnic and/or religious levels (may include language groups)

Gender level

Generation level (age and experience)

Social class (educational background, occupation or profession)

Organisational or corporate level (for those who are employed, the level of social interaction in the workplace)

(Adapted from *Cultures and Organisations*, by Geert Hofstede, HarperCollins, 1994. Reproduced with kind permission of Geert Hofstede)

Each person's cultural programming starts as a child when basic values are learned: the differences between good and bad, what is perceived to be right or wrong, normal or abnormal, rational and irrational, etc. If individual values and psychological cultural differences fail to match or are vastly different from that of the organisation they work in, this can create tension and conflict.

[Women working in non-traditional environments provide an example of how cultural differences lead to clashes and incidents of harassment in the workplace. Gender difference is very rarely viewed in terms of culture. Hofstede points out that women are not considered suitable for roles that men traditionally fulfil, even though they may be perfectly capable of carrying out these roles. Women do not carry the symbols, stand up to the hero images, participate in the rituals or sustain the values dominant in the men's culture; and vice versa. [The same intensity of feelings and fears about behaviours exist about ethnic groups as they do about the opposite sex.]

[Research indicates that women in non-traditional environments are subjected to sexual harassment at a higher rate than women in other areas. When women adopt such roles, they are unwittingly confronting institutionalised sexism, based on an ideology of male superiority, which has been going on for hundreds of years.]

Institutions that have recently opened their doors to women do not prepare the majority workforce for their arrival, and inadequate equal opportunities awareness training takes place. It is a difficult task for women to take on, and without the right support, they can often feel isolated, and find themselves in environments which are, in some cases, life-threatening.

Case Study

Women in Non-traditional Environments

The following case study examines the "deeply ingrained culture of hostility" in the fire service.

After a 23-day hearing in Shrewsbury, an industrial tribunal ruled that Tania Clayton's health was broken and her career destroyed by years of harassment and sexual discrimination from male colleagues with a "deeply ingrained culture of hostility". The hearing was told that she was one of the first two women in the fire service when she joined Hereford and Worcester Brigade in 1989 and that sub-officer Ronald East referred to her as a "cow" and told her to get a job in the kitchen. She was later subjected to a "deliberate" and "incredibly cruel" attempt by Gordon Perkins, another sub-officer, to frighten her by making her take a turntable ladder to 100ft and spin it for more than an hour.

She was also made to carry out dangerous drills as punishment and it was clear that male fire-fighters were not subjected to the same "harsh and unfriendly regime".

The tribunal also said that she was made to make tea for her male colleagues for 15 months to intimidate and demean her. She eventually retired.

The tribunal agreed that she had suffered sexual discrimination and that the general behaviour and verbal abuse of the two officers towards her was "quite extraordinary" and "her personality and self-confidence has been totally destroyed".

The tribunal chair, David Thompson, is quoted as saying that the brigade had done little or nothing to prevent sexual discrimination and its management was "totally ineffectual".

Tania Clayton will now claim compensation from the brigade for the loss of her career and for psychiatric trauma.

There had been virtually no equal opportunities training before Tania Clayton's complaints and an investigation into her complaint was conducted by intimidation and fear.

The Fire Brigade Union's general secretary, Ken Cameron, is quoted as saying: "This decision is a scathing indictment of the brigade management, who, unfortunately, are not untypical of the British Fire Service."

(Adapted from an article in *The Daily Telegraph*, 1 April 1995. Printed in the *Harassment Network Newsletter*, 1995)

Organisational climate

The different relationships between organisational culture and harassment are very crucial ones, because culture is reinforced through the system of rites and rituals, patterns of communication, the informal organisation, expected patterns of behaviour, power distances and perceptions of the psychological contract. In turn, this has a profound effect on the climate of an organisation – about how the organisation feels to work in, the level of staff morale and motivation. According to Laurie Mullins:

"Organisational climate is characterised by the nature of the people–organisation relations and the superior–subordinate relationship. These relationships are determined by interactions among goals and objectives, formal structure, the process of management, styles of leadership and the behaviour of people."

The extent to which power influences the people–organisation, and superior–subordinate relationships plays an integral role in analysing the type of organisational climate in which harassment and bullying thrives easily.

The influence of power in organisational culture and climate

Power is normally a concept that is seen merely as a characteristic which one person possesses over another. However, in its broader context, power forms the basis of the way things are done within organisations. As harassment is about an abuse of power, if the dissemination of that power is abused and unequal at the same time on an organisational level, then harassment and bullying will persist at most (if not all) levels within that organisation.

Out of Hofstede's research emerged a method of measuring power and inequality in society, based on value-related differences. **Power distance** can be defined as *"the extent to which less powerful members of institutions and organisations accept that power is distributed unequally"*.

In organisations where a large power distance is evident in its culture, relationships between superiors and employees are often loaded with emotions, superiors being viewed with suspicion or held in high esteem.

Employees are supposed to make contact with superiors "through the appropriate channels". These channels, of course, are normally established by superiors. If an individual is the target of harassment and bullying by their manager, it is normally considered to be part of the course of things, and structures are so hierarchical that it would be very difficult to get an even-handed resolution of the problem. In fact, it would be highly unlikely that a complaint could be made and dealt with fairly, because power is centralised at the top of the organisation and held by a chosen few.

Relationships between superiors and employees in organisations whose cultures exhibit a small power distance are based on respect for each other's roles and responsibilities. Superiors are freely accessible to employees, and consultation, participation and involvement take place at most levels in the organisation. An employee making a complaint of harassment or bullying by a superior will be able to use a formal, structured system set up by the organisation.

Table 5 highlights the main differences between small and large power distances in the workplace.

Table 5. *Power distances*

Small power distance	Large power distance
Inequalities amongst people in the organisation should be minimised	Inequalities amongst people in the organisation are both expected and desired
There should be, and there is to some extent, interdependence between less and more powerful people in the organisation	Less powerful people in the organisation should be dependent on the more powerful; in practice, less powerful people are stuck between dependence and counterdependence
Employees who are highly educated hold less authoritarian values than less-educated employees	Both higher- and lower-educated employers have similar values about authoritarianism
Narrow salary and benefits range between top and bottom of organisation	Wide salary and benefits range between top and bottom of organisation
Organisational structures are flatter, there is less hierarchy and forms of matrix management are popular	Hierarchy in organisations reflected in a steep, rigid structure, where higher demarcations between managers and subordinates are clearly defined
Less centralisation of systems and skills (for example, recruitment and selection dealt with by line managers)	Centralisation of systems and skills popular (for example, recruitment and selection for organisation dealt with by central department)
Decision-making is achieved through wide consultation, participation and employee involvement at all levels	Very little consultation and involvement takes place – subordinates expect to be told what to do and act on decisions made for them
The ideal manager is seen as being accessible, resourceful, democratic and diplomatic	The ideal manager is seen as being benevolent, autocratic, paternalistic and revered (through compliance)
Privileges and status symbols are viewed with suspicion and disapproved of	Privileges and status symbols for managers are expected and an important part of the norm

(Adapted from *Cultures and Organisations*, by Geert Hofstede, HarperCollins, 1994. Reproduced with kind permission of Geert Hofstede)

Power distances are a useful way of determining the type of climate that exists within an organisation, and the nature of the relationships between superiors and subordinates.

Harassment can therefore be seen in a corporate sense as an issue which is potentially woven into an organisation very easily and potentially diagnosed as being prevalent when it is ingrained and established through its cultural patterns of behaviour. These patterns of behaviour, as mentioned earlier, are found in almost every organisational practice, through its vision, goals and objectives, formal structures, the process of management, styles of leadership and the behaviour of people. Chapter 6 looks at the characteristics of each of these behaviours and how they can be improved, in order to develop a positive working environment.

The extent to which organisations embrace the value of equality is another key indicator of the level of harassment and its prevalence in culture and climate. An organisation can be representative of the community it works in, yet operate on a discriminatory level. As harassment, bullying and violence are the manifestations of prejudice and discrimination, the adoption of values which encourage fair and equal working practices and diversity amongst its employees is essential to eradicating discrimination.

The following questionnaire analyses the stage of development an organisation has reached in the process of valuing equality and achieving diversity:

DEVELOPING DIVERSITY IN ORGANISATIONS
Assessing Progress

Tick the statement that is true to (or very like) your organisation. Your responses should reflect what you think your organisation is like *now*, and not what it *should be* in the future. You may tick more than one statement for each item number, but not all three.

1. The organisation:
a expects you to adopt the formal dress code
b does not enforce a dress code; however most employees dress to convention
c encourages variety in employees' style of dress.

2. In this organisation:
a newcomers are expected to adapt to existing norms
b there is some flexibility to accommodate the needs of diverse employees
c norms are flexible enough to include everyone.

3. In this organisation:
a equal opportunities is an issue that stirs irritation and resentment
b policy development and meeting legislative requirements as a priority
c diversity amongst staff at all levels is seen as a strategic advantage.

4. Dealing with discrimination is:
a not a top priority
b the responsibility of personnel and/or HR
c every manager's responsibility, and considered part of his/her role.

5. People in this organisation:
a ignore or are negative towards differences amongst employees
b tolerate differences and the needs they imply
c value differences and see diversity as an advantage to be cultivated.

6. Monitoring of the organisation shows that:
a there is diversity amongst staff at lower levels
b diverse staff are at lower and middle levels
c there is diversity at all levels of the organisation.

7. Training programmes are designed to help employees:
a adapt to the organisation's culture and learn "the way we do things here"
b develop diverse staff's ability to move up the organisation ladder
c communicate effectively across gender and ethnic barriers.

8. Managers are held accountable for:
a motivating staff and increasing productivity
b avoiding discrimination grievances and tribunals
c working effectively with diverse teams.

9. Managers are held accountable for:
a maintaining a stable team and perpetuating existing norms
b achieving equal opportunities goals and actions
c building productive work teams with diverse staff.

10. Managers are rewarded for:
a following existing procedures and meeting financial targets
b solving problems in the system
c creativity and trying new methods.

11. This organisation:
a resists change and seeks to maintain the status quo
b deals with changes as they occur
c is continually working on improvement.

12. In this organisation, it is an advantage to:
a be a white male
b learn to be like the "old guard"
c be unique and find new ways of doing things.

Scoring directions:

Total the number of ticks next to each letter and fill in the amount below:

_____ a Mono-cultural
_____ b Non-discriminatory
_____ c Multi-cultural

(Adapted from *Managing Diversity: A Complete Desk Reference and Planning Guide*, by Lee Gardenswartz and Anita Rowe, McGraw-Hill, 1993. Reproduced by kind permission of The McGraw-Hill Companies)

An organisation moves through the following three stages as it changes to accepting differences in the workplace:

1. Mono-cultural.
2. Non-discriminatory.
3. Multi-cultural.

Mono-cultural

At the mono-cultural stage, the organisation acts as though all employees are the same. Whilst staff may be diverse, there is an expectation to conform to a standard that is, in most cases, a traditional "white male" model, which puts white men (normally middle class) at an advantage in the organisation. The "Old-Boys Club" or "Network" accurately describes the organisational political system here. Success is achieved and measured by following the expectations and norms of this model, and meeting the criteria for membership of "the club".

The power distances of these organisations tend to be very large, with little room for questioning the power base of the dominant group. Hierarchical structures that are in place ensure that members of "the club" maintain their hold on power within the organisation.

Women, ethnic minorities, people with disabilities, gay and lesbians and other minority groups are expected to assimilate and adopt the dominant style of the organisation. There will be a small representation of minority groups, but they will be found mainly in the lower levels of the organisation. Tokenism is common amongst minority groups, and stereotypes are reinforced by the dominant group in the workforce in an attempt to make it difficult for minority groups to conform and therefore progress within the organisation.

The saying "When in Rome, do as the Romans" has a ring of truth here. Differences are underplayed, and this is a culture which tolerates discrimination and prejudice. Integration of minority groups is not seen as important or encouraged, and there is a tendency to be "colour-blind".

Non-discriminatory

This is the second stage in the development of managing diversity. Because of legislative requirements and the threat of employee grievances and tribunal cases, organisations begin to pay attention to equality policies and positive-action initiatives. The main aim is to eliminate past discrimination and redress the balance for groups with a perceived disadvantage.

Recruitment and selection is concentrated on first of all, and training is devised to raise awareness on disability, gender and race issues. Organisations will adapt models for equal opportunities policies, create plans of action and set up monitoring systems to evaluate the progress of the policies. There is very little concentration on the development of skills to manage diversity, as this has not yet been identified as a priority.

For diverse employees, there is a conflict between the need to assimilate and a desire for the organisation to accommodate their needs. There is also a conflict between the culture differences and values an individual may hold and those of the organisation. Tokenism may still exist. However, there will be more of a backlash because of the implementation of positive-action initiatives, which are seen by the dominant groups in the workforce as positive discrimination.

Although diverse groups are being recruited within the organisations, they find themselves up against "the glass ceiling" – an invisible barrier encountered as they seek advancement towards senior management and executive levels at the top of the corporate ladder. Compromise is the usual method of resolving these conflicts, with each side giving in a little in order to gain.

Multi-cultural

Eventually, the organisation moves into the multi-cultural stage. This third stage comes about due to the influence of demographic changes in the workforce, lifestyle and a shift in personal values. At this stage, there is not only a recognition that there are clear differences of culture, background, preferences and values, but a valuing of those differences. Assimilation is no longer the model for success. Rather, new norms are created that allow more flexibility for employees to do things their own way. Concentration is on the development of the needs of the individual, and not on redressing the balance for "disadvantaged" groups.

Power distances in the organisation at this stage are reduced. Employees are comfortable with the concept of empowerment at all levels within the organisation, and the need for hierarchical structures is removed.

Strategy development is a key feature of this stage. The organisation's values and vision are seen as an essential part of a multi-cultural organisation, and gaining commitment from all employees to these is a priority. Levels of awareness of cultural differences are high, and are viewed in the light of individual culture instead of group culture (often viewed in terms of ethnicity, which concentrates on group differences and reinforces stereotypes).

Organisational policies and procedures are flexible enough to work for everyone, and no one is put at an exploitative advantage. The mood of the organisation is one of synergy and interdependence, in pursuit of the organisation's vision.

There seems to be a major shift from the mono-cultural stage and most organisations within the UK are at the non-discriminatory stage. The challenge now is how to move smoothly from the non-discriminatory stage to the multi-cultural stage where diversity exists.

What impact does all of this have on eliminating harassment, bullying and violence? Organisations which have little or no commitment to equality and diversity, and whose cultures encourage dominant groups to hold power, are more likely to have climates where harassment and bullying thrive. Behaviour breeds behaviour, and creates a climate at work which could permit and encourage incidents of harassment. Chapter 6 looks at testing the working climate and creating a positive work environment.

The sliding scale

It seems that in some professions harassment is more prevalent than in others. This could be due to the extraordinary nature of the work concerned and the traditions that have built up around it.

A good example of this is the high level of bullying in the City environment – particularly in stockbroking, dealing rooms and insurance houses. Historically, recruits are generally in the 17- to 24-year-old age bracket, fresh from school or from university. Due to their lack of interpersonal skills and awareness they find it difficult to relate to others in the work environment and are often easy targets for harassment and bullying by older, more experienced members of staff who are usually perpetuating their own experiences as new recruits.

In addition, the nature of the work is that time = money, and there is a pressure to make and seal deals, etc. This pressure often overrides the need to develop the kinds of interpersonal relationships which would be vital in other professions. Therefore, the dominance of the task and the need to achieve targets override the need to develop the individual and build the team. This is often seen in sales and marketing, which has similar stress levels with regard to performance.

Other professions where harassment is prevalent include:

● Education.
● The health service.
● The law.

- The building industry.
- Journalism and media.
- The armed forces.

This is not to say that harassment does not exist in other professions; however, the nature of the work in these sectors can lend itself more easily to harassment and bullying.

How does this come about?

Education

The power relationship in education has not always been well defined. Its most common manifestation involves lecturers sleeping with students or using quid pro quo (results in return for sex) agreements. However, in schools, there is increasing evidence of harassment working top–down (head teacher → teacher) and bottom–up (pupil → teacher). The teachers are often caught in the middle as a result of the failure by head teachers to control pupils and admonish parents for fear of tarnishing the school reputation. This is reinforced by a more bullish approach by pupils and parents whose educational expectations and increasing demands for schools to provide a social service are creating pressures and stress.

Again, in Geert Hofstede's research, value differences in schools give rise to some of the behaviours described. The rise in bullying and aggression in schools is the small power distance situation in the extreme, where students treat teachers as equals and vice versa. Teachers are often bullied by parents, who tend to side with the children when they misbehave. The increased aggression at school has created an environment where bullying is more likely to thrive.

The health service

Similar issues affect the health service and whilst staff frequently have to contend with violence and harassment from patients, families and colleagues, some hospitals have introduced policy guidelines relating to hospital staff harassing patients.

Two surveys highlight the extent to which doctors and nurses experience harassment by patients. A survey of 300 GPs conducted by *Pulse* revealed that nine out of ten female GPs were subjected to verbal sexual harassment and one third of female GPs felt threatened by sexual advances from patients. (Three-quarters of male GPs were also subjected to sexual innuendoes from patients.) Some, however, said that harassment by colleagues was more of a problem. A study compiled by the Policy Studies Institute and commissioned by the Department of Health found that black and Asian nurses suffered racial abuse on a large scale, and that "racially abusive behaviour is considered the 'norm' and is part of the culture of the workplace."

The law

The legal profession is taking action on harassment, following complaints from within the profession that they were not taking the issue seriously. Whereas the education system and health service have had to respond to constant socially and legally provoked change, the legal profession and its regulatory bodies have had to change very little. Despite attempts by government to introduce change, the profession seems to be remarkably resistant to these demands.

Membership of this particular club is very stringent and although there has been an increase in the number of women and ethnic minority entrants to the profession, decidedly few remain. According to a survey (1996) commissioned by the Council for Legal Education, two-fifths of women barristers have experienced sexual harassment at the Bar. As Charles Handy points out, in *Gods of Management*, in order to stay within the club, sometimes it is required that entrants sell something of themselves to assimilate. This "something" could be their diversity and/or cultural identity.

The building industry

The building industry is renowned for perpetuating bullying inside its ranks. This behaviour spreads externally and is transformed into sexual harassment via remarks made by an overwhelmingly male workforce to women members of the public. One issue to consider is that one of the provisions of the Criminal Justice Act relating to public or intentional harassment as an offence means that the days of scaffold banter might be numbered:

"A woman who regularly walks past a construction site may now be able to say to the perpetrators, 'your sexual remarks really bother me and if it happens again, I'm calling the police.'"

(*Equal Opportunities Review*, No. 58, November/December 1995)

Internally, this macho environment makes it difficult for women working within it, and they currently make up less than 10% of the 1.77 million people in the construction industry, according to research by the Institute of Employment Studies in 1995. Not surprisingly, the majority of these women are in administrative roles and few hold manual or technical positions.

Racial harassment is also prevalent in this industry, and may explain why many ethnic minority builders are self-employed, few remaining with established companies, and even fewer in managerial positions.

Case Study

Racial Abuse in the Building Industry

Martin, a construction manager, has worked with his organisation for over 18 years now. Despite his length of service and excellent performance record, he still remains as a construction manager, training young white men for promotion. His current line manager is someone he trained five years ago.

"I have accepted the fact that I will never get the recognition I deserve – not in position, anyway. My bonuses are good, and my salary is amongst the highest, but I know this is a way of the company keeping me sweet, without giving me the promotions.

I feel as a black construction manager that I am resented for holding this position. I can remember on many occasions where I was resented by the white traders or employers. There have been occasions when things have been done incorrectly by tradesmen and I had to draw this to their attention. As a result, in one particular incident, I was referred to as a 'coon'. I could not tolerate this. I lost my temper and sacked the scaffolder and told his boss I did not want to see him on my site again."

(Martin, a construction manager)

The following case study also highlights the prevalence of racial harassment in the construction industry.

"Black Bastard" Not Words of Camaraderie

Eugene Sutton, who was of mixed-race parentage, began working as a general labourer on a construction site for Balfour Beatty construction in October/November 1989. Shortly after Christmas, the general foreman, George Gladwell, started abusing him by calling him a "black bastard". He did so at least 20 times over a period of some months. The site manager, a Mr Sindle, knew about the abuse but failed to do anything to prevent it until Mr Sutton complained, whereupon he told Mr Gladwell not to use such language. In May 1990, Mr Sutton had a meeting with the employer's industrial relations manager, Mr Cummings, who appeared to suggest that the words "black bastard" could be treated as camaraderie and "were not unusual in his industry". Mr Sutton claimed that the persistent abuse amounted to unlawful discrimination.

An industrial tribunal upheld the complaint. It rejected the suggestion that such words should be treated as camaraderie. "In our view, it is not correct to regard the use of such words as camaraderie and this tribunal does not accept that it is usual to call people who are black 'black bastards'. If that has been the situation in the past it is no longer a tolerable situation and we strongly disapprove of any employers and particularly industrial relations managers who seek to sustain such language." It found that Mr Sutton had been less favourably treated on the grounds of his race and that Mr Gladwell had subjected him to a detriment by abusing him with the words "black bastard". As "Mr Sindle failed in his duty in not stopping Mr Gladwell from using such language much sooner than he actually did", the company could not avoid liability for Mr Gladwell's actions.

The tribunal awarded compensation of £2,000 for injury to feelings.

(Sutton v Balfour Beatty Construction, Case No. 21650/90, June 1991. Reproduced from Equal Opportunities Review: Discrimination Case Law Digest, No. 12, Summer 1992. With kind permission from Eclipse Group Publishing Ltd)

Journalism and media

The media have fed off numerous harassment cases, but their own profession is in disrepute. A mix of unrelenting pressure to deliver stories to tight deadlines amidst a tough competitive environment, combined with the contradiction between new technological systems and old-style attitudes and behaviour, can give rise to cases like the one outlined in the following case study.

Case Study

Bullying in the News Room

When Fran, aged 41, returned from maternity leave to her old job on a daily provincial newspaper, the new editor had been in place for one week. Despite an established reputation as a skilled features writer, her professional ability was immediately called into question. After twenty years in journalism she was reduced to relatively menial tasks usually reserved for trainee reporters.

"The atmosphere at work had become quiet and hostile. We were discouraged from chatting and having the usual office banter – in fact there was practically a no-talking rule. Even on the telephone we were not expected to spend any time establishing any sort of rapport with the public. I had come back to work expecting reasonable status as a writer, but not only was I assigned to jobs like golden weddings and press releases, I was put under someone fifteen years younger who wasn't even properly qualified.

Initially I felt insulted, but when I asked to see the editor, he told me he was under no obligation to honour any previous agreement. 'We're doing things my way now,' he said, 'and you will do as you are told.' He was very difficult to confront because he used to remove himself from the office, and when he was there, he was surrounded by people who sided with him.

As the pressure built up, I could see other reporters looking strained and upset, but I didn't know why because nobody said anything. Those who were picked on and humiliated in public very quickly got out.

Then I received the first of many memos, which would sometimes run to two pages of A4 paper, criticising the standard of my work and pointing out that my stories were having to be knocked back and rewritten. In all my experience, under three previous editors, this had never happened, and when I read that first memo I literally had a physical reaction. I was sweating, my scalp prickled and I had this feeling that the whole office was staring at me. The memo made it clear that copies had gone to six other senior members of staff, so I was terribly shaken, but I didn't tell anyone because it was embarrassing. I think it was a bit like a woman who's been raped not telling the police in case they think it was her fault.

It was more than a year later before I became aware that others had received memos like this too. Those memos were obviously designed to intimidate from the outset, and they succeeded. At the time, each of us thought we were the only one because nobody told, nobody stood up and waved them about. They upset me so much that I couldn't even bear to put them at the back of a drawer, or even in a dustbin, because that meant that they not only still existed, they would go on festering. Instead, I burnt them. Looking back that was wrong. It meant I had no evidence, and that was a mistake.

As I went on getting copy thrown back at me, I began to think it was all my fault. One correspondent became so overloaded on top of all his specialist work that it was quite ludicrous, but when he complained to the editor, he was told not to carp. Everything I did was repeatedly criticised, and even if I wrote an intro to a story exactly as I'd been instructed, a sub-editor would come over to me later and say, 'Why have you written it this way, surely this is the obvious angle?' Then I would have to re-do it. It was very undermining, especially when the editor was sitting in the middle of the room while all this was going on, swivelling in his seat and fixing me with a stare. Whatever I did seemed to be wrong. On one occasion I drove a few miles from the office to cover a story which needed a personal interview, and was later accused of incurring unnecessary mileage. Another time I collected a quote over the telephone and was promptly told off for not doing the 30 mile round trip to collect some personal quotes. Time and time again it seemed as if I was being set up to get it all wrong.

Other people were publicly dressed down for things they genuinely hadn't done, and at the end of each week the editor would go over our copy, word by word, inch by inch, to assess the quality and quantity. I can remember frantically rummaging through drawers in search of press releases to re-write so that I wouldn't be accused of sitting there twiddling my thumbs. From the moment I arrived in the office on Monday morning, it was like being in a cage with an unpredictable animal.

Once people started to leave, there was a general feeling that senior management would notice that good journalists were pouring down the drain and wonder why. Then we began to realise that the salary bill must be a fraction of what it had been, so perhaps they liked it like this. Even so, the paper's circulation had dropped dramatically, so we would still think: it can't go on for ever, someone is bound to put a stop to it. But it didn't stop of course, and here I was, a one-time union official, without the strength even to put pen to paper to make a complaint. I knew I couldn't cope with the confrontation at an industrial tribunal. I didn't want to leave because I'd always loved local journalism, and in that area there were no other jobs around for journalists.

In the end, my health suffered so much that after thirteen months I decided to leave. As soon as I knew I wasn't going back I felt personally released. My health improved in leaps and bounds over the following weeks, and relationships at home relaxed."

(Adapted from *Bullying at Work*, by Andrea Adams, Virago Press, 1992. Reproduced with kind permission from Virago Press)

The armed forces

The armed forces have long had a tradition for turning new recruits into highly skilled, disciplined professionals. However, with this tradition comes the unenviable reputation of being a breeding ground for bullying and harassment. In a culture where assimilation is the norm, differences are difficult to accept. The controversy that surrounds gay men and lesbian women joining the armed forces is an example of the fears and prejudice that are ingrained in a culture which perpetuates discrimination. Anti-harassment policies (excluding sexual orientation) have now been established, amidst some criticism and hostility from those in the forces' higher ranks.

In response to the Royal Navy publishing rules discouraging sexual harassment, sexist language and pin-up posters, one admiral of the Fleet is quoted as saying: *"I don't believe sexual harassment is harassment. It has merely been made to appear to matter."* Another admiral of the Fleet, who remarked that *"the politically correct creeps behind this ludicrous action are stupid"*, is also quoted as saying: *"The Wrens probably suffer sexual harassment. It is what you would expect in a working place with a lot of virile men."* With this level of resistance and antagonism, it will take a long time to change the culture of harassment and bullying in the armed forces.

Case Study

Breaking of the Thin Black Line
Army roll-call of shame

In 1990, Richard Stokes, the first black member of the Household Cavalry and first black soldier to take part in the Changing of the Guard at Buckingham Palace, quit after sustained racial abuse. He received hate mail and during rehearsals for Trooping the Colour had a banana thrown at him by a fellow soldier. His decision to leave embarrassed the Army as Prince Charles had complained about the lack of black soldiers in the Household Cavalry and urged that more soldiers be recruited from ethnic minorities.

In 1991, Stephen Anderson, a black private, was awarded £500 after suffering four years of racial abuse. The High Court overturned the initial decision by the Army not to grant him any compensation. The court heard that Anderson was punched and called "nigger" by fellow members of the Devon and Dorset Regiment. The only black soldier in his platoon, he joined the Army in 1983 and complained of constant abuse.

In 1994, Geoffrey McKay was awarded £8,000 compensation because of racial abuse. A former member of the Queen's Royal Irish Hussars, he was considered one of the brightest recruits to undergo basic training but was driven out because of racism. An Army board of inquiry heard how, during his first parade, the sergeant said, "we've got a nigger in the troop, lads".

The case of Mark Campbell, the first black trooper to join the Life Guards, dealt another damaging blow to the Army's race relations record. Campbell, 28, made history when he became the first black soldier to ride as one of the Queen's escort. Described as a model trooper, he was moved from the Guards' central London barracks to Windsor following a skin complaint, but close friends say he is being driven out because of racism. "He could leave any day," says one. "He's under a lot of stress."

(From an article by Vivek Chaudhary, *The Guardian*, 5 March 1996. Reproduced with kind permission from *The Guardian*. © *The Guardian*)

Reflection

Ultimately, an organisation's culture should serve the needs of the business. We have seen how organisation culture and climate can impact on personal behaviour. However, this can happen at corporate levels and bullying can take place between organisations. When senior and executive management condone harassment and bullying as behaviour which is appropriate to use with customers and competitors, the short-term gains are soon cancelled out by the long-term effects of these actions on profit margins. Whilst it may appear acceptable to instruct employees to obtain business at all costs, the risk of tarnishing the organisation's public image and losing future business is high.

The much-publicised case of British Airways and Virgin Atlantic in 1993 has been the focus of discussions and analysis of senior management behaviour and business ethics. Gerard Egan, in his book *Working the Shadow Side: A Guide to Positive Behind-the-Scenes Management*, said of the behaviour of employees, "It was discovered that some of the airline's employees were using unethical, if not illegal, methods to filch passengers from Virgin Airlines. If these 'dirty tricks', as they were called in the press, were not condoned by higher authorities – the dynamics of that might be well hidden forever – then some rogue operators within the company apparently decided to take competitive matters into their own hands. The economic impact of such idiosyncratic shadow-side behaviour has been quite negative for *'the world's favourite airline'*. The image of the airline was tarnished, at least for a while, and a cloud of suspicion drifted over its senior managers."

Alan Kitson and Robert Campbell, in their book *The Ethical Organisation: Ethical Theory and Corporate Behaviour*, explore the impact of such behaviour, and note a change of public mood in relation to unethical behaviour in business. To protect organisations' long-term interests and future business, Kitson and Campbell advocate the adoption of a corporate code of ethics which establishes ethical forms of conduct, reflective of a healthy organisational culture and a positive working climate. A commitment to reducing the impact and occurrence of harassment, bullying and violence in the workplace, and improving organisational culture, is also an ethical issue, and one which should not be ignored when creating codes on business ethics.

References

Cultures and Organisations: Software of the Mind – Intercultural Co-operation and its Importance for Survival, Geert Hofstede (HarperCollins, 1994).

Gods of Management, Charles Handy (Pan, 1985).

Managing Diversity: A Complete Desk Reference and Planning Guide, Lee Gardenswartz and Anita Rowe (McGraw-Hill, 1993).

Managing People at Work, Peter Makin, Cary Cooper and Charles Cox (The British Psychological Society and Routledge, 1993).

Beyond Race and Gender, R Roosevelt Thomas Jr (AMACOM, 1992).

Managing the Mosaic: Diversity in Action, Rajvinder Kandola and Johanna Fullerton (Institute of Personnel and Development, 1994).

Working the Shadow Side: A Guide to Positive Behind-the-Scenes Management, Gerard Egan (Jossey-Bass, 1994).

Teambuilding: A Practical Guide, Alastair Fraser and Suzanne Neville (Manager's Pocket Guides Series, The Industrial Society, 1993).

The Ethical Organisation: Ethical Theory and Corporate Behaviour, Alan Kitson and Robert Campbell (Macmillan Business, 1996).

Management and Organisational Behaviour, Laurie J Mullins (Pitman Publishing, 1996).

Nursing in a Multi-ethnic NHS, Department of Health/Policy Studies Institute, BEBC Distribution, 1996.

Women in the Construction Industry, The Institute of Employment Studies, 1995.

Bullying at Work: How to Confront and Overcome it, Andrea Adams (Virago Press, 1992).

Quotes of Navy admirals, *Sunday Telegraph*, 12 November 1995.

CHAPTER 6

Creating a harassment-free environment

This chapter defines a positive work environment which is harassment free, and sets out the practical actions which can be taken to achieve it, through auditing the organisation's culture, carrying out a harassment audit or survey and dealing with its outcomes. The chapter also emphasises the importance of management and leadership in creating a climate in which diversity is valued, and gives practical advice on helping organisations achieve the changes needed to create a more positive work environment.

Chapter 5 explored the role of culture and climate on the existence of harassment in the workplace.

The unwillingness of organisations to acknowledge the impact that organisational culture has on behaviour means that not enough analysis and research takes place to discover what the organisation is really like, where the problems lie and what actions need to be taken in order to create a positive working environment free of harassment.

What is a positive work environment?

The term is fashionable at the moment, and is often used without much thought as to what it really means in relation to the workplace.

A positive work environment is one which, quite simply, allows employees to work to the best of their ability, in pursuit of an organisation's goals, aims and objectives.

Characteristics of a positive work environment

The main characteristics of a positive working environment are as follows:

- A high level of trust and support exists at all levels in the organisation.
- The pursuit of organisational goals is a common aim, and individual targets and performance are no longer the drivers.
- Unhealthy stress levels are low and occupational health hazards are minimal.
- There is a genuine concern for the quality of working life.
- Creativity springs from teamwork and individual/departmental competition is non-existent.
- The climate is warm and friendly, and allows for free expression of diversity.
- There are opportunities for personal development and career progression.
- The behaviour of managers and leaders is appropriate and reflects best practice.
- Conflict is discussed openly and resolved speedily.
- Empowerment dominates over individual power politics.
- Exclusive clubs and informal cliques do not exist.
- There are equitable systems of rewards and there is justice in treatment in employee relations and HR practices.
- There is a strong sense of loyalty to the organisation, with the feeling of being integral to the organisation and a valued member.

Is it possible to have a "harassment-free" work environment? Organisations can certainly aim for it, even though in some circumstances it may be considered an impossibility. Starting from the premise that it is conceivable lays strong foundations for the work needed in order to achieve it. A positive, "harassment-free" work environment can be achieved by:

⇒ auditing the organisation's culture and
⇒ managing the audit outcomes by:

- exploring different approaches to maintaining the value of equality
- testing the temperature of the climate
- acknowledging the role of leadership and management styles
- setting standards of behaviour through good policy development
- examining the organisation's capacity to change
- finding ways of gaining commitment to change.

⇒ adopting a strategic approach to change the working environment.

The rest of the chapter looks into each area, and, more importantly, outlines how a positive work environment can be maintained.

Auditing the organisation's culture

Culture – *"the way we do things around here"* – is often taken for granted, and it is assumed that everyone in the organisation knows what it is. However, misreading the culture, paying little attention to it, or knowing what it is but being unsure of how to operate in it, are common problems that can lead to conflict and discrimination within the organisation.

As culture is integral to every aspect of the business, its patterns of behaviour are reflected in such organisational practices as:

● strategy and vision
● formal structures – modes of operation; ways of communicating decision-making, quality processes, etc
● HR systems
● leadership styles.

If negative patterns of behaviour are evident in these areas, harassment can easily thrive and limit the effectiveness of the organisation. Gerard Egan describes accurately how such patterns of behaviour manifest themselves through these practices, and assesses the impact of cultural "shadow" in the organisation. Adapted from his book *Working the Shadow Side*, the following are examples of how negative patterns of behaviour perpetuate harassment and bullying:

● **Strategy**: "A strategy was developed by an external consultant, we only had two months to complete it, and as we have no consultation methods, it's difficult to get everyone to work effectively from it."
● **Formal structure**: "We only release information to those who we feel will use it appropriately – if we gave it out to everyone it would take for ever to make a decision and get on with running a business."
● **HR systems**: "We have an excellent recruitment and selection policy, but it is never taken seriously – managers will still recruit and promote who they want when they want without adhering to the guidelines."
● **Management**: "You don't need 'people' skills here. If in doubt, be tough. No manager has ever been fired for not listening to good ideas from subordinates."

- **Leadership**: "It is evident that the power in the company is at the top. We can't question what is done by them, it's more than your job's worth."

In contrast, a positive work environment is one where the patterns of behaviour enhance the performance of the organisation and would be reflected in the following ways:

- **Strategy**: "Our strategy was created by consulting with every employee in the organisation – with the particular help of the management group who will be responsible for implementing it. The managers now own it and sell the benefits to their teams."
- **Formal structure**: "Consultation and employee involvement at all levels is integral to the way we get things done here. We try to encourage employees to give open and honest feedback upwards, as well as across and down the organisation."
- **HR systems**: "We have developed a system to prevent harassment and bullying purely because we value our employees and want them to work in a safe, healthy environment."
- **Management**: "We choose managers with *savoir faire*. They appreciate and understand the balance between productivity and the quality of work life. They are excellent at developing staff and building positive work relationships."
- **Leadership**: "Everyone around here tries to improve the work in her or his unit, and is not afraid to take accountability if things don't work out right. Improvement is thriving, power politics seems to be a thing of the past here . . ."

(Adapted from *Working the Shadow Side*, by Gerard Egan. © G Egan 1994. Published by Jossey-Bass)

It is essential that the culture of an organisation enhances the business, and when harassment or bullying negates this objective, an organisation stands to lose more than its customer base: it will eventually become static, and lose good, talented employees, leaving others to fight between themselves.

The foundation of any culture consists of the assumptions, beliefs, values and norms that drive organisational behaviours. Assumptions and beliefs develop values; norms are developed as a result of the assumptions and values of the organisation. Those norms also determine the patterns of behaviour in an organisation.

Egan also points out the difference between the "preferred" culture which serves the business and the "covert" culture – beliefs, values and norms that are not publicly named and quite often hidden but which still drive patterns of organisational behaviour. What is necessary is to identify the "covert" behaviours that are negative and limit the effectiveness of the organisation, and identify the positive behaviours that form part of the "preferred" culture – one which is publicly recognised as having values which support business objectives and the quality of working life.

The objectives, then, of a culture audit are:

● to identify the key assumptions, beliefs, values and norms that are fundamental to the organisation
● to identify the negative patterns of behaviour they generate
● to determine which behaviours support or hinder the organisation
● to determine which behaviours to keep in place
● to determine the preferred culture which serves the needs of the business.

The type's of issues to consider when undertaking culture audits include:

✓ What is our business focus and is the culture helping or hindering this focus?
✓ What are the recurring problems and issues that keep rising to the surface, and yet remain undiscussed?
✓ To what extent are leaders and managers carriers of the culture, and how is this perpetuated?
✓ What aspects of negative cultural behaviour are rewarded, and how?
✓ Is there complacency and inertia in the organisation?
✓ Is there recruitment "in your own image"? How flexible is the recruitment system?
✓ Do staff have faith in existing HR systems? Are they fair?
✓ What systems are in place to prevent discrimination occurring?
✓ How would you describe the culture currently – strong, weak or flexible?
✓ Are internal communications adequate? If not, what needs changing?

As part of the process, an audit or survey to discover the extent of harassment in the workplace should take place, as shown below:

Ascertaining the reality of the situation – carrying out a harassment audit/survey

It may be necessary to carry out an audit or survey to find out the extent to which harassment, bullying and violence is an issue within the organisation. A survey will give background information as to the current climate (an audit is a more rigorous process).

The very fact that a survey is to take place amongst staff can either encourage them to be open and honest about their experiences, or make them wary or cautious about their responses. Therefore, it is important that the survey is conducted in a confidential, objective manner, as this will play a great part in the quality of information received. The questionnaire must be completed anonymously, in order to gain candid, honest information. Most organisations commission audit and survey consultancies to conduct the whole process, so that it remains fair and impartial.

There are other methods of diagnosing the organisational climate, including focus groups, one-to-one interviews, monitoring of exit interviews, performance appraisal ratings, feedback and evaluation from training activities, etc. However, some of these methods can be used in conjunction with a questionnaire as part of the survey process.

A survey that incorporates good practices needs to cover three specific areas to establish whether harassment is an issue in the organisation. The three areas are:

1. Questions which determine the range of behaviours employees may consider to be harassment.
2. Questions that evaluate the depth of experience, from identifying the perpetrator to the effects of the behaviour.
3. Questions that scrutinise the organisational environment, from the systems which exist to combat harassment to the actions employees take to confront it.

A classification section (looking at factors such as gender, age, department, length of service, job level, grade, etc) enabling statistical analysis of the survey findings must be included.

Example survey questions:

Have you ever experienced harassment or bullying at work?
Yes
No
Don't know

Which of these behaviours do you consider to be unwelcome or unwanted?
Turning discussions to sexual/racial topics
Making innuendoes
Teasing, jokes and remarks which you found offensive
Winking, leering, throwing kisses
Staring
Suggestive gestures

Displaying pornographic or racially offensive material
Unnecessary touching or patting
Unwanted attention, letters, telephone calls
Physical abuse or intimidation
Threat of job detriment/benefits in connection with sexual favours
Threatening behaviour
None of the above

Who demonstrated this behaviour?
Immediate manager/supervisor
Higher-level management
Subordinate
Peer
Customers/clients

How often does this happen?
Never
Once
Once a month or less
2–4 times a month
Once a week or more

Who did you go to in order to get something done about it?
Your manager
A friend or relative
A work colleague
Someone in personnel/HR
A counselling service
Another manager
The person harassing you
That person's manager
Your union
Your lawyer/solicitor
Another external organisation
You didn't go to anyone at all

What other action did you take?
Didn't do anything about it
Ignored the behaviour
Made a joke about the behaviour
Avoided the person(s)

Asked/told the person to stop
Threatened to tell others
Reported to union representative
Reported to management
Made an informal complaint
Made a formal complaint

How effective is your organisation at taking the following actions?
Establishing clear policies prohibiting harassment
Carrying out thorough and impartial investigations of complaints
Enforcing penalties against managers who take no action
Enforcing penalties against harassers
Communicating the informal and formal system
Providing support and counselling services for harassment
Providing awareness training for all staff at all levels

Managing the audit outcomes

The culture audit is only the beginning of the process – implementing the changes and gaining commitment to the development of a new culture are the most challenging parts of the process.

These will reflect, quite directly, the issues paramount to staff members and cannot be pre-judged. Once this process is complete, you are in a better position to set clear aims and objectives for necessary action. To recap, the following issues are the ones which are most usually highlighted as ready for development:

- the approach to maintaining equality
- the climate of the organisation
- management and leadership styles
- policy development
- the organisation's capacity to change
- ways of gaining commitment to change.

Maintaining the value of equality

The culture audit will reveal the way an organisation values equality and prevents discrimination, and also the stage of development it has reached in its creation of a multi-cultural workforce.

Developing aims, objectives and visions to take the organisation forward, having completed the audit, will depend on where the organisation is at in terms of equal opportunities practices, its culture and its climate. As mentioned earlier, the audit outcomes should reveal the types of practices prevalent in the organisation. Having established these, you are in a better position to keep that which is positive and amend the negative.

Part of the problem organisations face is the lack of research and analysis carried out before choosing and adopting the most appropriate approach to achieving equality. In the past, finding the most appropriate approach to creating a harassment-free work environment proved difficult for organisations committed to the value of equality. Those who were in the forefront of breaking down the barriers of discrimination introduced equal opportunities initiatives designed to eliminate discrimination in systems, practices and procedures (such as recruitment and selection, pay and reward). However, whilst some of these initiatives were successful in some organisations, others had difficulties in implementing their action plans, and, consequently, equal opportunities policies became ineffective, and were viewed cynically as pieces of paper meeting the requirements of legislation.

Background

Legislation in the early to mid 1970s (the Equal Pay Act 1970, the Sex Discrimination Act 1975 and the Race Relations Act 1976) brought about the introduction of equality principles and led to the adoption of equal opportunities measures in the workplace. These were characterised by a reliance on the formation of policy, the introduction of positive action initiatives aimed at recruiting previously excluded groups of people, statistical and evaluation methods linked to recruitment, selection and progression, and were primarily designed to reduce and/or eliminate discrimination.

These practices were developed by increasing awareness levels amongst managers and HR professionals by a simultaneous recognition of the ethics of valuing difference and social responsibility as well as the need to eliminate harmful industrial relations disputes. Many organisations were also concerned about their public image and their ability to recruit and retain the best people as increasing numbers of black people and women came through the education system, and social and demographic changes meant that organisations had to take this seriously.

Valuing differences became paramount to the attainment of an environment which supported these changes. Such an approach differed from equal opportunities in that it looked more deeply at the moral and ethical reasoning. It is a fluid concept which has feet in both equal opportunities and managing diversity camps. Based on equal opportunities in its qualitative characteristics, its focus is on developing different and more appropriate behaviour relevant to managing diversity – an area not specifically covered by equal opportunities. Table 6 (opposite) illustrates these differences and progressions more fully.

Creating a harassment-free environment means acknowledging your organisation's current culture and changing it to suit. Which of your practices match the characteristics in the table? The position of your organisation in the table will determine the kinds of actions you will need to take as a result of your audits.

The climate of the organisation

In Chapter 5, we mentioned that, according to Laurie Mullins: *"Organisational climate is characterised by the nature of the people–organisation relations and the superior–subordinate relationship."* What follows is a method of testing your own organisational climate. Remember, climate is a reflection of the culture of the organisation and is an important element of reducing harassment and bullying in the workplace. It is a mix of the psychological and the physical environment people have to work in. Therefore, it is a vital component of the psychological contract which exists between the employer and employee.

Testing the temperature

Go through the following checklist (continued on p. 158) and see how many of the examples are true of your own organisation:

A POSITIVE WORK ENVIRONMENT?

1. Is the early-morning, late-evening syndrome common in your organisation?
2. If yes, are staff encouraged to take breaks and holiday entitlements?
3. Are targets/income generation the main way to measure success?
4. Office banter – is it lewd and crude?
5. Is bad language (ie dirty jokes, swearing, innuendoes) commonplace?
6. How heavy are individuals' workloads?
7. Are working practices within your organisation inflexible?
8. What is the current turnover rate of staff, and how does it compare to previous years?
9. Are you losing well-trained, experienced staff at a higher rate?
10. Is stress a common complaint amongst staff?
11. What training, counselling and support is provided for employees who are suffering from stress?
12. Are personal conflicts between staff frequent?
13. Has there ever been an incident of physical violence between staff?

Table 6.

EQUAL OPPORTUNITIES	VALUING DIFFERENCES	MANAGING DIVERSITY
Quantitative characteristics – Equality of opportunity in the work environment is achieved by ensuring fair representation of all groups. This eventually changes the make-up of the workforce and is monitored by statistical analysis and evaluation reports.	*Qualitative characteristics* – The appreciation of differences and creation of an environment in which all employees feel accepted and valued. Attitude surveys and audits are used as a form of monitoring and evaluation.	*Behavioural characteristics* – Concentrate on skill building and the creation of policies which enable all employees to work at their fullest potential. Performance management and appraisal mechanisms, which set goals and objectives, form the basis of monitoring and evaluation.
Legislative characteristics – Policies and action plans are based on legislative requirements, and meet the provisions outlined in the Codes of Practice operated by the Commission for Racial Equality (Race Relations Act 1976) and the Equal Opportunities Commission (Sex Discrimination Act 1975). The provisions of the Disability Discrimination Act 1995 will also have to be met.	*Ethical characteristics* – Moral, ethical and value reasonings are behind this cultural change.	*Strategy characteristics* – Aims and objectives are integral to the organisation's overall strategy, and are internally driven. Behaviours and policies contribute to an organisation's productivity and results and are linked into reward and benefits.
Remedial characteristics – Positive action initiatives and targeting are introduced as measures to reduce the impact of past discrimination for "disadvantaged" groups.	*Visionary characteristics* – Everyone benefits in some way and all feel valued and accepted in an inclusive environment.	*Pragmatic characteristics* – The organisation benefits through increased morale, greater creativity, increased productivity and a healthier bottom line.
Assimilation model – Assumptions are often made that disadvantaged groups will adapt comfortably to the existing organisational culture, climate and behavioural norms.	*Differences model* – Assumptions are made that individuals retain their own characteristics, contributing to changes in the organisation and its culture, creating a common set of values.	*Diversity model* – Assumes that individuals find new effective ways of working together in a positive work environment.
"Open door" characteristic – Equal opportunities open doors to minority groups to enter organisations, changing recruitment, selection and progression systems.	*"Open hearts and minds" characteristic* – Valuing differences affects the attitudes of employees and attempts to change core values.	*"Open system" characteristic* – Changes managerial practices and procedures in an attempt to improve them.
Perceptions of positive discrimination – Resistance may come from majority groups who feel that minority groups are at an advantage to them.	*Fear of change* – Resistance may come from those who have discomfort with differences, and who want to return to the "good old days," of a mono-culture.	*Denial of reality* – The need to change and learn new skills, alter existing systems and find time to work towards achieving synergy may lead to a reluctance to face the task ahead and the enormity of it.

(Adapted from *Managing Diversity: A Complete Desk Reference and Planning Guide*, by Lee Gardenswartz and Anita Rowe, McGraw-Hill, 1993. Reproduced by kind permission of The McGraw-Hill Companies.)

14. If yes, how many times has this happened?
15. Are employees reluctant to make complaints for fear of reprisal?
16. What is the level of sickness and absence in the organisation?
17. Have sickness and absence levels increased dramatically within a particular department or area in your organisation?

If you have answered yes to five or more of the questions, this may be an indication of problems within the organisation's climate.

If you have recognised some of the instances as occurring in your workplace, it is likely that the climate and culture need attention. The examples given are common indicators of an environment conducive to bullying and harassment, in which expected behaviours and boundaries are not properly defined and are being transgressed.

To improve the climate of the organisation, employers need to establish the psychological barriers which exist, such as lack of openness – is the political environment conducive to raising issues of harassment and bullying? Do people fear retribution if they make a complaint? Do they feel that they belong to the organisation: are they "in" or "out"? What type of work ethic is in operation? What is the view towards family and life outside work? Can people be open about their differences?

Amy J Zuckerman and George F Simons created the following exercise in their book *Sexual Orientation in the Workplace* to test how receptive organisations would be to the issue of sexual orientation. We have adapted it to include the issue of diversity as a whole:

Where does the organisation and the people within it stand on issues of diversity? Are they warm and welcoming to employee differences or cold and threatening?

Write in the temperature to the left of the thermometer on the items that are true of your workplace. Then calculate the temperature at the bottom of the thermometer.

Figure 13.

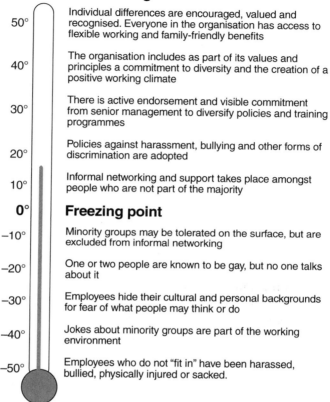

Warm and welcoming

50° — Individual differences are encouraged, valued and recognised. Everyone in the organisation has access to flexible working and family-friendly benefits

40° — The organisation includes as part of its values and principles a commitment to diversity and the creation of a positive working climate

30° — There is active endorsement and visible commitment from senior management to diversify policies and training programmes

20° — Policies against harassment, bullying and other forms of discrimination are adopted

10° — Informal networking and support takes place amongst people who are not part of the majority

0° — **Freezing point**

−10° — Minority groups may be tolerated on the surface, but are excluded from informal networking

−20° — One or two people are known to be gay, but no one talks about it

−30° — Employees hide their cultural and personal backgrounds for fear of what people may think or do

−40° — Jokes about minority groups are part of the working environment

−50° — Employees who do not "fit in" have been harassed, bullied, physically injured or sacked.

Cold and threatening

Temperature rating:
To calculate your organisation's temperature, total the degrees above freezing and subtract the total degrees below freezing:

Degrees above freezing: _____

Degrees below freezing: _____

Our organisational temperature: _____

If the climate is warm:

● What actions need to be taken to harness the temperature?
● Can more be done to make it warmer?
● What aspects of the climate help to prevent harassment and bullying?

If the climate is cold:

● Why is the climate cold or colder than expected?

● What actions need to be taken to make the climate warmer?
● What aspects of the climate hinder the prevention of harassment and bullying?
● How can the climate be improved?

Organisational climate will have an impact on the morale and attitude of employees, and consequently will influence employees' work performance and relationships – with both working colleagues and at home. It is therefore essential that attention is given to basic ergonomics, creating a non-intrusive environment which encourages high levels of involvement, and one which sees family and domestic life as an integral part of individual and organisational life.

Leadership and management styles

Leadership and management styles play a vital part in creating the right climate for the prevention of harassment and bullying.

As outlined previously, some leadership and management styles are themselves forms of bullying, and if valued as a behaviour which brings in the business and increases profitability, become the norm. This norm is then perpetuated throughout the organisation, and bullying and harassment thrive.

However, the negative effects on the organisation of poor leadership and poor management behaviours are greater than the perceived financial benefits of, for example, pushing for high targets. These effects are described more fully in Chapter 8.

Leaders must stand firm as the creators and promoters of the "preferred" culture, and cannot shirk the responsibility of providing the vision needed to prevent harassment and bullying. Not only must they be exemplars of appropriate behaviour, they must be firm in stamping out the behaviour in managers and other staff. In the following case study, Rachael Ross and Gill Jackson of Schneider-Ross, a consultancy firm experienced in the implementation of diversity strategies, reflect on the importance of senior management commitment to creating a positive work environment.

Case Study

Beyond Lip-service – Senior Management Commitment to Eliminating Workplace Harrassment

"Organisations are realising that developing a culture which values diversity is no easy task. The greatest challenge is that of translating a well-meaning equal opportunities policy into practice. It is in the area of cultural change that leadership from senior managers, including the Board, becomes critical.

Often it is the gaps between intended policy and actual behaviour that reveal the extent of the challenge. One anecdote tells of the chairman who, on being asked about an equal opportunities initiative, referred to the 'girls' at work. Sadly, this kind of comment (perhaps made with no intention to offend) does a great deal to undermine organisations' 'good intent'.

If creating a diverse culture is about developing an environment where the potential of people from all backgrounds is realised, then eliminating harassment is clearly a critical element. Harassment is often, therefore, one of the key initiatives organisations choose to tackle following the development of an equal opportunities vision and strategy.

The launch of a harassment policy, and the associated support required for its successful integration, often symbolises an organisation's desire to change its culture. However, as with any equal opportunities initiative, the policy alone is not sufficient. A critical element in changing the culture is the role played by senior managers, but what should this role be?

In Schneider-Ross' book *From Equality to Diversity: a Business Case for Equal Opportunities*, we stress the need to be conscious of the different leadership styles appropriate to building ownership of equal opportunities. Many aspects of building ownership require consultative or selling modes rather than telling modes. The area of harassment is, however, one of the exceptions. It is entirely appropriate for senior managers to tell the organisation what is or is not appropriate. New standards of behaviour may be required.

'The tell style is wholly appropriate where top management need to wear their values on their sleeve . . . they should issue . . . a disciplinary procedure which makes explicit reference to sexual and racial harassment as examples of misconduct.'

Just as with any cultural change, this one is best signalled clearly from the top of the organisation. In our work with top teams, we are often asked to focus on leadership skills. Since there is no doubt (see Chapters 4 and 5) that harassment has much to do with abuse of power, it is important that those in powerful positions within the organisation take their leadership role seriously.

Directors are sometimes surprised to learn that their own actions send out strong signals to their organisations. If their own behaviour is at odds with the harassment (or any other) policy, this will clearly undermine its standing with the organisations.

Modelling acceptable behaviour and dealing effectively with harassment are two ways of demonstrating commitment to the development of a 'diversity culture'. They are examples of 'symbolic leadership'. To fully support a new Harassment or Dignity at Work policy, though, what initiatives should senior teams consider?

1. Redraw the lines of acceptable behaviour

In this area more than any, a strong message needs to be sent to the organisation that it will no longer tolerate behaviour which is bullying or offensive. Examples include rethinking the annual conference speaker who specialises in offensive racist or sexist comedy, or writing a supporting statement in the harassment leaflet sent to employees.

A harassment policy may require the questioning of your own behaviour too. Clearly, if you fail to respond to unacceptable behaviour at, for example, a public function, employees might infer that you are colluding with the behaviour. We know of one senior executive who started an annual social do with a pretty raunchy joke which he alone thought was funny. His senior managers laughed supportively but more junior women (and men) were merely embarrassed. (So were the senior managers' wives!) This wasn't just a misjudged joke. Due to his seniority it sent the worst possible signals. It is in that sort of example that you can almost hear the head-on collision between policy and practice, between talk and walk.

2. Link the policy to other organisational change

Set out to managers the positive reasons for pursuing a harassment policy, and how it contributes to the development of a healthier organisation. Make the links with leadership initiatives and 360 degree feedback.

3. Be prepared to punish transgressors

If harassment by an individual has been established, the disciplinary route (and perhaps ultimately dismissal) must be followed through. Often the line of action is difficult, particularly when a senior colleague is involved. However, if the problem is not dealt with seriously, and is perhaps 'swept under the carpet', then the credibility of the policy is called into question.

4. Review progress

Ultimately, it is important to make it clear that challenging harassment in the organisation may not be easy. It is an emotive subject and will require skilful handling. However, it represents only one aspect of a broader shift in organisational values. The old-world 'macho' management is moving towards a more open teamworking style, organisations are rightly re-examining their values on many fronts, and ethical responsibilities have been rising up the business and political agenda. Innovation and creativity are prized in the new world organisation, but if they are to thrive as living values, then harassment and bullying must be eliminated.

It is in the parts of the organisation where 'mono-cultures' thrive (see Chapter 5), where people who are different stand out and are few in number, that harassment is most likely to thrive. Examples include the predominantly male fire-fighting, or City analyst, teams, or the all-female and white factory packing team with few male or black employees.

Innovation and creativity cannot survive where harassment is an accepted norm. Individuals will simply stop coming up with new ideas and suggestions. Organisational 'ghettos' will continue, as the 'minority group' steers clear of joining parts of the organisation where they feel they won't be accepted, and stays put in the more mixed team.

Seen as part of an overall shift in ethical standards and a re-examination of values, harassment becomes a critical issue for senior managers. It is therefore important to build harassment case figures and indicators of cultural change into your monitoring process and also set (and review) some personal leadership objectives.

Creating an environment where harassment cannot thrive should therefore be seen as part of a wider shift in values and organisation culture. Sold internally, it will not be seen as a 'being nice to each other' policy, but an essential part of the development of the organisation into the 21st century."

Rachael Ross and Gill Jackson, Schneider-Ross

The link between management and leadership is a vital one. As quoted by Peter Drucker, *"Management is doing things right; leadership is doing the right things,"* a view echoed by Warren Bennis: *"Management is efficiency in climbing the ladder of success; leadership determines whether the ladder is leaning against the right wall."* The role of providing clear vision and commitment to creating a positive culture falls on leaders; managers enact that vision and commitment, and in so doing, set the working climate through their relationships with subordinates and peers.

It is clear, then, that the most fundamental element of a manager's role is the ability to handle people effectively. Laurie Mullins, in his book *Management and Organisational Behaviour*, states:

"The style of managerial behaviour has an obvious and direct effect both on the well-being of staff and on their level of work performance . . . Different styles of management may be appropriate in managing different people in different circumstances. And a more autocratic management style many not necessarily be a bad thing.

However, the environment of the work organisation and the nature of the manager–subordinate relationship can cause tension and stress. Increasing attention is being given to health problems that are classified as stress-related and affected by working conditions. It is important to remember both the effects on organisational performance and the potentially high human cost of inappropriate management . . . Managers [should] have a highly developed sense of 'people perception' and understand the feelings of staff, and their needs and expectations. It is people who are being managed, and people should be considered in human terms."

(From *Management and Organisational Behaviour*, by LJ Mullins. Reproduced by kind permission of Pitman Publishing)

As mentioned in Chapter 4, managers who have a high concern for people as well as for production are more likely to be effective, and less likely to be perpetrators of harassment and bullying. Blake and Mouton's Leadership Grid (Figure 14) builds on the principles of concern for people and production, and with vertical and horizontal axes on a scale of 1–9 has produced seven combinations revealing styles of management.

Figure 14.
Blake and
Mouton's
Leadership Grid

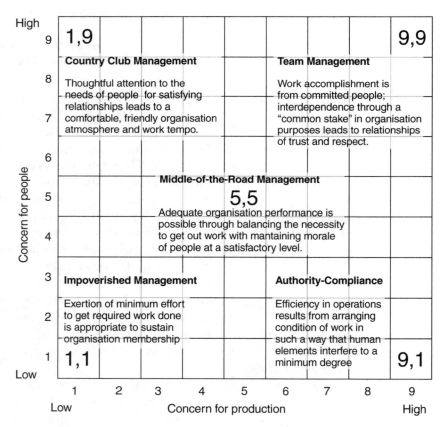

(From *Leadership Dilemmas – Grid Solutions* p. 29 by Robert R. Blake and Anne Adams McCanse. Copyright 1991. © by Robert R Blake and the estate of Jane S Mouton, used with permission. All rights reserved)

The grid provides a useful framework for managers to examine their attitude and behaviour, and helps them identify their current style of management and which areas need improving.

The seven combinations of the grid
The five basic combinations

1,1 Impoverished management

Often referred to as *laissez-faire* leadership. Managers in this position have little concern for people or productivity, avoid taking sides and stay out of conflicts. They do just enough to get by.

1,9 Country club management

Managers in this position have great concern for people and little concern for production. They try to avoid conflicts and concentrate on being well liked. To them the task is less important than good interpersonal relations. Their goal is to keep people happy.

9,1 Authority–compliance

Managers in this position have great concern for production and little concern for people. They desire tight control in order to get tasks done efficiently. They consider creativity and human relations to be unnecessary.

5,5 Middle-of-the-road management

Managers in this position have medium concern for people and production. They attempt to balance their concern for both people and production, but are not committed to either.

9,9 Team management

This style of leadership is considered to be ideal. Such managers have great concern for both people and production. They work to motivate employees to reach their highest levels of accomplishment. They are flexible and responsive to change, and they understand the need to change.

Although not shown on Figure 14 the Grid also covers two additional styles, 9+9 Paternalistic management, and Opp Opportunistic management.

| **9+9 Paternalistic management** | Known as "father-knows-best" management, this is a style in which reward is promised for compliance, and punishment threatened for non-compliance. |
| **Opp Opportunistic management** | The style utilised depends on which style the leader feels will return him or her the greatest self-benefit. "What's in it for me" is the key phrase here. |

(Source L Mullins – Robert R Blake and Jane S Mouton – The Managerial Grid III. Reproduced with kind permission from Pitman Publishing)

Managers with a 1,1 or 9,1 rating may be in danger of developing a style which could be interpreted as harassment or bullying, and need to take great care with interpersonal relationships.

More emphasis has to be placed on an integrated style of management which involves and empowers employees, rather than a dictatorial, authoritative style which is controlling. It is clear, then, that "team management" is the style that managers need to aim for, in order to prevent harassment and bullying becoming an issue within their teams.

Incidents of harassment often occur when managers do not have a clear understanding of how to "flex" their management style, particularly when managing people who do not necessarily have the same cultural background. The phrase "manage different people differently" aptly describes how to manage diversity; however, the following simple guidelines show that applying good management practice is the key to managing diversity effectively:

Guidelines for managing diversity
To manage diversity managers need to:

● Approach every employee as an individual.
● Understand that cultural differences such as language, mannerisms and communication patterns are not necessarily indicators of an employee's performance or capabilities.
● Recognise and confront the issue of discomfort – your own and others' – in dealing with a diverse workforce.
● Appreciate and utilise the different perspectives and styles of diverse workers.
● Convey clearly your expectations for the work unit, whilst at the same time recognising group differences in communication and perspective.
● Use equal performance standards for all workers.

- Provide feedback often and equally to all members of your team (and other employees).
- Openly support the competencies and contributions of employees from all groups.
- Know the legislation that underpins equality in employment, and the responsibilities that lie within them.
- Be aware of subtle and systematic institutional discrimination, intentional or unintentional, that pigeonholes and limits opportunities for members of groups other than those in the dominant culture.
- Confront racist, sexist or other stereotypical or discriminatory behaviour – in yourself as well as in others.
- Be comfortable asking questions about preferred terminology or interactions.
- Assume responsibility not only for the behaviour and attitudes of your team/department but for trying to influence change in your organisation.
- Act as a role model at all times.
- Understand that it is you, the manager, who ultimately holds the key to unlocking and releasing the full potential of each person in your team.

(Adapted from *Voices of Diversity*, by Renee Blank and Sandra Slipp, AMACOM, 1994. Reproduced with kind permission from AMACOM)

Setting standards of behaviour through good policy development

A policy has to serve the needs of the business and is a guideline for organisational action. Policy creation and revision is one way of updating and working towards the "preferred" culture of the organisation. Therefore, it is essential that it is clearly linked to organisational vision, goals and objectives. The vision of a diverse workforce in a healthy working climate is one which must be communicated clearly and with genuine commitment, in order to eradicate harassment, bullying and violence in the workplace.

Policies also set the standards for the way employees behave in an organisation. A control system for improving the work environment and combating harassment must be set up in order to give employees clear guidelines on the type of behaviour expected within the organisation. Not only will the system set guidelines for individual behaviour, it will measure the level of control over employees, and how well the organisation is doing in terms of performance.

The level of power and influence within the organisation will also be measured by the control system, as well as the types of social relationships that exist within the organisation's structure. How leaders use (or abuse) power will give a clear indication of the level of institutional discrimination within the organisation, and the extent to which covert cliques and clubs that exclude individuals or certain groups of people exist.

Gerard Egan suggests that organisations should conduct a political audit to assess how far the practice of power and political influences adversely affects organisational achievement. The types of questions to ask include:

● How would we describe the political culture, and to what degree does it limit our effectiveness?
● What are the rules of "combat" and conflict management? How do we manage conflict?
● How do we feel about employee empowerment and involvement? To what degree are we a paternalistic organisation?
● What are the principal sources of power in the organisation?
● To what degree do people in the organisation glory in the use of power?

A good control system needs to be fully understood by all employees, and so the importance of good communication should not be underestimated.

Chapter 8 looks in detail at developing policies and systems to combat harassment, and Chapter 11 looks at the role of training and development, which reinforces the standards of behaviour required to make the policy work.

Examining the organisation's capacity to change

How will the organisation react to the changes needed in order to create a more positive work environment?

The deeper the cultural values, the more ingrained the behaviours and practices, the more difficult it is to change. Organisations are more capable of change than individuals or the societies they live in. However, the difficulties of change in organisations should not be underestimated.

It is not unusual to encounter tough resistance to changes in the workforce, particularly when implementing equality initiatives. If the climate of the organisation is cold and frosty towards equality, people may feel that adopting harassment policies is a waste of time, or see little benefit in trying to use a system which they do not believe will work for them.

Below are some common reasons why individuals and organisations resist change.

Individual reasons for resisting change
● *Selective perception* – Creating a unique picture of the "real world", which can lead to a biased view of a particular situation that fits most

comfortably into a person's own perception of reality and can cause resistance to change.

● *Habit* – Habits may serve as a means of comfort and security, and as a guide for easy decision-making. Proposed changes to habits, especially if they are well established and require little effort, may well be resisted. However, if there is a clearly perceived advantage, there is likely to be less, if any, resistance to change.

● *Inconvenience or loss of freedom* – If the change is seen as likely to prove inconvenient, make life more difficult, reduce freedom of action or result in increased control, there will be resistance.

● *Security in the past* – There is a tendency for some people to find a sense of security in the past. In times of frustration or difficulty, or when faced with new or unfamiliar ideas or methods, people may reflect on the past, and there is a wish to retain old and comfortable ways.

● *Fear of the unknown* – Changes which confront people with the unknown tend to cause anxiety or fear. Many major changes in a work organisation present a degree of uncertainty.

Organisational reasons for resisting change

● *Maintaining stability* – Large-scale organisations often invest a lot of time in maintaining stability and predictability. The need for formal structures and established rules and procedures can result in resistance to change.

● *Investment in resources* – Change often requires large resources which may already be committed to investments in other areas, and assets such as buildings, technology and people cannot easily be altered.

● *Threats to power or influence* – Certain groups in the organisation may see the introduction of change (particularly those changes which affect their control over decisions, resources or information) as threatening. Where a group of people have, over a period of time, established what they perceive as their "territorial rights", they are likely to resist change.

(Adapted from *Management and Organisational Behaviour*, by LJ Mullins. Reproduced with kind permission from Pitman Publishing)

Gaining commitment to change

If an employee is to be committed to the changes required to create a positive working environment, that employee must believe wholeheartedly in the organisation and its goals and objectives. They must also exhibit a willingness to work with and help the organisation challenge discrimination – not just because it is part of their role, but as an act of faith and integrity.

As commitment is very personal, organisations must first understand how individuals go through change, and realise that the process is a much slower one than that of the structure of the organisation. The following transition curve (Figure 15) indicates the stages of change that individuals go through in their lifetime. The process is not smooth and there may be many deviations; however, the curve acts as a good guide.

Figure 15.
The Transition
Curve

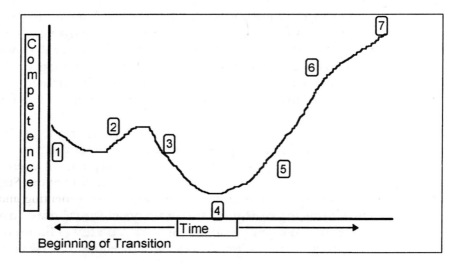

(Adapted from "Transitions", by J Adams *et al.* Source: Elizabeth Kubler-Ross)

The transition curve

The curve applies to any kind of change, positive or negative, expected or unexpected, and wanted or unwanted. Examples of major life changes are births and deaths, marriage, divorce, promotion, redundancy and retirement. The curve applies to grief as well as other emotions. Elizabeth Kubler-Ross used it originally to describe the stages that terminally ill people went though.

The stages

1. **Immobilisation**. *Shock.* Overwhelmed mismatch between high expectations and reality, which may cause a temporary paralysis and/or disbelief. Positive changes bring this state as well, eg when you are unable to believe your good luck.

2. **Denial of change**. *Temporary retreat, false competence.* This stage marks an attempt to return to pre–Stage 1, which represents a denial that anything has happened. Some people attempt to continue as

before, and get "stuck". Elizabeth Kubler-Ross discovered this in people who find it difficult to accept that a loved one has died and hold back their grief and freeze at Stage 2.

3. **Incompetence**. *Awareness that change is necessary. Frustration phase. How to deal with change.* Stage 3 is the downward slope. It is the stage of emotionality, of fear, grief, anger and blame. There is no point being logical here, or reasoning. To help someone in this stage, just support and accept their emotionality. Eventually they come to a point of acceptance.

4. **Acceptance of reality**. *"Letting go" of past comfortable attitudes and behaviours.* Stage 4 is where they are drained and empty, ready to rebuild. This represents the bottom of the curve. This can apply to alcoholics. They have to admit they are one (Stage 2+) and then face up to their problems until they reach Stage 4. Sometimes it is necessary when people are capable of it to help them go through Stage 3.

5. **Testing**. *New behaviours, new approaches.* The tendency here is to stereo-type, i.e. the way things should be done. Lots of energy. Begin to deal with new reality – a lot of anger and frustration. Stage 5 is one of trying new ways of doing things, of experimenting and learning.

6. **Search for meaning**. *Internalisation. Seeking to understand why things are different.* Not until people get out of activity do they understand their lives better. Stage 6 involves trying to understand what lies at the basis of the new behaviour.

7. **Integration**. *Incorporate meanings into new behaviours.* Stage 7 marks the coming together of new behaviours and meanings and a return to effectiveness.

The curve is very similar to a learning curve. It entails risk. We do not know what is going to happen; we may fail and have to revert back. It involves cost and stress. However, going through the curve gives us the opportunity to gain "experience" and "wisdom". Having got used to change, we can do it again. The curve also helps to make change exciting and fun – once we are aware of it.

 Once employees are given the opportunity to analyse their response to the changes made, in order to gain their commitment, organisations need to:

● Develop a clear vision of the change and communicate it – often and well.
● Communicate the aims and objectives of the change, and help individuals set personal goals to cope with it.

● Help people accept change by considering how they will be affected.
● Involve people in the change process through consultation and giving them information frequently.
● Never rush changes through quickly – give people a reasonable amount of time to get used to what is happening, and allow them the time to learn new behaviours to cope with the changes.
● Monitor the changes and publish the results – even if there is very little activity.
● Leaders and managers must, at all times, demonstrate their commitment to change and act as role models.

Case Study

When Management Commitment Is Misplaced . . .
The effects of management behaviour when gaining commitment to eradicating workplace harassment are far-reaching. Samantha, a management consultant in an HR advisory firm, describes how her belief that the organisation she worked for was committed to equality was dashed:

"I was over the moon. I had just put the telephone down from a client who had connections with a firm in Hong Kong, and had confirmed over £75,000 worth of consultancy business with them.
    I rushed to tell Christopher, my manager, the good news. He was supportive, and we began to sit down and plan how best we could complete the project.
    Imagine my surprise the next day when I heard Christopher talking on the phone – obviously to my client. His conversation went: 'Of course, we understand, it's a different culture out there and we wouldn't want to offend them in any way.' What was going on? Christopher had put down the receiver with a promise to 'sort things out'. He got up from his seat, without giving me any eye contact, and went immediately to Robert's desk (Robert and I work closely on similar projects). I saw Robert lift his head up and he looked over to me in shock. 'I'm not getting involved in this unless you tell her directly,' he said firmly.
    Christopher called me over to Robert's desk. By this time, I had a vague idea what was going on, but the butterflies in my stomach told me that this was going to be a confrontation that I would suffer from greatly. Christopher, looking very uncomfortable, shifted his weight from side to side, and looked at me with sheepish eyes. 'Samantha, remember the call we received from your client yesterday? Well, I took the call from them this morning because you were not around, and well, we thought it best not to put you in the position of having to deal with the whole load of this project, and so I have asked Robert to do the training in Hong Kong, whilst you make sure the project runs smoothly from this end.'

I could tell by Robert's expression of shock that Christopher was lying through his teeth. By this time, I was so angry that I blurted out my version of events. 'Do you think I was born yesterday? I was standing right in front of you when the client asked specifically for you. What's wrong? Don't they want a woman to stand in front of a group of Asian men?' At least Christopher had the decency to look embarrassed at this point. 'Am I not good enough at my job, or am I quite simply the wrong sex?'

'It's nothing like that Samantha. You'll have plenty of other opportunities to travel abroad, and besides, we have to look after the client's needs. They like you, but they would prefer to have a contact that they can rely on here in the UK, and when I suggested that you wouldn't mind staying here, they were happy with it and agreed.'

I couldn't look at him in the face, and walked away. Robert caught up with me later, and told me straight. The client had second thoughts and did not want a woman for their male colleagues in Hong Kong, and Christopher had gone along with their sexist behaviour, without even challenging it or sticking up for me.

What hurt me more was his lack of commitment towards me, and his condoning of their discriminatory behaviour. How is this company going to show real commitment to equal opportunities, and get rid of the harassment and bullying that occurs, when managers like Christopher espouse lip-service?

I didn't manage that client's account. I found another job instead, and left a lengthy explanation of how I felt in my exit interview."

(Samantha)

Tying all the strings together – developing strategies to create a positive work environment

Developing strategies to implement organisational processes is a fundamental part of organisational development. Bartlett and Ghoshal, in an article written for the *Harvard Business Review* in 1990, state: *"the surest way to break down insularity is to develop and communicate a clear sense of corporate purpose that extends into every corner of the company and gives context and meaning to each manager's particular roles and responsibilities"*. Without a clear strategy for improving the working environment, very little will be gained from the activities outlined in this chapter.

A good strategic approach will facilitate a change in culture and influence environmental conditions. The key elements of such an approach are:

● Diagnosis and analysis of the organisation to get a true picture of its current situation (the culture audit is a key activity here).
● Defining vision, and setting clear aims, goals and objectives as a benchmark for monitoring and evaluation.
● A focus on maximising opportunities as opposed to minimising risks.
● A thorough involvement, participation and consultation exercise which is aimed at gaining the commitment of employees to change, and to influence behaviour by selling the positive benefits of the strategy.
● Good planning and control system development, with structures in place for learning, in order to make the policy work.
● Continuous evaluation and monitoring against a quality framework, to ensure continuous improvement.

A successful strategy for eradicating workplace harassment, bullying and violence relies on a balance being struck between "quick wins" (immediate and effective opportunities for improvement) and more challenging long-term targets for creativity and changing the character of the organisation.

Reflection

So far, we have looked at the theories as to why discrimination occurs at varying levels within organisations, as well as giving some suggestions on how to improve certain contributory factors of organisational life. Eliminating workplace harassment is a continuous process, and as an organisation's culture changes and becomes more flexible, so the need to implement different levels of harassment awareness is necessary. However, there are basic steps an organisation needs to take in order to meet its responsibilities.

The rest of the book will now concentrate on: the practical issues of creating policies; using the law as a guideline; training and development as well as dealing with cases of harassment and bullying when they arise.

References

Managing Diversity: A Complete Desk Reference and Planning Guide, Lee Gardenswartz and Anita Rowe (McGraw-Hill, 1993).

From Equality to Diversity: A Business Case for Equal Opportunities, Rachael Ross and Robin Schneider (Pitman Publishing, 1992).

Managing the Mosaic: Diversity in Action, Rajvinder Kandola and Johanna Fullerton (Institute of Personnel and Development, 1994).

Working the Shadow Side: A Guide to Positive Behind-the-Scenes Management, Gerard Egan (Jossey-Bass, 1994).

Management and Organisational Behaviour, Laurie J Mullins (Pitman Publishing, 1996).

"Matrix management: not a structure, a frame of mind", CA Bartlett and S Ghoshal, *Harvard Business Review*, July–August 1990.

Sexual Orientation in the Workplace: Gay Men, Lesbians, Bisexuals and Heterosexuals Working Together, Amy J Zuckerman and George F Simons (Sage Publications, 1996).

Voices of Diversity: Real People Talk about Problems and Solutions in a Workplace Where Everyone Is Not Alike, Renee Blank and Sandra Slipp (AMACOM, 1994).

CHAPTER 7

Harassment and bullying: the law

This chapter describes the current state of UK law and the impact of EU legislation on harassment and bullying. It also makes comparisons between the law in the UK and USA, and describes some of the key decisions of courts and tribunals, and the influence of developments in European courts.

Racism and sexism in the workplace affect everyone and not just those who are the target of the offensive behaviour. This view has been reflected in discrimination legislation, where there has been a major shift towards making employers responsible for the discriminatory behaviour of their employees at work. The laws designed to counteract discrimination in the workplace are being used with increasing vigour to assist employees who suffer racial or sexual harassment, and behaviour that once went unchecked is now deemed to be unlawful.

The law around sexual harassment is far more developed than that of racial harassment. This is because there is a wider acceptance of sexual harassment as an issue of concern, whereas racial harassment complainants still have a hard job proving their cases before a tribunal and only the clearest cut, most serious cases are ever successful. However, the growing number of sexual and racial harassment cases that reach tribunals each year reflects an increase in public awareness. As more claimants are successful this will encourage more people to challenge all forms of harassment in the courts and thereby increase the pressure on employers to pay more attention to their legal responsibilities in this area.

There is a considerable body of anti-discrimination law which prohibits sexual and racial harassment. This chapter will examine the legislation, the decisions of courts and tribunals and the influence of developments in European courts. In the case of bullying at work, however, there is very little protection for employees. Employees suffering from bullying in the workplace can only rely on the unsatisfactory provisions of the Health and Safety at Work Act 1974. Also, an employer who fails to take steps to prevent bullying at work is likely to be in breach of the implied contractual duty of mutual trust and confidence. This may lead an employee to resign and bring an action for constructive dismissal. This is explored further at the end of this chapter.

In the area of employment law, the main statutes are the Race Relations Act 1976 (RRA) and the Sex Discrimination Act 1975 (SDA), amended in 1986, which contain similar provisions relating to discrimination on the grounds of race, sex and marital status.

The legislation prohibits discrimination but does not mention racial or sexual harassment specifically. Three kinds of discrimination are prohibited by the legislation:

Direct racial and sexual discrimination

This is what most people consider as discrimination. Direct racial or sexual discrimination happens when somebody is treated less favourably because of their race or sex. Direct sex discrimination can also occur on grounds of marital status: e.g. if a married woman is treated less favourably than a single woman.

Indirect racial and sexual discrimination

It is also discriminatory when a requirement or condition is applied to all workers but results in a disadvantage to one race or sex. It can also be indirect discrimination when people from one race or sex find it harder to comply in practice with a particular requirement than other people: for example, to work full time may be harder for women than men. However, employers may be able to justify requirements or conditions which have a discriminatory impact.

Victimisation

It is unlawful to penalise anyone for bringing proceedings, making allegations or complaints or giving evidence in relation to a racial or sexual discrimination case. This was included in the law to protect people who complain of racial or sexual discrimination and take action against their employers.

The meaning of harassment

There is no legal definition of harassment in either the RRA or the SDA. Protection against harassment is provided indirectly, since there is actually no offence of racial or sexual harassment specifically identified in the legislation. This means that there may be some acts which might be considered as harassment by victims that will not necessarily amount to discrimination under the law.

The European Commission's Code of Practice on sexual harassment has one of the most widely acceptable "non legal" definitions and states that sexual harassment means: *"unwanted conduct of a sexual nature or other conduct based on sex affecting the dignity of women and men at work"*.

The Commission's definition can usefully be extended to cover racial harassment also, and the Code makes the link with harassment on the grounds of race by pointing out that sexual harassment is often combined with racial harassment.

The Commission for Racial Equality (CRE) state in their guidelines *Racial Harassment at Work: What Employers Can Do About It* that *"there is no hard and fast definition of racial harassment. It is a general term covering a wide range of unacceptable, and often unlawful, behaviour"*, and adapts the EC Code of Practice definition of sexual harassment to racial harassment.

Although there is no express prohibition in the legislation against harassment, both the RRA and the SDA offer legal remedies to people who have been harassed at work, where that harassment amounts to discrimination under the Acts. It is clear from the decided cases under both Acts that racial and sexual harassment can constitute direct discrimination and are therefore potentially unlawful. Thus if a person is harassed for a reason which relates to their sex or their race, and this constitutes less favourable treatment or is to his or her detriment, then this would constitute unlawful discrimination. The same principle would apply to the Disability Discrimination Act 1995 (DDA), in relation to harassment of a disabled person. This is explored more fully below.

The CRE can give advice and assistance on racial harassment, whilst the Equal Opportunities Commission (EOC) provides a similar service in relation to complaints of sexual harassment.

What the law says about harassment

Harassment as less favourable treatment
S1(1) of the RRA states that *"a person discriminates against another if on racial grounds he treats that other person less favourably than he treats or would*

treat other persons." (S1(1) of the SDA is similar except that it prohibits discrimination against a woman "*on the grounds of her sex*").

Sexual and racial harassment have been found in the courts and tribunals to be a type of direct discrimination that amounts to less favourable treatment on the grounds of sex or race.

Thus, if an employee wishes to make a claim about racial or sexual harassment, they must show that as a result of the behaviour they have been treated less favourably on the grounds of race or sex. So, for example, if a man sexually harasses a woman, she will be able to claim that the harasser is treating her less favourably than he would a man, and she is thereby subjected to direct discrimination.

In the same way if a black or Asian employee is harassed and the particular insult or abuse of behaviour is expressly racial, the harasser will be held to have treated that employee less favourably than a white colleague. Furthermore, the harasser cannot avoid liability under the RRA by saying that white employees would have been treated in an equally insulting manner, because of the explicitly racial nature of the behaviour involved.

Harassment as a detriment or disadvantage

The legislation outlines the type of behaviour that will amount to discrimination. The RRA s4(2)(c) states that: "*It is unlawful for a person to discriminate against an employee by dismissing him or subjecting him to any other detriment.*" (An identical provision is contained in s6(2)(b) of the SDA, making it unlawful for an employer to discriminate against a woman on similar grounds.) Any other detriment here means "putting under a disadvantage" (*Ministry of Defence* v *Jeremiah*, 1980).

For example, the detriment might be in the form of lack of promotion or other advancement due to a refusal to accept sexual advances. It is not necessary for there to be a sacking or for the employee to feel forced to resign. For an action to constitute a detriment there does not even have to be any direct repercussion following the harassment. A black or Asian person would be put at a disadvantage simply by working in a hostile environment, which for their white counterparts would not present a threat.

Sexual harassment – how the law has developed through cases

Sexual harassment is becoming increasingly widespread in the workplace; indeed, many would argue that this has always been the case. As discussed in Chapter 1, it can take many forms, from leering, sexual remarks or abuse to unwanted and repeated physical contact. To succeed before the employment tribunal, a woman being harassed must show that she has been treated less favourably on the grounds of her sex than her comparable male colleague and that she has suffered a detriment or has been dismissed as a result. If the treatment she is complaining of was on the basis of her sex this will still constitute sexual harassment even if an equally disliked male would have been treated equally badly. This was established in the ground breaking case of *Strathclyde Regional Council v Porcelli* (1986).

In this case Mrs Porcelli was a school laboratory technician who alleged that male colleagues sexually harassed her as part of a campaign to make her leave, by deliberately brushing against her and making suggestive sexual remarks. As a result of their behaviour she was forced to apply for a transfer to another school. She complained that she had been unlawfully discriminated against and that she had been subject to a detriment contrary to s6(2)(b) of the SDA.

It was claimed by the council that Mrs Porcelli's treatment was not due to her sex but because she was disliked, and that a male employee in the same position would not have been treated any differently. The tribunal which heard the case agreed with them and rejected her claim on the grounds that although she had suffered, a man would have suffered just as much if he had been similarly disliked by his colleagues.

On appeal the case went to the Scottish Court of Session, which concluded that Mrs Porcelli's treatment was due to the fact that she was a woman. The Court stated that the real issue was whether she had been treated less favourably on the grounds of her sex than a man. It was irrelevant that an equally disliked male colleague would have been treated just as unpleasantly, because he would not have suffered the sexual element of his colleagues' behaviour:

"This particular part of the campaign was plainly adopted against Mrs Porcelli because she was a woman. It was a particular kind of weapon, based on the sex of the victim, which would not have been used against an equally disliked man."

It was decided that Mrs Porcelli had indeed been subjected to unlawful discrimination. The Act is concerned with less favourable treatment and not motive. In fact it is important to note that there is no need to show an explicit sexual motive, and an employer will not be able to argue, as was tried in Porcelli, that the woman's treatment was not based on her sex, but simply because she was disliked.

Whereas in most cases the behaviour complained of will form part of a pattern or course of conduct over time, there are cases which indicate that sometimes just a single act or remark is sufficient to constitute harassment.

In *Bracebridge Engineering Ltd v Darby* (1990), a worker was sexually assaulted by two of her supervisors. The employer argued that a single act was not enough to constitute harassment, as it was not possible, after only one occasion, to say that the act was unwanted.

The Employment Appeal Tribunal (EAT) rejected that argument and held that a single act of sexual harassment, provided it was serious enough, will constitute a detriment under s6(2)(b) of the SDA and is therefore unlawful: *"whether or not harassment is a continuing course of conduct, there was an act of discrimination against a woman because she was a woman."*

Also in *Heads v (1) Insitu Cleaning Co Ltd* and (2) *Brown* (1995), Ms Brown's manager greeted her with "Hiya big tits" when she walked into a meeting. This single remark was held to be sufficiently serious to constitute a detriment and was therefore discrimination.

Many of the cases have considered the impact of the complainant's sexual morality, mode of dress and emotional state of mind on the issue of whether there has been discrimination. The courts' view is that it is necessary to show subjectively that the particular employee was disadvantaged in her working circumstances and that objectively a reasonable worker of the same sex or race would have been disadvantaged. The nature of the workplace, the employee's status and vulnerability are likely to be relevant.

In *Wileman v Minilec Engineering Ltd* (1988) the courts refused to allow evidence that Ms Wileman had posed in a scanty costume for the newspaper to back a claim that she had not really suffered any detriment as a result of the harassment.

The court also refused to allow evidence that the harasser had made sexual remarks to other women:

"If this gentleman made sexual remarks to a number of people, it has to be looked at in the context of each person. All the people to whom they are made may regard them as wholly inoffensive: everyone else may regard them as offensive. Each individual has the right, if the remarks are regarded as offensive, to treat them as an offence under the Sex Discrimination Act."

This case underlines the subjective nature of sexual harassment by establishing the principle that it is for an individual woman to determine what offends her and what she is prepared to accept. So, the fact that a woman may accept or even welcome one male colleague putting his arm around her does not give *carte blanche* for every man in the organisation to do so: *"A person may be quite happy to accept the remarks of A or B in a sexual context and wholly upset by similar remarks made by C."*

A typical example of behaviour that many women would regard as harassment is the display of pictures of nude women in the workplace. One case which considered this issue is *Stewart v Cleveland Guest (Engineering) Ltd* (1994). In that case the Employment Appeal Tribunal (EAT) held that on the facts presented to them the employer had not discriminated against a woman employee who complained that the display of pin up pictures of women was offensive to her.

They accepted that she had been subjected to a detriment by having to work in an area where there were pin ups of nude women and that it was reasonable for her to find this offensive. They ruled that this did not amount to discrimination however because a hypothetical man might also have made similar complaints. She had not shown therefore that she had been treated less favourably than a man would have been treated.

The EAT also made a curious finding that the display of nude pin ups was "gender neutral" because a man might also find them offensive. It is clear however that such pictures offend women because they are women more so than they offend a man. It is also well documented that nude pin ups can poison the working environment for women.

The EAT did point out however that their decision did not mean that... "it is never an act of sex discrimination for a company to allow its male employees to display pictures of that kind in the workplace." This depends on the particular facts of every case and it is clear that displays of nude pin ups falls within the scope of the European Commission's definition of sexual harassment. So whilst this is an unfortunate decision from a woman's point of view, employers need to be aware that despite the outcome, there was a finding of fact that working with pin ups did subject Miss Stewart to a detriment and it is unlikely that the "hypothetical" man's objections will always prevail against the demonstrable harm suffered by a woman.

Quid pro quo harassment involves the exchange of any kind of employment benefits in return for express or implied sexual favours. S6(1) of the SDA makes it unlawful for employers to discriminate on the grounds of sex in the provision of access to opportunities for promotion, transfer or training, and thus prohibits quid pro quo harassment.

Difficult issues arise when the harassment takes place outside of the workplace or where the perpetrator of the harassment is not an employee of the organisation. In the latter case the courts have found that an employer can be guilty of unlawful discrimination where the employer had knowledge or foresight that the employee would be exposed to discriminatory acts (*Go Kidz Co Ltd* v *Boudane*). This issue is explored in detail below (liability for third parties) but some of the problems that can arise are illustrated by the following case study.

What happens when the alleged harasser is external to the organisation?

There have been occasions when members of staff have been harassed by contractors, clients, customers, service users or volunteers. Although the organisation might need the services, support and assistance of these parties or have a duty to provide services, this does not absolve the employer from taking action. Often organisations have nothing in their policies to cover such situations. So what can you do when the situation in the following case study arises?

Case Study

The Harassing Client

Lena Davis was a top account manager for a large firm specialising in computer software.

To launch the release of a major desk-top publishing package, a champagne lunch was arranged at a top City venue for key and new accounts. Lena hosted a table with her team and their major clients, one of which had recently made a £200K pre-order for the new software.

As the champagne flowed and the event progressed, Lena moved around the table, ensuring that her clients were enjoying themselves, and dealing with any questions and queries they had about their accounts, as well as the new software package. Lena finally reaches David Freman, software purchasing manager of a large dealing firm. "I'm annoyed with you Lena!" David teases. "I placed some good business your way this year, and you leave me until last!!" Lena is embarrassed, but keeps her calm – she does not want her guests and team to recognise her unease. The client whose firm made the £200K pre-order was a new account, and Lena did not want him to witness a scene, and withdraw his order.

David Freman's firm was developed as a key account by Lena's predecessor. When she was first introduced as the new account manager, David's reaction was one of pleasant surprise, and he commented to Lena's predecessor that "he was at last getting the special treatment he deserved, and thank you to your firm for introducing the prettiest software seller in the business!" He often invited Lena to dinner (usually in small cosy restaurants based in hotels). However, Lena handled him professionally by occasionally meeting David for lunch with one of her team, and dealing with his account mainly by telephone.

Although Lena was fully aware of his intentions, she never considered his behaviour to be a serious threat (she saw him as a nuisance, and felt the situation was manageable). But, he had been knocking back the champagne at an incredible rate, and now his behaviour was unpredictable.

To pacify him, Lena looked at David and said, "I'm sorry if you felt neglected David. Let me make amends. I am sure you wouldn't say no to a free demonstration copy of the desk-top publishing package." David responded quickly. "Come on, let's show these people why I can't say no to you every time you come into my office" – and promptly grabbed Lena around the waist, pulled her over his lap, and kissed her forcefully, whilst keeping Lena in a firm clinch.

Half of the guests on the table laughed – probably from embarrassment – and the others looked on in shock. Lena felt humiliated, made an excuse, and rushed off to the toilets.

One of Lena's team, Richard Preston, challenged David quietly. "Mr Freman!" Richard said – jokingly. "You've managed to render Lena speechless. I know what she's like though, when Lena gets her breath back, she'll make mincemeat out you!"

Lena came back, just in time to hear David retort "You are kidding? How is she going to explain to your director that because of one little kiss, she wants to close my account? Lena is a sensible girl and I'm sure she won't complain. Besides, I am her client, and this is one of the hazards of the job!"

Lena instantly felt depressed. "He has harassed and embarrassed me in front of my team and my guests, and I'm supposed to put up with this?"

What action could Lena take?

It is clear that Lena is in a difficult situation. Her employers would be concerned at the prospect of losing such a valuable account. She should not be expected to put up with this appalling harassment, however, and there are a number of options open to her:

● First, Lena must inform her managers, who should institute an investigation into what happened through the company's complaints procedure.
● She could consider criminal action for assault or for intentional harassment and should seek the support of her employers in doing so.
● She should press her employers to take up the matter with Mr Freman's firm, who may consider taking action against him.

Lena's firm would be in a difficult position if they did not take appropriate steps to deal with the situation. They could end up being liable for the harassment she has suffered because they have either failed to provide her with a safe place of work or take her complaint of harassment seriously.

It is now clear that employers can be legally liable for the behaviour of third parties, such as clients, if the situation was sufficiently under the control of the employer that he could, by applying good employment practices, have prevented the harassment or reduced its extent. The *Burton* v *DeVere Hotels* (1996) case, outlined later on in this chapter, is a prime example.

Racial harassment – how the law has developed through cases

Fewer cases of racial harassment have reached the higher courts, which reflects the greater difficulty involved in establishing a claim.

In the case of *De Souza* v *The Automobile Association* (1985) a secretary overheard a manager telling a senior clerk to "give some typing to the wog" and claimed racial discrimination. It was held that a racial insult in itself may be a detriment under the RRA if the employee was thereby disadvantaged in their working conditions. However, the Court of Appeal also took the view that for a racial insult to amount to less favourable treatment the person making the statement must have intended the complainant to hear the remark or anticipated that they would hear it. This is very difficult to prove in everyday working conditions, as often the behaviour will be subtle and obtuse, but none the less intentional and painful for the recipient.

In *Patel and Harewood* v *T & K Home Improvements Ltd* and *Johnson* 2 (1994) incidents of racial harassment went unchecked in a friendly and informal work environment. First of all a notice appeared on the factory notice board carrying the heading "Application for Employment, Minorities Division". It was a mock application form which was described by the tribunal as "*the most offensive, insulting and degrading*" example it had ever seen. The second incident happened a week later when Mr Johnson, the production director, gave Mr Patel and Mr Harewood a notice reading "Help wanted – a small black man for mudflap – must be flexible and willing to travel".

The foreman treated it as a joke and no action was taken, but both men were very distressed by this and they complained of racial discrimination. The tribunal rejected the respondents' explanation that the notices were a joke and part of normal workplace banter, and the applicants were awarded a large sum in compensation which included aggravated damages. The tribunal commented that: *"it defies belief that such offensive material could be considered humorous."*

The company's attitude was also criticised by the tribunal:

"The respondents have made matters worse by the attitude which they have displayed both before the tribunal and indeed throughout these proceedings. They have maintained their position that this was a joke. Not once has any form of apology been offered."

In *McAuley v Auto Alloys Foundry* (1994), Trevor McAuley, an Irishman who had lived in England for 20 years, complained to an industrial tribunal about the incessant and vicious campaign of Irish jokes that he was subjected to in his work as a machinist in a Derbyshire foundry. He was often called a "typically thick paddy" and if he made a mistake his workmates would retort, "What do you expect from an Irishman?"

The tribunal's decision in his favour, awarding him £6,000 compensation, was a landmark decision which caused intense media interest, much of which was unsympathetic.

In *Jenkins v Burney and Others* (1993), Mr Jenkins, a black lecturer, claimed that he was being racially abused by students. Each time he complained the college authorities refused to believe him and passed off his complaints as "misunderstandings".

Mr Jenkins finally decided to take his case to an industrial tribunal and he brought three complaints against the college: two of racial discrimination and one of victimisation. The tribunal upheld his complaints and criticised the fact that nothing had been done despite the persistent nature of the racial harassment.

In the case of sexual harassment it is clear that for someone to be treated less favourably "on sexual grounds" the treatment complained of must relate to their sex. Thus a man cannot claim that he was discriminated against because of behaviour that was directed against a woman. The definition of "racial grounds" in the RRA is given a much wider meaning however in the case of *Weatherfield Ltd T/A VAN v Sargent* (1997).

In this case it was held that a white woman was discriminated against on racial grounds when she resigned after she had been given an instruction to discriminate against prospective customers of Black and Asian origin. The Court of Appeal in that case rejected the notion that for a person to be treated less favourably on racial grounds, the treatment had to relate to their own race. They contrasted the words of the SDA which states explicitly that the less favourable treatment must be on the grounds of "her" sex, whereas the RRA is capable of a broader interpretation.

Harassment issues and disability

According to research estimates there are over 6.5 million disabled people in the UK. However, legislation in this area has traditionally imposed a very limited obligation on employers. The Disability Discrimination Act 1995 is an attempt to change this. For the first time, employers have a duty not to discriminate against disabled people in their employ. The provisions are identical to those in the RRA and SDA. S4(2) of the Act makes it unlawful for an employer to discriminate against disabled employees in terms of employment opportunities for promotion or by dismissing or subjecting them to *"any other detriment"*.

The Act will therefore cover cases of harassment of people with disabilities by the able-bodied. Behaviour which is likely to constitute harassment will include asking intimate questions about a person's disability, name-calling or "jokes", unwelcome interference in an attempt to "help" with work and uninvited touching or patting on the head.

Whilst the Act can be welcomed for bringing in a specific prohibition against discrimination on the grounds of disability, many groups which represent the disabled have complained that its provisions do not go far enough and are too vague to make a real difference to the lives of the majority of disabled people.

Gaps in the legislation – gay men and lesbians

The anti-discriminatory legislation in the UK does not specifically cover discrimination on the grounds of sexual orientation, which can also be a focus for harassment in the workplace. However, in his manual *Preventing and Remedying Sexual Harassment at Work*, Michael Rubenstein argued that there are instances where sexual harassment of gay men and lesbians by heterosexuals could be covered by the SDA. He also argued that offensive remarks which are specific to either lesbians or gay men, such as "dyke" or "puff", could be viewed in the words of the court in *Porcelli* as *"a weapon based on the sex of the victim"*. Similarly, if a man is harassed because he is HIV positive, it could be argued that this is sex discrimination because of the association of HIV and AIDS with gay men.

In the EC Code of Practice the definition of harassment specifically includes harassment on the grounds of sexuality.

However in the 1998 case of *Grant v South West Trains Ltd* (SWT), both the UK courts and the European Court of Justice missed a historic opportunity to expand the rights at work of lesbians and gay men throughout the European Union.

Miss Grant was refused a travel pass for her female partner with whom she lived in a stable relationship. She made an application to the European Court of Justice (ECJ) for a determination as to whether under European Community Law (Art 119 of the EC Treaty) discrimination based on sex included discrimination based on an employee's sexual orientation. The ECJ held that as at the time of the decision European discrimination law did not protect a lesbian from less favourable treatment than a heterosexual. The court also stated that protection against discrimination based on sexual orientation was a matter for national governments. It is likely therefore that pressure for legislation that specifically addresses this issue will intensify as a result of this case.

A similarly restricted view was adopted by the court in this country in the 1998 case of *Smith* v *Gardner Merchant* where the Court of Appeal held that dismissal on the grounds of sexual orientation did not amount to discrimination under the SDA. In a situation where a homosexual man claimed discrimination, the correct comparator in deciding whether he had been subjected to less favourable treatment, was with a lesbian woman. In *Chessington World of Adventures* v *Reed* (1996) however the EAT upheld the tribunal's decision that sex discrimination does cover less favourable treatment of a person undergoing or having undergone "gender reassignment" (sex change). A direct comparison of treatment between a biological male and a biological female was not necessary when interpreting the SDA with the Equal Treatment Directive.

Case Study

Homosexual Harassment

A security officer subjected to homosexual harassment was awarded £4,500 by a Cardiff industrial tribunal in 1993. Matthew Gates, employed at Alphasteel, said the site supervisor directed sexual remarks at him, attempted to simulate anal sexual intercourse with him, and simulated sex with another worker in front of him. The tribunal referred to the EC recommendation and Code of Practice in its judgment.

Vicarious liability of employers

Most sexual and racial harassment cases are brought against the employer rather than the individual employee(s) responsible for the act or acts in question. This is because of the vicarious liability conferred on employers by s32 of the RRA and s41 of the SDA: *"Anything done by a person in the course of his employment shall be treated for the purposes of this Act as done by his employer as well as by him, whether or not it was done with the employer's knowledge or approval."*

A similar provision is contained in the DDA in s58. Thus an employer is legally responsible for the discriminatory actions of an employee, whether or not they were done with his or her knowledge or approval, provided that they were done "in the course of employment".

It is not always clear however whether discriminatory behaviour has occurred "in the course of a person's employment" or not. This is because the phrase has a well established meaning in common law or tort which is much more restrictive than the meaning envisaged by the Acts. A distinction has now arisen between cases decided under discrimination legislation and cases decided under general principles of common law.

In the case of *Jones* v *Tower Boot Co Ltd* (1996), the Court of Appeal applied a very wide definition to this phrase, extending the employer's responsibility for harassment perpetrated by an employee to an unprecedented degree. In this case, Mr Jones (a man of mixed race) was subjected to serious racial abuse by his fellow employees. One employee burned his arm with a hot screwdriver, metal bolts were thrown at his head, his legs were whipped with a piece of welt, someone stuck a notice on his back bearing the words "Chipmunks are go" and he was called names such as "chimp", "monkey" and "baboon".

The employers argued that the actions of the harassers could not be regarded as within the course of their employment, as the phrase had been defined under the common law. The court rejected this argument however stating that the RRA goes further than the common law and imposes a higher level of liability on the employer because of the words "whether or not it was done with the employer's knowledge or approval".

However, the EAT ruled that these acts were not "in the course of employment" and that the employer was not liable for the racial harassment inflicted on Mr Jones. In discussing the implications of this decision, Linda Clarke, in her book *Discrimination*, states:

"The phrase has a well-established meaning in law, developed in the law of negligence, which draws a distinction between actions that fall outside the course of employment and actions that are unauthorised modes of doing what the employee was employed to do. The EAT held by a majority that actions such as branding someone with a hot screwdriver could not by any stretch of the imagination be described as an improper mode of performing authorised tasks."

The decision of the EAT, which was criticised for taking too narrow a view of what "the course of employment" involves, was overruled by the Court of Appeal, which stated that the words "course of employment" are ordinary and readily understandable, and should be interpreted *"in the sense in which every layman would understand them"*. The Court of Appeal then went on to suggest that the layman would understand "course of employment" to mean that the discriminatory act was done by the perpetrator *"while working"*. On the surface, this would cover any act during working hours, at the place of work.

The reasoning in this case was followed in the case of *Chief Constable of the Lincolnshire Police* v *Stubbs* where it was held that a male police officer who subjected his female colleague to inappropriate sexual behaviour at a work social event in a public house was acting "in the course of his employment". His employer was therefore vicariously liable for his actions under s41(1) of the SDA. The tribunal in that case held that "these incidents were connected to work and the workplace. They would not have happened but for the applicant's work. Work related social functions are an extension of employment and we can see no reason to restrict the course of employment to purely what goes on in the workplace."

The employers' defence – how to avoid vicarious liability

S32(3) of the RRA and s41(3) of the SDA provide the same defence for employers, whereby they may not be held responsible for the unlawful discriminatory acts of employees if they *"took such steps as were reasonably practicable to prevent the employee from doing that act or from doing in the course of his employment acts of that description"*. (See also DDA s58.)

So if an employer can show (and the onus of proof will be on the employer) that reasonably practicable steps were taken to prevent the harassment, they will avoid vicarious liability and the employee concerned will be personally liable.

In *Balgobin and Francis* v *London Borough of Tower Hamlets* (1987) two women were subjected to sexual harassment by a male cook who worked with them in a council-run hostel. The cook was suspended and an inconclusive investigation was carried out, following which the employers allowed him to return to work with the two women. The women claimed that the management had ignored problems in the staff canteen and that staff supervision was inadequate. The employers argued that management had not been informed of the problems, that there had been adequate staff supervision and that they had made known to employees their equal opportunities policy.

The majority of the EAT, whilst accepting that there had been sexual harassment, decided that the employers were not liable. The court ruled that since the allegations were not made known to the management *"it was very difficult to see what steps in practical terms the employers could reasonably have taken to prevent that which occurred from occurring"*.

In the *Balgobin* case the London Borough of Tower Hamlets did not have to do a great deal to avoid liability for the actions of their employee. This was in spite of the fact that at that time their equal opportunities policy did not mention specifically that sexual harassment was unlawful and little or no guidance was given to employees about the operation of the policy. In recent cases the courts have placed a more onerous burden on employers to show that they adopted a positive policy to prevent harassment before they can take advantage of the defence.

In *Cooley* v *British Road Services* (1994) Mr Cooley was told to "forget it" the first time he made a complaint of racial harassment. The second time, although his grievance was heard formally, the company felt that the jokes were not malicious and decided not to take any disciplinary action. British Road Services had what the tribunal described as an "excellent" equal opportunities policy, but this did not prevent the tribunal deciding that its actions did not measure up to the standard required when it came to applying that policy. The tribunal concluded that British Road Services did not have a defence under s32(3) of the RRA because they had not taken the appropriate steps to put the policy into practice.

In *Graham* v *Royal Mail and Nicholson* (1993) Ms Graham and her colleague Mr Nicholson were leaving work when Ms Graham, referring to Mr Nicholson's receding hairline, shouted, "I'll see you later you white bald-headed bastard". Mr Nicholson in his turn shot back that he preferred to be a white bald-headed bastard than a black bastard. Ms Graham took exception to the remark and despite Mr Nicholson's immediate apology she reported the matter to her supervisor. In line with the Royal Mail's harassment procedures Mr Nicholson was immediately transferred to another area and given a formal written warning.

When Ms Graham complained to a tribunal, they did not find any racial discrimination, bearing in mind the relaxed and informal relationship that existed at work which included occasional office banter. The tribunal were at pains to point out, however, that *"in most cases of racist banter in the workplace there can be no degree of acceptability"*.

What is noteworthy about this case is that even if the tribunal had found racial discrimination it is unlikely that the Royal Mail would have been held liable for its employees' discriminatory actions. The tribunal specifically commended the Royal Mail on its policy and the speed with which it had acted upon it.

Failure to deal with harassment may itself be a discriminatory act

In some cases an employing organisation will not only be vicariously liable for the discriminatory actions of employees but may also be guilty of discrimination because of failure to respond adequately to a complaint of harassment.

The discrimination could occur either in the way that the complaint is investigated (or in a failure to do so) or in the subsequent action taken: e.g. transfer, dismissal or alteration of the duties of the employee. Employers can also be liable if they fail to take action, delay in taking action or fail to keep the employee informed of the progress of their complaint.

To prove discrimination the employee would have to show that if the complaint had been brought by a white person in race cases, or a man in the case of sex discrimination, it would have been treated more seriously or investigated more thoroughly and would have been dealt with more favourably. If this is the case it would constitute a detriment under the RRA or the SDA and the employee would be able to take action.

In addition an employer may be guilty of direct discrimination if the handling or response to the complaint and the treatment of the worker concerned amounts to victimisation of him/her for raising the issue.

Liability for third parties

Where the actual abuser is a third party, and not an employee of the employer, the test is whether the event was something which was sufficiently under the control of the employer so that he could, by the application of good employment practices, have prevented the harassment or reduced the extent of it. It is likely that tribunals will find employers directly liable if they fail this test.

In the case of *Burton v DeVere Hotels* (1996), the EAT held that an employer subjects employees to the detriment of racial harassment *"if he causes or permits harassment serious enough to amount to a detriment to occur in circumstances in which he can control whether it happens or not"*. Whether or not the harassment was foreseen might be relevant to the issue of control, but even in cases where the harassment occurs unexpectedly, if the employer could have exercised control, a tribunal may well find him liable.

In *Go Kidz Co Ltd* v *Boudane* (1995) a children's party organiser was sexually harassed by one of the children's parents and complained to her employer who knowing of the harassment nonetheless encouraged her to return to the situation without taking any action. The woman was later dismissed when she made a complaint about the matter and insisted that the incident should be reported to the police. The tribunal held that the employer was directly liable for the harassment because they did not take all reasonable steps to prevent the discrimination taking place whereas it was within their power to do so.

Case Study

Burton v DeVere Hotels (1996)

Two black waitresses brought a claim against a hotel for being subjected to racist jokes by Bernard Manning. *The Times* reported that Freda Burton and Sonia Rhule told an industrial tribunal that 500 men at a Round Table dinner at The Pennine Hotel, Derby, cheered as Bernard Manning told sexist and racist jokes about them, and guests at one table continued the abuse after the performance. The hotel representative told the tribunal that the real guilty parties were Bernard Manning and the Round Table, and that staff had sympathy with the women for the abuse they had suffered.

The Chair of the tribunal, Mr David Sneath, said that the hotel could have done more to stop the women being exposed to the racist jokes but did not find it responsible for discrimination.

An appeal was brought on behalf of the two women by the Commission for Racial Equality, which they subsequently won in October 1996.

In this case the hotel manager should have anticipated the problems and instructed the relevant supervisors to be alert to any such difficulties. If that had been done, the waitresses could have been withdrawn from the hall at an early stage.

(Original article from *The Times*, 2 November 1995
[quoted in the *Harassment Network Newsline*, February 1996].
Reproduced with kind permission from *The Times*. © The Times Newspapers Ltd 1995)

Constructive dismissal

An employee is entitled to resign without notice if there is a breach of one or more of the fundamental terms of the contract of employment. The breach may be of an express term or of one of the implied terms which have been developed and formulated by the courts and form part of each and every contract. This is known as "constructive dismissal".

In sexual and racial harassment cases the complainant will usually allege that the employer's failure to deal adequately with a complaint of harassment amounts to a breach of the employer's implied duty of mutual trust and confidence. Alternatively, an employee may claim that there has been a breach of the duty to provide a safe and healthy workplace or competent and safe employees.

Being subjected to sexual or racial harassment is regarded by the courts as conduct by an employer which will justify the employee bringing the contract to an end.

In *Milovanovic* v *Hebden Dyeing and Finishing Co Ltd and Others* (1995) Mr Milovanovic had complained on numerous occasions of persistent harassment which was based on his Serbian origin, particularly after the start of the war in Bosnia:

"We don't use a No. 7 like that. You're not in f. . .ing Bosnia now . . ."

"Don't you think it would be a good idea . . . if you go back to Bosnia and fight and die like a dog instead of our lads."

"If all the foreigners and blacks go back to their own country we would have a better environment in this country."

This finally proved too much for Mr Milovanovic, who left the company and phoned in to say he was giving a week's notice. The tribunal accepted that Mr Milovanovic had no choice but to leave his employment, because he *"ultimately felt so oppressed by what happened that he felt quite unable to continue in his employment since the relationship of trust and confidence between him and the employers had been destroyed"*.

In *Western Excavating Ltd* v *Sharp* (1978) the court recognised that *"persistent and unwanted amorous advances by an employer to a female member of staff"* would be an example of conduct by an employer which would justify a finding of constructive dismissal.

Employers who fail to deal with issues of bullying may find themselves defending claims of constructive dismissal, as discussed later on in the chapter.

Criminal sanctions against harassment

The Criminal Justice and Public Order Act 1994 introduced a criminal offence of "intentional harassment, alarm or distress" which is punishable by up to six months' imprisonment. The new offence covers all forms of harassment including racial and sexual harassment in the workplace, as well as harassment on the grounds of disability, age or sexual orientation, and grants the police an immediate power of arrest.

To show that the offence has been committed it is necessary to prove beyond reasonable doubt that the harassment was intentional and that someone was actually harassed, alarmed or distressed.

The language of the Act is very wide and it should be relatively easy to prove intentional harassment in most racial and sexual harassment cases, but there are some difficulties and limitations. First, its effectiveness will depend on how the police and the Crown Prosecution Service interpret the provisions, in terms of the decision to arrest and prosecute. Also, it is unlikely that it will be any easier for a vulnerable employee to take criminal proceedings than it has been to pursue the matter through the internal complaints procedure or before a tribunal.

Employers need to ensure that their harassment policies take into account the impact of this offence however.

Protection from Harassment Act 1997

The Act's main aim is to deal with stalking, though targets of all forms of harassment suffered at work now have an additional remedy to resolve unacceptable behaviour.

The Act creates four criminal offences:
(1) harassment (2) putting another person in fear of violence
(3) breach of a restraining order (4) breach of an injunction.

In comparison with the amended Criminal Justice and Public Order Act 1994, the Act does not define harassment. However, it does refer to harassing a person as "*a course of conduct*" which includes but is not limited to "*alarming the person or causing the person distress*". S7 of the Act states that a "course of conduct" must involve conduct on at least two occasions, and that "conduct" includes speech. This precise definition was adopted specifically to widen the Act's scope to deal with other "anti-social behaviour", as well as stalking.

The main provisions of the Act do not require proof of intention to harass. It concentrates on the conduct of the harasser and prohibits conduct which amounts to harassment of another and "which the harasser knows or ought to know amounts to harassment of the other". There is thus no need to prove "beyond a reasonable doubt" – which would be the usual criminal burden of proof that a person intended to harass.

The Act states that a person knows or ought to know that their conduct amounts to harassment if "a reasonable person in possession of the same information would think it amounted to harassment of another".

The Act also creates a new offence of "putting someone in fear of violence". This too is defined in terms of "a course of conduct" which causes someone to fear that at least on two occasions violence will be used against him or her.

Proceedings must be started in the Magistrates court where the maximum penalty is a fine of £5,000 and/or six months imprisonment. A person accused under the Act can however elect to be tried in front of a jury in the Crown Court where the chances of being found guilty may be reduced but the maximum penalty is an unlimited fine and five years' imprisonment.

The Act also gives the courts power to impose a restraining order on the harasser once convicted, to protect the victim from further conduct which amounts to harassment or causes fear of violence. Breach of a restraining order is a criminal offence as is breach of an injunction imposed by the civil court to prevent further harassment.

What are the implications of this Act for an employer?

The provisions made in the Act would mean that an individual making a claim would have to bring it against the alleged harasser, rather than the employer. This could mean, however, that an employee who is suffering from harassment in the workplace could make a claim of discrimination against their employer at an employment tribunal, whilst seeking an injunction against the alleged harasser.

The emphasis in the Act on the conduct of the harasser knowing what amounts to unreasonable behaviour and, as a reasonable person, being aware of the effects of harassment, reinforces further the responsibility of employers to use training to raise employees' level of awareness about what constitutes harassment. Chapter 11 looks at this issue in depth.

Impact on UK law of EC legislation

Legislation from the EC continues to have a far-reaching impact on UK employment practice, particularly in the area of sexual harassment. In May 1990 the EC Council of Labour and Social Ministers adopted a resolution relating to sexual harassment at work. This was followed in November 1991, as part of its third action programme on equal opportunities, with the "Recommendation on the Protection of the Dignity of Women and Men at Work" and a Code of Practice on sexual harassment. There is also a recent EC directive which recommends reversing the burden of proof in sexual discrimination cases. If adopted this means that the presumption will be in favour of discrimination whenever it is alleged and it will be for the employer to disprove that discrimination occurred. It is envisaged that this directive will be implemented for both sex and race discrimination in the UK.

The Code is not a legislative measure in itself, but it is now used by tribunals to clarify issues such as the definition of sexual harassment and the duty of employers to have a coherent harassment policy.

The European Commission is also considering further legislation in this area and has published a consultation paper "The prevention of sexual harassment at work" (1997).

Comparisons with US law

In the USA the law prohibiting sexual harassment and imposing a duty on employers is much stronger and more wide-reaching than in the UK.

In 1964 the US Congress passed the Civil Rights Act which prohibits all forms of discrimination on the basis of race, colour, national origin and sex in all aspects of employment. Just as in the UK, the development of a specific prohibition against sexual harassment developed in a piecemeal fashion, led by guidelines established by the Equal Employment Opportunity Commission and case law in the Supreme Court.

There have been a number of high profile US cases which certainly left UK employers with something to think about. The decision in the Rena Weeks case where record damages of $7.1 million were awarded was a salutary message to all employers and to individual workers that sexual bullying will not be tolerated by the courts.

Miss Weeks was a secretary in the law firm of Baker & McKenzie, the largest commercial law firm in the world. Her boss, Mr Martin Greenstein, a partner in the firm, subjected her to a campaign of sexual harassment which included comments on the size of her breasts and ordering her to strike titillating poses. The award to Miss Weeks, which was made up largely of punitive rather than compensatory damages, was viewed by commentators to be a punishment to the firm for having a culture which allowed such harassment to happen.

Whilst the decision in the Weeks case represents an extreme reaction to an extreme form of harassment, employers cannot afford complacency in this area. The laws on sexual and racial harassment are now firmly established and other forms of harassment are coming increasingly to the attention of legislators. This can only mean that organisations must examine ever more closely their policies and procedures in this area in order to avoid potentially damaging and expensive claims.

Compensation for sex and race discrimination in the UK, including harassment, has no upper limit, and tribunals are increasingly willing to award large sums.

Case Study **Behaviours Recognised in US Legislation**

Behaviours related to sexual harassment in the United States are more clearly defined and specifically referred to in legislation. The three main areas which have impacted on case law are as follows:

● **Unwelcome conduct** – Conduct that is not welcome and the target does not want it. It is unsolicited, and the target considers the behaviour to be undesirable or offensive.
● **Quid pro quo (this for that)** – Sexual harassment involves the exchange of a job benefit for express or implied sexual favours. If you sleep with me, you will keep your job, get a salary increase, guarantee job promotion, etc.
● **Consensual relationships** – A manager with a promotion opportunity available chooses to bestow that job benefit on a subordinate he or she is sexually involved with. The test will be whether that involvement is mutually welcome.

The landmark case of *Meritor Savings Bank* v *Vinson* set a precedent for sexual harassment cases in the US.

Mechelle Vinson was hired as a trainee bank teller, and was promoted on the basis of her abilities to the position of assistant branch manager before being sacked for excessive use of sick leave.

About one year later, Ms Vinson sued the bank and Sidney Taylor, her then supervisor, alleging *hostile-environment sexual harassment*. Ms Vinson claimed that during her four years at the bank, she had sexual intercourse with Mr Taylor. He also followed her into the women's toilet, fondled her in front of her work colleagues, and raped her several times.

Although Meritor Savings Bank had an anti-discrimination policy and an internal complaints procedure, Ms Vinson did not complain, as she feared reprisals and victimisation.

The Supreme Court ruled that although Mechelle Vinson had voluntarily participated in a sexual relationship with her supervisor for several years, the conduct was unwelcome (undesirable or offensive) to her, and she consented only out of fear of losing her job and fear of retaliatory action should she refuse to comply with Taylor's sexual demands.

What the law says about bullying

Health and safety legislation

There is no health and safety legislation that specifically prohibits bullying in the workplace. Employees are given some protection against bullying indirectly, however, by the Health and Safety at Work Act

1974 and by the regulatory regime set up by the Act. The central aim of the Act, as described in Chapter 3, is to provide a safe place and system of work for employees.

The Act imposes a duty on employers to ensure as far as is reasonably practicable the health, safety and "welfare at work" of its employees. What is meant by "welfare at work" is not defined anywhere in the Act, however. The Act does make the employers specifically responsible for preventing "personal injury" to employees, which is defined as "any disease or impairment of a person's physical or mental conditions". Although it is not specifically stated, it could be implied that the duties on employers relate to both the physical and psychological well-being of their employees and would therefore cover a situation where an employee is experiencing bullying.

In addition to the duties imposed on employers the Act also imposes on the employee a general duty to *"take reasonable care for the health and safety of himself and other persons who might be affected by his acts or omissions at work"*. Whilst this falls far short of a prohibition against bullying, it imposes an individual duty of care on the perpetrator of the bullying which mirrors the duty on the employer.

Carrying out a risk assessment

Every employer has a legal duty to carry out a suitable assessment of the risks to health and safety that any employee is exposed to whilst at work and to take the appropriate protective and preventative measures to deal with them. This is contained in Regulation 3 of the Management of Health and Safety at Work Regulations 1992 (MHSW).

Good practice dictates that this assessment should include risks to both the physical and mental health of the employee. The Health and Safety Executive has published guidance for employees on preventing stress at work which makes it clear that bullying could be a cause of stress and that preventative measures must include action to eliminate bullying where it exists.

Below is a summary of HSE guidelines to help identify and reduce bullying at work:

- identify potential/actual causes of stress in the workplace
- determine the perceived level of stress among employees
- examine existing protective measures and evaluate their effectiveness
- examine organisation and other relevant policies to see whether they are adequate or whether more needs to be done.

Once any problems have been identified remedial action must be taken. This may require a longer term strategy to tackle organisational and management problems as well as the work environment. The guidelines recommend that "if what is needed is a change in organisational culture, a review of management practices, the development of training or the improvement of internal communications, then these changes must be implemented according to an agreed timetable".

In addition to the legislation an employer has a common law duty to take reasonable care for the health and safety of its employees. This too covers physical and mental health and thus an employer might be liable for negligence if a breach of this duty causes a reasonably foreseeable stress-related mental illness or breakdown.

Discrimination legislation – is bullying covered?

The RDA and the SDA do not cover a situation where bullying is taking place. It is important to note, however, that where the bullying centres on the race or sex of the person, then this will usually amount to unlawful sex or race discrimination. A similar test may now also apply to disabled people under the Disability Discrimination Act.

Reflection...

As this chapter shows, the legislative framework with regard to discrimination in the UK is complex and contrasting. Employment legislation and case law is continuously changing, sometimes quite radically, and the impact of European law is steadily growing. It therefore becomes essential for organisations to do more than simply what is required by legislation to tackle harassment and bullying effectively.

The law relating to harassment and bullying should be used as a starting point for employment practice. Combined with a sense of social responsibility, adopting a non-discriminatory approach to creating strategies and policies to prevent harassment and bullying will reduce the need to use legislation punitively.

References

Equal Opportunities Review, Nos: 50–74.

Preventing and Remedying Sexual Harassment at Work: A Resource Manual, Michael Rubenstein (IRS, 1992).

Sexual Harassment: A Trade Union Issue, MSF booklet, 1991.

Racial Equality Means Business, CRE booklet, 1995.

Combating Sexual Harassment in the Workplace, Rohan Collier (Open University Press, 1995).

Employment Law: An Adviser's Handbook, Thomas Kibling and Tamara Lewis (Legal Action Group, 1994).

Sensitive Issues in the Workplace, Sue Morris (The Industrial Society, 1993).

Sexual Harassment: Women Speak Out, Amber Coverdale Sumrall and Dena Taylor (Crossing Press, 1992).

Sexual Harassment in the Workplace, Ellen J Wagner (AMACOM, 1992).

Discrimination: Law and Employment Series, Linda Clarke (Institute of Personnel and Development, 1995).

CHAPTER **8**

Meeting the organisation's responsibilities

To reduce and eliminate unacceptable behaviours in the workplace, organisations have several responsibilities to meet – not just compliance with the legislation, but ensuring that effective measures are in place to deal with any issues, and to facilitate the creation of a healthy culture. This chapter explores the different responsibilities that organisations face, and takes you through steps which will assist in meeting them.

Taking responsibility

The responsibilities that organisations are accountable for are challenging, yet when taken seriously can have a positive effect on the climate in the workplace. Unfortunately some organisations refuse to face the problem of harassment, and not taking their responsibility seriously can have alarming consequences, as the following case study reveals.

Case Study

The Repeat Harasser
A female colleague in a Hampshire college relates this catalogue of blunders.
Rosalyn (the colleague) met Peter (the harasser) when she took up her first teaching post in the college. Peter was her head of subject.
Soon after Rosalyn started work, she had countless complaints about Peter from women students. The women who approached her seemed to conform to a pattern: they were vulnerable, and had gone to Peter

for advice, and he had used this position of trust to manipulate them sexually. He had already been disciplined for an alleged liaison with a 17-year-old student whilst on a field trip. The student concerned happened to be the daughter of the principal's personal assistant (possibly a key factor in the decision to take action against Peter). He later boasted about his sexual escapades to male colleagues, and the union representative supporting Peter, though reluctant, felt duty-bound to assist him because the college failed to follow correct procedures when dealing with Peter's case.

Rosalyn had one ally in her situation. Her head of faculty (a woman) knew all about Peter. Following another relationship with a young 18-year-old woman – a student in Rosalyn's tutor group – Peter made the mistake of confiding in a colleague about his activities. The teacher concerned was not sympathetic to Peter, and as she was leaving the college, decided to go to the principal on Rosalyn's behalf and told him about the situation that Rosalyn was facing. Rosalyn kept the faculty head informed of all the events too. The outcome was that the principal informed Peter that he would be advised to look elsewhere for employment and advancement as he would not get any promotion in this particular college. His days were marked. Eventually he left – with an excellent reference – and joined the teaching staff at another local, but much bigger, college.

Whilst this was happening, Rosalyn had taken up a new position at the same college, and was appalled to see Peter, not only at the college but that he was once again her boss.

Peter started another relationship with an evening-class student soon after joining the college. However, student complaints about Peter escalated, culminating with classes writing to the principal about his lack of professional ability, as well as the comments he made to women students regarding their appearance, boyfriends and personal life. Parents (obviously receiving complaints from their children) also wrote to the college.

The college did not have a harassment policy, and their recently re-negotiated contracts did not cover any reference to relationships between teaching staff and students. Rosalyn felt that she was powerless to act, that the union would do nothing, and that the failure to take disciplinary action against Peter was also due to the fact that many other male colleagues behaved in a similar way to Peter. There was an almost tacit acceptance of Peter's behaviour, which was underpinned by the lack of policy, training and contractual alterations. To date, the college has only issued a strong verbal warning to Peter – relating to his lack of professionalism with regard to his work, and not to the harassment he has meted out.

What are the main responsibilities an organisation faces?

The following "Ten steps to beating workplace harassment" clearly define the main responsibilities an organisation needs to face in order to stamp out harassment:

Ten steps to beating workplace harassment

1. Carry out an audit to analyse the extent to which harassment is a concern, identifying any particular issues which may need to be addressed.
2. Draw up a harassment policy (preferably as an extension of the main equal opportunities, diversity or dignity at work policy).
3. Make harassment of any kind a disciplinary and grievance offence.
4. Educate line managers and make them responsible for implementing the policy.
5. Ensure that employees can make a complaint without fear of reprisal or victimisation.
6. Set up an informal support system made up of independent volunteers to assist employees complaining of harassment.
7. Communicate and publicise the organisation's stance on harassment, and inform all staff of their rights and responsibilities. Communicate that the policy applies to everyone – including contractors and clients.
8. Provide awareness and skills training on dealing with harassment.
9. Monitor and review the procedures and complaints system.
10. Where possible, provide independent, confidential counselling for the target and witnesses, and coaching for the harasser.

(Adapted from *No Offence?*, The Industrial Society, 1993)

Effective policies against harassment

The largest task an organisation has to complete in order to help meet all of these responsibilities is the creation of a policy.

Any policy, whether health and safety or equal opportunities, is developed in order to set standards of behaviour in the organisation. As behaviour is the outward manifestation of an individual's core values, the only way of facilitating change is to be clear on the behavioural standards required in an organisation. The onion skin diagram (Figure 16 overleaf) shows how policy can impact on values. We can only guess at the values and beliefs a person holds by their attitude, and their attitude is reflected in their behaviour.

Similarly, an organisation's values are reflected in the behaviour of its workforce. Policies, particularly equal opportunities policies, need to be designed in order to send a clear message to its employees: "This is the way we want you to behave in this organisation – this is the standard of behaviour required in order to maintain our values."

Figure 16.
The link between
policy development
and behaviour

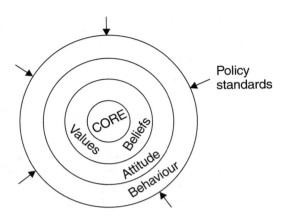

"The way we want you to behave . . ."

Harassment policies are extensions of an organisation's equal opportunity, diversity or dignity at work policies. They also link into grievance and disciplinary procedures; however, some of these procedures are not far-reaching enough to deal with complaints of harassment, and may need to be revised and updated.

Some of the best and most effective policies embody general good practice by extending beyond what the legislation requires. They are created in consultation with all employees, unions and staff association groups and deal with specific issues which are designed to combat the problems that occur in the organisation's culture. An example of this may be the inclusion of a couple of paragraphs in a written policy outlining why the installation of pornographic images on computer systems would be a disciplinary offence.

Attitude surveys and audits often reveal any such problems, and must be conducted before a policy is created to help to make it more active (see Chapter 6).

What should a policy include?

● A clear, up-front statement of commitment to eradicating workplace harassment, bullying and violence, and an assurance that it will not be tolerated within the organisation at any level.
● Definitions of harassment, examples of behaviours that constitute it and clear messages about what is unacceptable behaviour.
● A clear message that conveys that harassment can be unlawful.
● A clear statement that harassment is a disciplinary offence.

● An outline of the responsibilities that individuals and managers have to ensure that harassment does not occur.

● Clear, concise procedures for resolving issues and complaints, ie:
  – an informal system (including details of support and advice)
  – a formal system (including details of the complaints procedure, investigations, grievance, disciplinary and appeal procedures).

● A message that complaints will be taken seriously, that confidentiality (as far as possible) will be adhered to and that victimisation will not be tolerated as a result of making a complaint or witnessing an incident.

● Details outlining the provision of awareness, skills and knowledge training in support of the policy.

● A list of contact points, with telephone numbers and/or location addresses, for help and/or further advice.

The Consumer Association – A model policy
The policy was created in consultation with the Consumer Association's union representatives from the NUJ and MSF, and is an excellent example of best practice. Simple, effective language has been used to put across the Consumer Association's stance on harassment and bullying, the definitions are clear and concise, and the guidelines for making informal and formal complaints are portrayed in practical steps.

(Reproduced by kind permission of the Consumer Association)

Figure 17.

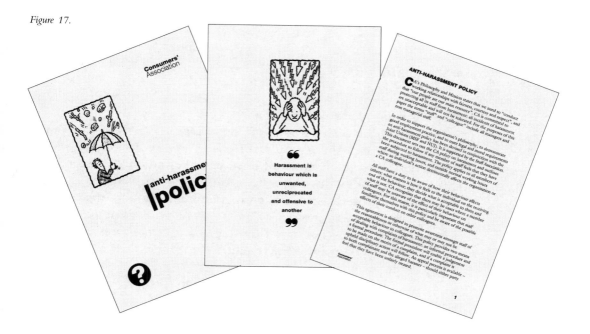

Many organisations produce a "policy statement" outlawing harassment of any kind. However, experience has shown (particularly with equal opportunities policies) that this is not enough and does not send sufficiently serious messages about the organisation's commitment to eliminating harassment.

Dedicated time and resources need to be allocated to ensure that the policy is properly established and communicated throughout the organisation. A timetabled action plan, from the policy development stage to the launch of the policy, can be created to aid implementation. Included in the plan should be arrangements for communicating the rules and procedures of the policy, as well as training plans which would include sessions raising employees' awareness of harassment.

Procedures for dealing with harassment and resolving harassment complaints

The test of a good policy is the practicality of the procedures within it and the guidelines for making those procedures work. Time and time again, tribunals comment on the lack of adequate procedures within organisations and the mishandling of complaints. Tribunals also note that organisations which do have well-written harassment policies sometimes fail in their responsibility to communicate the procedures within the policy to their employees, and train those involved in their implementation.

The procedures for resolving issues and making complaints fall into two areas:

● the informal route
● the formal route.

The informal route

An informal mechanism creates the opportunity to resolve harassment problems without the formality of the grievance procedures. Most people just want the harassment to stop, and an informal route allows this to happen smoothly. Informal mechanisms were created out of a recognition of the nature of harassment complaints, and the fact that most people feel embarrassed or guilty about their situation. Making a complaint formally can be off-putting and in some cases appear too heavy-handed, so an informal resolution to problems is a more cautious, sensitive approach.

It also offers the alleged harasser the opportunity to correct unacceptable behaviour. It is important to recognise the fact that most people who harass do not intend to, or realise the effect of their behaviour. An informal resolution to a problem is often the best way of meeting a complainant's needs and setting new standards of behaviour for the harasser, giving them the opportunity to develop.

Expediency is vital when dealing with complaints, and the informal route also offers a way of resolving complaints quickly and concisely. In some cases, however, an informal resolution may not be appropriate and it should be remembered that complainants still have a right to go through the formal route to get their problems resolved. No pressure should be placed on a complainant to use an informal route, particularly if the complainant wants to make a formal complaint.

It is important to note that the way a complaint is handled in the informal system may have a bearing on any future formal investigation.

A network of contact points normally forms the basis of an informal mechanism. Along with this, guidelines for helping a target take action by themselves (if it is appropriate) and the option to have a line manager or appropriate representative intervene informally on behalf of the complainant also form part of the informal mechanism.

The role of the supporter in an informal system

The supporter plays a vital role in the successful running of an informal mechanism. In the recommendations outlined in the European Commission Code of Practice for the Protection of the Dignity of Women and Men at Work, employers are advised to *"designate someone to provide advice and assistance to employees subjected to sexual harassment where possible, with responsibilities to assist in the resolution of any problems . . ."*

The supporter provides good quality guidance and help to employees complaining of harassment. The helping relationship between complainant and supporter needs to be one of guidance, information-giving and problem-solving – not of advice or instruction – as the complainant needs to feel comfortable and able to follow through on the actions agreed as a result of the relationship.

One of the main roles of a supporter is to help the complainant regain their confidence, self-worth and a sense of power. This can be achieved by the use of good counselling skills and assertiveness techniques, which the supporter must be well trained in. Chapter 4 explored how victims and targets experience harassment, and how they recognised what was happening to them. The supporter plays a vital part in this process, and by assisting the complainant to recognise which level they are at the supporter has an idea how best to help them through the process (see Table 7 overleaf).

The supporter must also have a good understanding of harassment

Table 7.

Level	Behaviour recognition	Possible support
First level	Able to identify behaviours as harassment, has inner resources and coping mechanisms to deal with the situation	Give guidelines on confronting the harasser by using assertiveness
Second level	Non-recognition of behaviours as harassment; however, once identified as such, has inner resources to deal with the situation	May need help to identify what is happening to them, and how to use inner resources to confront harasser by themselves
Third level	Non-recognition of behaviours as harassment, does not have inner resources to handle the situation	Needs assistance in identifying unacceptable behaviours and establishing inner resources by raising self-worth and confidence. If they want to confront the harasser, suggest they do so with a colleague
Fourth level	Recognition of behaviours as harassment, yet does not have inner resources to handle the situation	Needs assistance and encouragement in establishing inner resources by raising self-worth and confidence. Depending upon the circumstances of the incident, you may need to suggest they seek additional professional support externally, before confronting the harasser

and related legislation, a familiarity with the formal complaint procedures, and an understanding of the disciplinary and grievance procedures of the organisation they are working in. In essence, supporters must be properly trained and highly skilled to carry out this role effectively (see Table 8). Chapter 11 looks at this in more detail.

Supporters can also give assistance to alleged harassers and witnesses. For the alleged harasser, the supporter can help them see the effects of their behaviour and give a different perspective on the situation they are in. They can also develop an action plan to help the harasser change their behaviour and develop coping strategies for themselves to prevent further occurrences of harassment. The logistics of this must be clearly defined, as it would be inappropriate for the same supporter to help both the alleged harasser and complainant in the same case. For witnesses, supporters can listen to concerns and support them in giving evidence about the alleged incident. Supporters can also take a proactive

Table 8.

The Supporter/Adviser's role	
Informal	• helps victim/target to find an informal resolution to the situation • actively listens to the victim/target's concerns and uses counselling skills to deal with emotional consequences • discusses the situation openly and objectively, and helps the target come to their own conclusions and solutions
Core functions	• to draw the victim/target's attention to the differences between informal and formal action • to explain thoroughly to the victim/target the complaints procedure and the impact of using it • if role permits, to give assistance to the victim/target in filing a grievance • to draw the problem to the attention of the managers (if recipient wishes)
Facilities needed	• accessible and safe area for listening and supporting, where issues can be dealt with confidentially • deals with the target/victim alone • separate and confidential telephone lines should be set up where possible.

role in the education and training of the workforce by raising awareness on harassment issues internally, at all levels in the organisation.

Organisations should aim to have a network of volunteer supporters in key operational areas. Supporters should be representative of the workforce, and a fair mix of people representing minority groups (e.g. women, ethnic minority men and women, etc) should be aimed for wherever possible. The ideal person specification of a supporter could include the following:

● *someone well trusted and respected in the organisation*
● *someone who is easy to talk to and actively listens*
● *someone who is able to keep confidentiality and is known for this ability*
● *someone who is objective and empathetic*
● *someone who understands and knows the organisation well*
● *someone who is accessible and approachable*
● *someone who is sensitive to cultural, gender and minority group needs*
● *someone who is assertive and able to challenge discrimination*
● *someone who has the ability to recognise and manage stress in themselves and others.*

Choosing a label for the supporter is key to the message that is given by employers to employees about the role of the supporter, and needs to be done with thought and care. For example, "confidential counsellor" is a title that is frequently used. Whilst in some cases it may be appropriate to use the name (some organisations can employ professional counsellors to fulfil the role), it may give the impression of a fully trained counsellor willing to give a complainant 20 sessions of psychoanalysis! As well as the term "supporter", other common descriptions include "adviser", "confidential adviser", "contact officer" (often used in government and public services), "listener", and "listening ears".

Supporters themselves need support in order to carry out their roles effectively. Continuous development is necessary, and line managers must give open support by respecting the need for supporters to retain confidentiality at all times. Line managers must also ensure that supporters are given the time to carry out their roles, in recognition of the fact they are volunteers, and assist in helping them manage their normal workloads.

Above all, the role of the supporter must be clearly defined and publicised. Discussions between supporters and complainants are confidential, and supporters should not be required to give any evidence in formal proceedings; the supporter plays no part in the formal process, nor in disciplinary and grievance proceedings.

The following case study illustrates how a supporter helps an individual to challenge harassment informally.

Case Study

Helping Others Help Themselves

"Tony, a manager in a London local authority, called me one afternoon to ask my advice.

'Asha, I'm getting fed up of this. Since Caroline saw me in a restaurant with a man, the gossip about me being gay is getting out of hand. Even Frank, my boss, gives me the cold shoulder. How can I deal with this?'

Tony was very angry. I asked him why this had upset him so much. 'It's because I am gay, and I made the decision not to disclose my sexuality to anyone in the workplace. But I'm really angry – the man I was with is my brother, who is straight and works in the neighbouring council, and Caroline's vindictive mouth will have spread rumours which will not just affect me, I'm sure it will affect him too.' I told Tony that I was free at 5.00pm, and he agreed to meet me to talk through the situation that evening.

As I reflected on Tony's complaint, I realised that he was understandably sensitive about his sexuality, and that he must have gone to lengths to hide it. Tony had been working with the council for at least ten years, and I had no idea he was gay until now. Caroline, whether she meant to or not, had touched his Achilles' heel.

What I needed to do was to calm him down first, establish the reality of Caroline's actions, and come up with a way of handling the issue that Tony felt comfortable with.

By the time Tony came into my office, he had already calmed down. 'I'm sorry about my ramblings earlier, Asha. I just needed to get it all off my chest.' I reassured Tony, and asked him to tell me about his working relationship with Caroline, and to give any reasons why she should behave in this way. 'I think Caroline overheard me talking to my partner on the phone once. It wasn't an explicit conversation, though. Caroline has always been asking about my love life, and I've never given her any information. She had the opportunity to be promoted to team leader in the regeneration department, but said the only position she wanted was mine, and she didn't feel ready for a move.

Caroline is always sweetness and light to my face. What gets to me is the manipulative bitching she does behind my back. She's never up-front in her criticisms of me. Once, she complained to Frank that I caused her to miss a deadline for a report by not giving her the full information that she needed to complete it in time. Luckily, someone else backed up my story – I had given it to her in advance. Caroline didn't look at it until the very last moment, and had to change a lot of the report because it didn't match with my advice. I suggested that she involve other members of the team to help her out after that incident, but she didn't like that very much.'

It was obvious to me that Tony needed to confront Caroline with her behaviour and ask her to stop. The council's harassment policy is quite comprehensive, and we take a hard line against people who harass on the grounds of sexual orientation, so Tony's complaint would be well supported. Tony is quite capable of confronting her; however, he would have to make a decision about how he dealt with the issue of his sexuality. I posed this question to Tony. 'Well, having had time to think, and after talking it through with you, what I will do is talk to Frank first. I'll tell him how I feel about Caroline's behaviour and the rumours, but I won't answer the question that they are all asking. My sexuality is none of their business – but Caroline's behaviour is, and if she doesn't stop, it will ruin the morale of the team, and progress on the project. I'll talk it through with Frank, tell him about confronting Caroline, and then I will speak to Caroline straight after. I don't care if she denies it – I'll take it further if I have to – but she's got to understand that I'm not taking any more from her, and I want an apology!'

Tony seemed in control of the situation. He asked me for some leaflets about harassment and our policy – 'I'll distribute them around the office!' he said to me, and I asked him to let me know what happened.

> Although I was worried about his decision to keep his sexuality hidden, I had to respect his right to do so. At least he is confident about making the first step, and that first step might just be enough to stop what was happening to him, and prevent the matter going further."
>
> (Asha Malik, a local authority "listening ear")

The formal route

The main aim of an informal route to resolving complaints of harassment must be to ensure that all complaints are dealt with fairly, sensitively and seriously, whilst protecting the rights of both the complainant and the alleged harasser.

The formal route to resolving complaints of harassment can be used when:

● the seriousness of the incident is such that only the formal route is appropriate
● attempts to resolve the situation informally have not been successful
● the complainant prefers to use the formal route for a resolution to the incident.

One of the difficulties in resolving issues of harassment is that targets are, more often than not, reluctant or afraid to make a complaint for a variety of reasons. These include: being afraid that their complaint will not be taken seriously, having little or no confidence that any action will be taken against the harasser, and that they will be victimised for making a complaint. It is for these reasons that complaints must be handled sensitively. The steps of the complaints procedure need to be widely publicised so that every employee understands the process, and the message that every complaint will be taken seriously must be prominent in any publicity material, and put into practice when cases are reported.

There is every likelihood that existing grievance procedures will not be adequate enough to deal with harassment complaints, as most procedures outline that a complaint must be made in the first instance to a line manager or supervisor. If the alleged harasser is an immediate manager or supervisor, this could mean that making a complaint becomes almost impossible. Complaints procedures should make provision for this, designating specific individuals (such as personnel officers, or equal opportunities officers) as points of contact for making a complaint. Their names should be published so that they can be contacted privately.

Investigating complaints is a crucial part of any formal procedure. It is important that any investigation is carried out by trained personnel within a reasonable timescale. The characteristics of good investigations into cases of harassment are discussed more fully in Chapter 9.

Once the investigation is complete, and recommendations for action are made, it is essential that any disciplinary measures are carefully carried out in order to maintain the rights of the harasser. Linking investigations to disciplinary procedures is a difficult area. However, to make the link distinct, the investigation should be viewed as a preliminary exercise, the purpose of which is to decide whether or not there is a case for disciplinary action. There are some cases in which incidents of harassment are considered to be gross misconduct, and the penalties for harassers need to be carried through – this is the stage where employees will assess the organisation's serious intent to stamp out discrimination. The conflicting messages between policy and practice can be damaging if an organisation does not act appropriately at this point.

The harasser's right to appeal needs to be acknowledged throughout the disciplinary process. Chapter 9 looks at the whole process of investigations and their recommendations in detail.

Malicious complaints are very rare. However, if one ever occurs, it should be treated as a disciplinary matter.

The complaints procedure must ensure that the complainant is not victimised in any way as a result of making the complaint. This may mean being careful about moving the target to a different area. Although it might be acceptable to do this (or suspend the alleged harasser on full pay) whilst the investigation is taking place, once an outcome has been established and actions decided upon, moving the complainant from their work area may be viewed as victimisation, and is not a viable option.

Generally, the decision to make a complaint lies with the target or victim of harassment. However, there may be circumstances where an employee is unwilling to make a complaint, and the employer has to step in – albeit gently – to resolve the issue and uphold their responsibility of creating a safe working environment for employees. Although this is difficult, every effort should be made to find a resolution to a problem, particularly as the rights of the alleged harasser may be infringed.

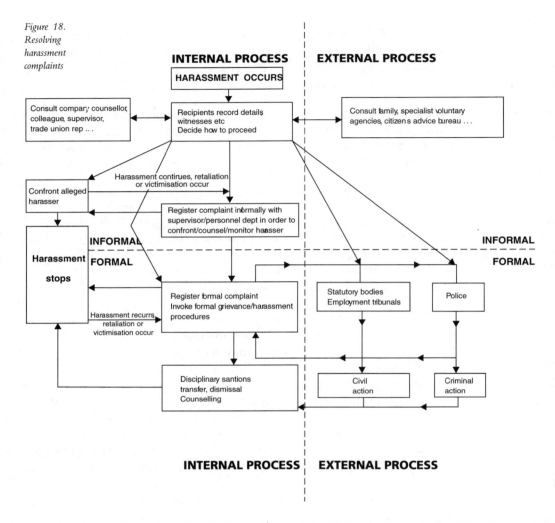

Figure 18.
Resolving
harassment
complaints

INTERNAL PROCESS | **EXTERNAL PROCESS**

HARASSMENT OCCURS

Consult company counsellor, colleague, supervisor, trade union rep ...

Recipients record details witnesses etc Decide how to proceed

Consult family, specialist voluntary agencies, citizens advice bureau ...

Harassment continues, retaliation or victimisation occur

Confront alleged harasser

Register complaint informally with supervisor/personnel dept in order to confront/counsel/monitor harasser

INFORMAL — — — — — — — — — — INFORMAL

Harassment stops | FORMAL — — — — — FORMAL

Register formal complaint Invoke formal grievance/harassment procedures

Harassment recurrs, retaliation or victimisation occur

Statutory bodies Employment tribunals

Police

Disciplinary santions transfer, dismissal Counselling

Civil action

Criminal action

INTERNAL PROCESS | **EXTERNAL PROCESS**

(Reproduced by kind permission of the Institute of Personnel and Development)

The key to resolving harassment complaints effectively is the speed with which the complaint is dealt with, the quality of advice and support given by supporters within the informal system, and the meticulous application of the procedures within the formal system. Above all, every complaint must be treated seriously and fairly, with a consistent approach being used.

The role of leaders and management

The role of leaders and management is vital in turning policy into practice, and making a harassment policy work. It is their responsibility to take harassment complaints seriously and deal with them effectively. The difficulty with this, however, is that most managers avoid addressing issues of harassment directly, because they feel uncomfortable about the topic and fear the consequences of dealing with it incorrectly.

It is for this reason that raising levels of awareness, gaining commitment to making a harassment policy work and developing skills for dealing with harassment need to be carried out at senior management level first of all. This will reduce some of the nervousness felt when handling cases of harassment. A climate must be created so that managers can freely admit ignorance and ask for help in certain areas, in order that they can develop the skills to deal with an incident effectively.

First line managers, in particular, have to juggle many responsibilities in order to fulfil their roles. The move from traditional personnel activities to HR management means that some personnel responsibilities now rest with line management. Thus managers are now having to deal with issues they have very little experience of. It is hardly surprising that there will be an element of resistance in management levels to taking on further responsibility. It is far easier to "abdicate" problems of this type to personnel, particularly as the sensitive nature of harassment is best addressed by those "skilled" to deal with it. Also, if managers are not sensitive to employees' feelings about harassment, and view the whole issue with cynicism, chances are they will brush aside a complaint and not take responsibility for the issue by confronting it.

Every manager in the organisation needs to understand and be aware of the potential consequences for the organisation if responsibilities are neglected. This includes appreciating the concept of "vicarious liability" (outlined in Chapter 7) along with its practical implications.

Understanding how the policy works in practice and the procedures for making complaints is a priority for managers. They must be able to communicate the policy and procedures to their teams, and follow through any queries team members may have. Managers must take complaints of harassment seriously, and if an incident occurs, they must handle it sensitively and swiftly, actively listening to all concerned. They also need to respect an individual's right not to complain; however, in certain circumstances it may be necessary to override this right to protect the individual being harassed.

Being an exemplar of good practice and challenging discriminatory behaviour at all times is essential in demonstrating visible commitment to the policy and its aims. This is crucial for leaders, who play a role in creating a harassment-free climate in the workplace. As Chapter 6 pointed out, certain management styles and behaviours can easily be interpreted as harassment, and routine "checks" on a manager's own personal style should be carried out to ensure that they are not – albeit unwittingly – perpetuating harassment themselves. Managers and leaders must be alert to unacceptable behaviour in their teams, and give clear messages that it will be dealt with fairly and firmly.

Do's and don'ts for managers

The following is a checklist (taken from an article in *Personnel Management*) on how managers can take responsibility for the issue of harassment in the workplace.

DO

● set a good example by treating all staff and customers with dignity and respect
● be alert to, and correct, unacceptable behaviour
● ensure staff know how to raise harassment problems
● deal with any complaints fairly, thoroughly and confidentially, respecting the rights of all the parties
● remember the impact of the behaviour determines harassment, not the intent.

DON'T

● assume that no complaints means no problems
● try to dissuade people from making complaints
● assume that complainants are over-sensitive or trouble-makers
● accept "I didn't mean any harm" as an excuse for harassment
● allow retaliation or victimisation.

(Kerry Hawkins (TMS Consultants), from "Taking action on harassment", *Personnel Management*, March 1994.)

The role of HR functions

In the 1970s, the traditional personnel role was that of primarily looking after the welfare of employees and advising managers on employment law issues. If there was a "difficult person" in the department, he/she would be sent along to the personnel officer to be sorted out. The role of personnel and HR functions has changed dramatically. The pressure on these functions to fulfil a more complex advisory role, and to ensure that policies, practices and procedures run smoothly within the organisation, means that the one-to-one handling of people problems has dwindled.

Difficulties arise when dealing with cases of harassment. It would be very easy to slip back into the "welfare" role, without fully meeting the needs of the organisation. There can quite easily be a conflict of interest between the needs of the individual being harassed and ensuring that the organisation meets its responsibilities. An example of this is when a personnel officer becomes a supporter in the informal system, and experiences a conflict of confidentiality when the matter becomes formal and they have to act on behalf of the organisation as well. It is for this reason that HR or personnel officers need to be very clear about their role in the informal system, and act as facilitators and back-up supporters, rather than be supporters themselves. In small organisations this may be difficult, so the rules on confidentiality should be absolutely clear and defined.

Harassment, in particular, must be treated as any other HR issue, with the same care and attention being given to the creation of policy and the implementation of plans as would be allocated to, for example, policy and plans for remuneration.

There is a tendency to view personnel and HR departments as the place for managers to "pass the buck" with employee problems and issues. Personnel specialists need to adopt a firm approach to ensure that managers take responsibility for eradicating harassment in the workplace, and not take on the problems on their behalf.

For this reason, it is essential that personnel and HR functions are seen as facilitators of policy into practice, rather than as owners of the harassment policy. Of course, they can be held accountable for the lack of policy development in this area; however, line managers are ultimately the ones who use the policy and put it into practice, and as such must be seen to be fully committed to it.

The role of personnel and HR functions is a crucial one here. They need to initiate and facilitate the development of a strategy to implement harassment procedures – creating the policy is only a small part of the process. Putting in place training and awareness sessions at all levels in the organisation, facilitating negotiations with unions and staff representation groups, making sure that the right support systems exist for managing change and resistance, and developing a communications plan and monitoring and evaluating the policy are all actions that should be initiated by personnel and HR functions, with the support of leaders in the organisation.

The question most HR and personnel functions ask is: "How do we get managers to take this matter seriously?" The following guidelines may help:

● Present them with statistical evidence of the extent of harassment and bullying in the organisation.
● Get management to "live in the real world", by explaining the reality of harassment and how it can impact in the workplace.
● Explain the potential costs to the business if harassment in the workplace is not confronted.
● Wherever possible, tell them about incidents involving organisations, particularly if a senior management colleague is involved.
● Ensure they are amongst the first to receive training and development, and always be on hand to give them the advice they need in order to handle issues.

Ultimately, HR and personnel functions need to ensure the organisation has the appropriate mechanisms in place to meet fully its responsibilities.

The role of the unions

The EU Code of Practice on the Protection of the Dignity of Women and Men at Work clearly states that:

"Sexual harassment is a trade union issue as well as an issue for employers. It is recommended as good practice that trade unions should formulate and issue clear policy statements on sexual harassment and take steps to raise awareness of the problem of sexual harassment in the workplace, in order to help create a climate in which it is neither condoned nor ignored.

Trade unions should also raise the issue of sexual harassment with employers and encourage the adoption of adequate policies and procedures to protect the dignity of women and men at work in the organisation. It is advisable for trade unions to inform members of their right not to be sexually harassed at work and provide members with clear guidance as to what to do if they are sexually harassed, including guidance on any relevant legal rights."

The role of trade unions is clearly defined in the recommendation. However, organisations still persist in excluding unions and staff representation groups from policy development, rather than using their expertise and ensuring their commitment to making the policy work. Harassment, bullying and violence are not issues that need to be "negotiated" in a "them and us" situation; it is essential that everyone in the organisation who has the skills and the expertise to create a harassment strategy is involved at every stage. The results of working in co-operation and consultation with unions for the greater good of the organisation can be very fruitful.

The MSF union has developed a reputation for creating practical policies in the area of harassment, and working alongside organisations to get them implemented. Its recommendations for combating bullying in the workplace have set the tone for other trade unions and staff representation groups to follow. MSF, along with the National Union of Journalists (NUJ), was one of the unions that worked with the Consumer Association to produce a policy and guidelines to help create a better working climate.

Case Study

MSF – Meeting its Responsibilities

In an interview with Ann Gibson, [then] MSF's equal opportunities officer, we explore MSF's work in this area, and their commitment to creating positive working environments in organisations.

1. How was MSF's campaign on combating racial and sexual harassment, bullying and violence in the workplace formed?

They were all subjects raised with us by members, and as we began to take up the issues, we realised we were touching the tips of icebergs.

2. What is MSF's national campaigning message(s) in these areas?

To turn to harassment first. We took up the matter of harassment in all forms and emphasised that it was/is a trade union issue because it affects a worker's life. Therefore as a trade union we were determined to fight it on behalf of members.

More recently our attention has been drawn to the question of bullying and even violence in the workplace. Again, the effect upon workers is horrendous, and we are determined to fight it in all its forms. The national messages are, therefore:

● Harassment, bullying and violence are trade union issues because they have a deep – and often lasting – effect upon workers.
● They are not acceptable behaviour and MSF will fight such activities wherever they are experienced.

3. What help is offered to the individual member who is suffering from harassment or bullying? (Can you give an example?)

We have comprehensive guidance for individual members, lay representatives and FTOs (full-time officers) on how to tackle these areas of discrimination, which has been widely circulated. In addition, schools, conferences and courses are run on the subjects. Our Education College runs excellent day and week schools for members, reps and FTOs. One example of harassment is where a young woman member had been subjected to sexual harassment over a period of months which bordered on indecent assault on one occasion. We took up the issue with management and were able to get her financial compensation for the harasser to be removed from the workplace. She has gone on to be promoted within the company. Once the case was raised, it was found that the harasser had been exercising his powers over young women workers for years. Women workers spoke for the first time of how they had faced similar situations with the same man. One woman employee had received similar treatment 15 years earlier when she had first joined the company. She had accepted it at the time because "it was something a lot of women had to put up with, I hadn't thought a trade union would take up such an issue, anyway". Thank goodness times have moved on!

4. *What help is offered to the individual member who is accused of harassment or bullying? (Can you give an example?)*

If a member is accused of harassment or bullying, we believe he/she has a right to representation by an MSF representative (lay or full time, as they choose) for their defence. After all, they have paid their subscriptions, and may be innocent. However, if the member is found guilty after investigation, we do not usually support them in appeals against the decision.

An example is where two female MSF members accused a male MSF member of harassment. One FTO represented the women and another FTO represented the man. The man was found guilty and he subsequently left the company. We did make it clear we would not support an appeal against the findings, but did give him advice about certain financial aspects when he left.

5. *What training is given to officials and union reps to enable them to support members being harassed and bullied and members accused of harassment and bullying?*

We are lucky in having our Education Centre at Whitehall College in Bishop Stortford and courses are run there for FTOs and lay representatives to enable them to support members being harassed and/or bullied and those accused of these actions. I think it fair to say we place more emphasis on the former than the latter. We also have extensive written guidance. Additionally, our legal department and the equal opportunities department are always willing to assist.

6. *Do organisations come to you for advice, and if so, how do you support them?*

We have good working relationships with the Equal Opportunities

Commission and the Commission for Racial Equality and also with organisations such as Women Against Sexual Harassment, the National Association of Citizens' Advice Bureaux, etc. We are also building up our relationship with organisations dealing with bullying or violence. We welcome the opportunity to work with other organisations on these issues, especially where we have members working in them.

With regard to advice, we do give out advice, especially on bullying, as we are the first union to work on this in any depth. We hand out any written information we have both to organisations and non-union members, as we believe it is important to raise the issues wherever possible.

7. Do you have any written guidelines for other areas of harassment (e.g. people with disabilities, heterosexist harassment)?

Yes. People with disabilities, lesbian and gay members, and youth. We are currently working on ageism guidelines. We have a general harassment statement also, which is for external use but which we also circulate within the union and at our annual conference to re-emphasise that we expect members to show each other respect too. We circulate an anti-harassment leaflet throughout our Education Centre also – in each bedroom and the main working areas – and if ever there is any suggestion of harassment etc when members are at the college, complaints are taken very seriously.

Three years ago, we did suspend a male member from office within MSF for five years, because of complaints about his behaviour from women members and we do have a clause in our rule book relating to this:

Disciplinary procedures
The National Executive Council shall have the power to terminate the membership of, or fine or remove from office, any member who, in its opinion, without reasonable excuse in his/her capacity as a member of the union, supports or speaks on behalf of organisations concerned with the dissemination of racist propaganda and/or himself/herself undertakes actions against others, whether members of the union or not, designed to discriminate on the grounds of race, creed, ethnic origin, nationality, sexuality or sex.

8. Have things changed in the workplace since starting the campaigns?

It is difficult to estimate and measure the improvement in workplaces, but what has definitely improved is the recognition of, and understanding about, harassment. Employers, by and large, now take this seriously and work with unions to ensure it either does not happen or is dealt with effectively if it does. Bullying is at an earlier stage but we already have some anti-bullying arguments.

9. *What projects do MSF have planned for the future?*

We have launched our latest anti-bullying guide and will be following these guidelines up by monitoring their use and effect. We are also considering helplines on harassment and on bullying, and in the future counselling services for members affected.

10. *What is MSF's message to organisations for preventing harassment, bullying and violence in the workplace, and for creating a positive working environment?*

Take the matters seriously, ensure that all your employees know you are serious and that harassment, bullying and violence are disciplinary offences. Work with us (trade unions) to eliminate these behaviours, by drawing up equal opportunities/harassment/bullying policies, sticking to them and monitoring their effects.

(An interview with Ann Gibson – equal opportunities officer until October 1996)

The cost of getting it wrong

Previous chapters should have left you in no doubt as to the serious effect that harassment has on the individual. The effects of harassment in the organisation should not be underestimated either. They may seem, at first, difficult to quantify; however, they will start to show through like cracks in a wall, eventually affecting the productivity and overall performance of the organisation.

The costs can be looked at in terms of:

● **Absence and sickness rates** – Long-term sick leave and inter-mittent absences break continuity in work. The Department of Health estimates that 360 million working days are lost each year through stress-related illness. Also 3.6% of salary budgets (national average) is paid to people absent from work due to stress-related illness.
● **Time** – It takes a considerable amount of time to handle complaints of harassment. Management resources are expensive, and the administrative costs of investigation are high.
● **Stress** – Levels of unhealthy stress increase and have detrimental effects on the organisation. Not only does the stress of harassment and

bullying contribute to serious illnesses, increased levels of stress make it very difficult for employers to meet the Health and Safety at Work Act 1974 requirement to provide a safe work environment. (In 1997, the Confederation of British Industry estimated the cost of stress and stress-related illness in the workplace to be approximately £12 billion a year.)

● **Costs of recruiting and retraining** – Recruiting becomes expensive, particularly when there is a high turnover in staff, and the investment in terms of training employees is wasted if they do not stay in the organisation. Harassment can also impact on an individual's career prospects, and levels of job satisfaction can reduce dramatically.

● **Tribunal proceedings** – In 1994/95, the average award paid out at a tribunal in respect of discrimination cases was £25,000. This does not include tribunal running costs such as administration time.

● **Loss of public image** – The effect of bad publicity from a very public, high profile case of harassment on the organisation is often underestimated. Not only does it reduce the morale and motivation of employees, but it brings into question the organisation's ethical stance (particularly if they purport to be supporters of equality) and tarnishes its reputation.

● **The hidden costs** – The psychological and social costs to the organisation are often hidden and very rarely talked about. The breakdown in relationships in the workforce, and the distractions that occur due to lapses in concentration, mean that the quality of work drops and expensive mistakes are made. This has a knock-on effect on the immediate team, and the organisation's performance as a whole.

At an Industrial Society conference on bullying, Tim Field, a survivor of bullying, estimated the cost to the organisation of his experience. The cost – comprising a redundancy payment, pension, personnel and occupational health time, a period of six months' sick leave, re-recruiting his position in the organisation, the loss of his knowledge and experience, the wasted training investment and the administration required to handle this situation – was well in excess of £200,000. The personal cost to himself was great. He suffered a breakdown, which took a year to recover from, and his career as a successful computer services manager ended.

A common complaint from management when attempting to implement any equal opportunities initiative is that "it costs too much". The cost of implementing a harassment policy and procedures is minimal in comparison to the detrimental costs of tribunal proceedings, the damage to the business due to a loss of public image and the loss of confidence that clients and customers may have in the organisation. "Customer Power" should not be undervalued: customers now have a wider and more diverse choice of service providers, and are becoming more discerning. Ethics also play an increasing part in the choice of where to spend their money, and bad publicity involving harassment and bullying may influence this.

Communication, training and monitoring

The success of a policy is dependent upon how well it is communicated, the level of awareness, skills and knowledge employees have to implement it, and the effectiveness of monitoring procedures.

Communication
Regular communication is important. Employees need to know:

● why the organisation is committed to eradicating harassment and how it plans to achieve this
● the progress of policy development
● the details of the policy and their individual responsibilities within it
● how to make a complaint and who to go to for advice and support.

This can be achieved by circulating posters in visible places around the workplace as well as notice boards, creating a booklet or leaflet and ensuring every employee has a personal copy of it, and printing a shortened version of the policy in staff handbooks.

Consideration should be given to informing contractors, clients, agencies and other associates of the organisation about the policy. The Local Government Management Board, in their guide to sexual harassment in the workplace, state:

"All employees should be informed of the policy alongside, for instance, elected members, agents, contractors and clients. While overall responsibility rests with the employer, there are clearly shared obligations between staff and management (and other associated parties) who may be personally liable for their behaviour."

A communication strategy can be devised, which would include plans for consultation with union groups and staff representatives and for publishing the outcomes of these discussions. It should also include details and dates of training and awareness events, such as presentations and roadshows, and information about the official launch of the policy, outlining when the policy comes into effect.

Training

To ensure the policy works effectively, training must take place at all levels in the workplace, particularly for those with designated responsibilities in both the informal and formal procedures. Chapter 11 looks at the process of education in the organisation.

Monitoring

The best way to find out how well the policy is working in practice is to put in place good monitoring and evaluation procedures. Effective monitoring can establish potential problem areas such as repeat patterns of behaviour and victimisation. It can also evaluate how effective training programmes are, and how well issues are resolved in both the formal and informal mechanisms. Monitoring can be carried out in the following ways:

- Reviewing the policy at regular intervals by holding meetings with supporters and managers.
- Keeping records of complaints made in the informal system.
- Keeping records of the outcomes of formal investigations and the time taken to resolve issues.
- Reviewing the nature of complaints, without breaking confidentiality guidelines.
- Checking exit interviews and performance appraisals for signs of bullying and harassment.
- Carrying out intermittent audits and surveys.

Reflection

In his article "Taking action on harassment" Kerry Hawkins states the prevailing view that *"the creation of a climate to challenge harassment begins with the policy"*. In practice, the reality of this statement is that a policy will not in itself change the climate of the organisation, nor is it the beginning of the process – examining the current culture and testing the temperature of the climate are the first steps, as already outlined in Chapter 6.

However, a good policy provides the framework to set standards of acceptable behaviour, supports and develops those who ensure policy guidelines are adhered to and, most importantly, facilitates the creation of a positive working environment.

References

Preventing and Remedying Sexual Harassment at Work: A Resource Manual, Michael Rubenstein (IRS, 1992).

Statement on Harassment at Work, Institute of Personnel and Development

No Offence? Sexual Harassment: How it Happens and How to Beat it (The Industrial Society, 1993)

Sexual Harassment in the Workplace: An Employment Guide, Local Government Management Board, 1993.

Bullying: Unacceptable Behaviour in the Workplace, paper from Industrial Society Conference, September 1995 (Tim Field, Success Unlimited).

"Taking action on harassment", Kerry Hawkins, TMS Consultants (*Personnel Management*, 1994).

CHAPTER 9

Conducting a harassment investigation: a step-by-step approach

Investigating complaints of harassment, bullying and violence is one of the most difficult tasks to complete. As organisations have an implied legal responsibility to investigate and resolve incidents of harassment, the employer must take complaints of harassment seriously, and therefore needs to carry out an investigation thoroughly, quickly and effectively.

As outlined in Chapter 8, investigating complaints of harassment is a crucial part of any formal procedure. The main characteristics of good investigations are:

- that they are carried out promptly and that timescales for resolution are strictly adhered to
- that they are conducted by highly skilled personnel who are impartial to the process
- that the rights of both the complainant and alleged harasser are protected until the outcome investigation (this includes their right to representation throughout the investigation)
- that details of the complaint are clearly outlined and the alleged harasser gets the opportunity to answer the charges
- that the rights and responsibilities of witnesses are clearly defined
- that the commitment to confidentiality and non-disclosure ruling is evident
- that accurate record-keeping and note-taking is carried out.

The objective of the investigation is to ascertain what took place, and come up with recommendations to resolve the issues in the most appropriate way. This will ensure that the complaint is taken seriously, and is dealt with in a sensitive and fair manner. Interviews must have a clear focus and concentrate on separating the facts from feelings and fiction. It is crucial that investigations are completely impartial at all stages.

Case Study

Harassment Complaint Not Taken Seriously
McGuiness v Finchale Training College

A female trainee whose complaint of threats of violence and harassment by a fellow male trainee was not properly investigated by the college principal was unlawfully discriminated against on grounds of sex.

Sarah McGuiness commenced a residential business administration NVQ course at Finchale Training College in County Durham in January 1992. Shortly before the Easter vacation, a male trainee was loudly abusive to Ms McGuiness and made various threats of violence, causing her "enormous fear and distress".

Ms McGuiness immediately reported the incident, which had been witnessed by others, to the college principal, Mr Goodman. During their meeting, no attempt was made by Mr Goodman to obtain a written report of the incident from her, even though, because of the vacation, she would be absent for any inquiry. He told her that she should return home to Hampshire to see her boyfriend and something to the effect that she was a tall, attractive redhead who would have to put up with harassment of this sort. However, before leaving she did provide a written statement of the incident to the college welfare officer who passed it on to the principal. Mr Goodman made no effort to interview any of the witnesses named by Ms McGuiness either in her meeting with him or in her written statement, and he did not make any real effort to make witnesses come forward. Nor did he carry out anything more than a perfunctory interview with the alleged harasser.

On her return to college Ms McGuiness formed the view that her complaint had not been taken seriously, been properly investigated or even believed, and by the middle of June her mental state had deteriorated very considerably. It became apparent that Ms McGuiness, who had a history of mental ill-health, required specialist medical help, which was unavailable at the college. In July, believing he had no alternative, Mr Goodman terminated her training. Ms McGuiness claimed that she had been discriminated against on the grounds of sex contrary to s14 of the Sex Discrimination Act.

The industrial tribunal upheld her claim. In its view, "the appropriate course would have been to ensure that at as early a stage as possible the applicant's account of the incident was committed to paper and an immediate investigation set in motion", which Mr Goodman had "plainly failed to do". Together with the "practically non-existent" attempts to find witnesses and the perfunctory interview of the harasser, the tribunal was convinced that "not only did Mr Goodman fail to carry out a proper investigation of the complaint but he also did not wish to carry out such an investigation". In so doing he subjected the applicant to a detriment in the course of her training, said the tribunal. It was satisfied that such treatment was probably on the grounds of sex and the likelihood was that had the applicant been a man Mr Goodman would have carried out a proper investigation. "Mr Goodman believed that the applicant was 'an hysterical woman' who was therefore inherently unreliable." It concluded that "even 'an hysterical man' would have received proper and appropriate treatment". In the tribunal's judgement, Mr Goodman's attitude towards the applicant and women in general was revealed by his comments to the applicant and in particular the comment about being red-haired and attractive, the "fact" that she would have to get used to harassment and the desirability of her returning home as soon as possible to her boyfriend. There was no question that similar remarks would have been made by Mr Goodman to a man.

(Case No. 28478/93, 14 June 1994, *Equal Opportunities Review: Discrimination Case Law Digest*, No. 23, Spring 1995. Reproduced by kind permission of Eclipse Group Ltd)

Creating an investigation plan

It is helpful to prepare a plan before beginning any investigation process. Planning helps reduce the time taken to conduct the actual investigation, ensures that the investigation is completed fairly and objectively, and meets the obligations set in your organisation's code of practice.

The plan should include:

● Agreement on who will conduct the interview and the role that each person will play in the process.
● A draft list of all the people involved in the situation, starting with the complainant, line managers and supervisors, the alleged harasser, witnesses (if any) and every person who might have any knowledge about the circumstances surrounding the incident. This list is only a starting point; as the investigation widens, more people may be high-lighted as witnesses, and therefore will be added to the list.
● The identification of any documents that may be helpful and where they are located. Create a file for these investigation documents, and

include dated copies of all relevant policy, procedural or handbook statements.
- If possible, arrangements to visit the place or scene where the alleged incident occurred. This may help to establish new facts, and corroborate (or exclude) evidence given by all parties concerned.
- Timescales for completing the investigation, with dates and times of interview meetings.
- Meetings with employee representatives or (where applicable) union officials to communicate progress on the investigation.
- Information and guidelines for evaluating the process and monitoring the recommendations that may come from the investigation.

Conducting the investigation

The investigation should be conducted by personnel who are highly skilled, and who are able to cope with the stress of this process effectively.

What skills are required to handle an investigation? The desired person specification of an investigator is someone who is:

- knowledgeable about the legal aspects of harassment and the conflicting rights and responsibilities of all those involved
- able to recognise what harassment is and what it is not
- experienced in handling general employee complaints and grievances
- familiar with the organisation's structure, policies, practices and management procedures
- outside the involved parties' immediate chain of command – ideally in an non-operational or service role
- credible to employees – the designated individual should have a corporate reputation for independence, honesty, professionalism, sensitivity and directness
- a trained facilitator, counsellor or someone whom others find it easy to confide in
- a neutral party, who is neither a friend nor colleague of either party
- able to recognise when their involvement might lead to issues of neutrality, impartiality and objectivity
- trained and experienced in dealing with the emotional aspects of an investigation.

It is recommended that investigators be as diverse as possible, giving the complainants the ability to select a listener with whom they will feel most comfortable.

Support for people who become investigators is an integral part of the investigation procedure. Investigators need to meet on a regular basis to discuss fears and concerns, and any problems they have encountered during the investigation. Development issues, both personal and organisational, may also be dealt with in this forum. Case studies (without breaking the guidelines on confidentiality) can be discussed for development purposes. These meetings should take the form of support groups, and will be confidential. An HR or personnel specialist, or trained counsellor, would act as a facilitator in these meetings.

Before the investigation starts, appoint the members of the investigation panel. A panel should consist of no more than three individuals, with fair representation of women, men, minority groups and people with disabilities. The role of each investigator needs to be clarified: for example, who will lead the questioning of the complainant? Who will carry out the research element of the investigation? Who will take notes, or nominate a note-taker? Will the investigation need a panel chair?

Begin your investigation at least three days after receipt of the complaint by:

- interviewing the complainant
- interviewing the alleged harasser
- interviewing witnesses.

Interviewing the complainant

The complainant has the right to representation. They can bring to the interview a trade union representative, supporter, adviser, listener or contact officer as part of the organisation's harassment process. A chosen friend or colleague can also attend.

Explain the process to them, including the role of the investigation panel, what the complainant's rights and responsibilities are within the process, how the investigation links into organisational policy and grievance and disciplinary procedures, and how the final outcome will be handled.

Put the complainant at ease, and be sensitive to any body language that may signify discomfort. The investigating panel may suggest that someone attends the interview with the complainant (if they have not already chosen to do so), in which case the interview can be suspended until a suitable person is identified by the complainant.

Discussions about the levels of confidentiality should be explained as soon as possible, so that the complainant is aware that the information they give will have to be shared with other people involved in the process. Confidentiality will be discussed later on in this chapter.

The interview should focus on the following points:

● finding out exactly what happened
● the extent to which the conduct was unwelcome
● whether the alleged harasser is a manager/supervisor, team member, a group of people or an outsider
● any existing patterns of behaviour
● corroborating witnesses and other evidence
● the emotional/physical state of the complainant.

Depending upon the system of note-taking used, the complainant should sign a copy of the notes after being given the opportunity to read and make changes to them if necessary, either directly after the meeting or not more than 24 hours later.

End the interview by reiterating assurances that the complaint is being dealt with seriously, and that they will be informed of the outcome as soon as possible.

As victimisation often occurs after a formal complaint is made, the investigators should inform the complainant that if there is any retaliation as a result of making the complaint, they should report the incident(s) immediately to the investigation panel.

Interviewing the alleged harasser

Remember, the alleged harasser is innocent until proven otherwise. It is essential that investigators are able to suspend all judgements – however difficult or harrowing the information received.

The same principles and structure involved in interviewing the complainant apply here – ensuring sensitivity and objectivity, and keeping in mind that the overall goal of the interview is to gain as much factual evidence as possible.

The alleged harasser should be encouraged to have a representative present at the interview, to ensure they are given a fair and complete hearing. Any refusal to have representation at the interview is important and should be noted. However, it should not be used against the alleged harasser when making a decision about the case.

The alleged harasser should be made aware:

● that the issue investigated is a serious matter, and that the process will be objective and impartial
● who is involved in the process and the roles that they play
● how long the process will take, how it will be concluded, together with a clarification of the decision-making process

● if appropriate, who the complainant is, and the nature of the complaint against them.

Review the facts of the case by presenting a brief summary to the alleged harasser. If a signed statement of events is available from the complainant, use this to go through the facts, step by step. Note areas of disagreement and agreement, and check the facts with any evidence received from witnesses.

In addition, the alleged harasser's position within the organisation is crucial to the outcome of the investigation. If they have any influence with any member of the investigation panel, the impartiality of the process is damaged. Provisions should be made to ensure that where the alleged harasser is a senior manager, investigators are of the same or higher level.

The failure to follow proper procedures when interviewing and dealing with the alleged harasser may lead to the alleged harasser making a claim of unfair dismissal against the organisation.

If the alleged harassers are a group . . .
Complaints against each individual in the group must be treated separately, even though the overall effect of the group's behaviour on the complainant is taken into account. Interview each member of the group concerned separately, and assess each allegation on its own merit to ensure that complaints against each individual are effectively answered.

If the alleged harasser is outside your organisation . . .
Most organisations feel that if an employee suffers harassment from a customer, visitor or other outsider, there is very little or nothing they can do about the incident.

Organisations are encouraged to bring the complaint to the attention of the alleged harasser's organisation, and request that an investigation into the allegations take place. Alternatively, a working partnership between the relevant organisations can be established in order that a joint investigation can take place to resolve the issue, and stop any reoccurrence.

Interviewing witnesses
Because of the abuse of power relationships involved in cases of harassment, bullying and violence, finding witnesses who are willing to speak up about incidents of harassment may prove to be a hindrance to the

investigation – particularly if the environment in which the incident took place is very hostile.

When publicising policy and procedures for dealing with cases of harassment, bullying and violence, it is a good idea briefly to outline the importance of coming forward when witnessing incidents. It is also essential to reassure potential witnesses that victimisation and harassment towards them will not be tolerated, and will be dealt with just as seriously as the incident itself. This gives the investigator solid background to help put a nervous witness at ease, and reminds them about their rights in the process.

Remember that although witnesses are providers of information, they may not necessarily be giving the true facts. Again sensitivity and objectivity is vital when interviewing witnesses, and concentration on the facts will keep the interview focused. It is not unusual to find, after a preliminary interview, that some witnesses may themselves be a target of harassment, but have never complained about their treatment. Also, the status of the witness may have a bearing on what they are prepared to reveal. The mood of the interview may make the difference between a witness revealing their experiences of harassment, or keeping quiet and saying no more than their level of confidence allows.

Make a witness feel comfortable enough to share the information that is needed to complete the investigation by using a variety of questions and a high level of listening.

What do you do if there are no witnesses?

Having no witnesses to an event does not mean that the harassment incidents did not occur. In fact, most harassment tends to happen in situations where the parties concerned are isolated and alone. This does not make the accusation of harassment unrealistic. When there are no corroborating witnesses, however, the examination of other evidence becomes all the more important.

Gathering and corroborating evidence

As well as interviewing the complainant, the alleged harasser and any witnesses, it will be necessary to gather as much documentary evidence as possible to support the complainant's claim, in order to carry out a full assessment of the situation.

Types of evidence may include:

● statements by witnesses on the effect of the harassment incident on the complainant

- changes in health, work performance (reviews and appraisals) and absence and sickness records
- relevant personnel files (complainant and alleged harasser)
- information about promotion, training and development opportunities and salary and grading rewards that links the alleged harasser with the complainant (was promotion or reward withheld by the alleged harasser if he/she was the manager of the complainant?)
- previous informal complaints from the complainant
- complaints from other witnesses or members of staff who have shared the same experience.

Disregard any evidence that:

- contains character assassinations (of both the alleged harasser and the complainant)
- contains emotive suppositions and innuendoes
- stereotypes the alleged harasser and the complainant in any way
- indicates that witnesses have been pre-informed of events or coached into relating what they should have seen or known.

Note-taking and record-keeping

Note-taking and record-keeping play a vital role in the process of investigating a case of harassment. Great care needs to be taken to ensure that every interview is properly documented, in order that a fair assessment of the facts can take place. The following points should be taken into account when note-taking and record-keeping:

- Ensure that the person nominated to take notes has been properly trained in minute- and note-taking.
- Wherever possible, try to have a member of the panel take written notes. If an administrator or secretary is asked to take notes, they should be far removed from the parties involved (from different departments or divisions) and reminded of the confidential nature of the interview.
- If interviews are to be taped, ensure you receive the full permission of all parties first and inform them of your intention. If possible, transcripts of the tapes should be made available to both the complainant and the alleged harasser if they request them.
- Records should be locked up, and shared only with authorised recipients who are involved in the investigation process.
- Signed statements of all interviews should be obtained, and copies given to all relevant parties. If any party refuses to sign such a statement, note the refusal and include your account of the interview.
- Any notes and papers received from the complainant, accused harasser(s)

or witnesses should be logged and kept on file – especially those which do not agree with or counteract evidence in signed statements.

The confidentiality trap

Confidentiality means keeping secret any information concerning the complainant revealed in the interview. Promising total confidentiality in an investigation process will make it difficult to keep. However, it is essential that confidentiality guidelines are established, to protect the rights of the complainant (or complainants) and those of the accused.

If guidelines about confidentiality are obscure and inconsistencies occur, the chances are that employer and personal liability will be seriously jeopardised, and claims of defamation or damage to reputation can occur. To prevent this, the following guidelines are suggested:

● Ensure there is a consistent message about confidentiality in all policy and procedural documentation, and that this message is communicated effectively throughout the whole organisation (not just to those who are directly involved in harassment cases).

● Clarify any confusion there may be about confidentiality in an informal support system (between client and counsellor/adviser/supporter) and the confidentiality guidelines required for formal investigation and grievance and disciplinary procedures.

● Never promise absolute confidentiality, but encourage all parties not to *disclose* information about the incident and/or investigation. A clear understanding of why a promise of total confidentiality cannot be made needs to be established, backed up with a guarantee by the employer to limit discussion to only those individuals who are involved.

● Be clear about "off the record" information – and carefully remind the individual before they start to speak that any information received may not always be considered off the record, but will, however, be treated with sensitivity.

● Only disclose information on a "need to know" basis – designate an investigator to ensure that details of the incident and the investigation are only discussed with those who are involved in the process, or with the personnel who have to make a decision about the outcome.

● Restrict the viewing and circulation of documents relating to the investigation to those involved in the investigation. Introduce tight document control by numbering and dating the number of copies issued, and keep a record of who holds copies of the information. Ask HR or personnel staff to type interview notes, rather than allowing departmental administration staff to view the contents.

The skills of interviewing

Good interviewing skills consist of:

- active listening
- the use of appropriate questioning
- reflecting and summarising information
- challenging conflicting messages sensitively
- appropriate use of body language
- dealing with emotions.

Active listening

Listening is a skill which is undervalued – it is the skill most used, however, we are not taught to use it at school.

Active listening is the process of understanding meaning as well as receiving information.

The key to active listening is to:

- accept what the talker is saying without judging it
- respond in ways that show he/she has heard and is trying to understand
- notice underlying feelings, attitudes, values
- be aware of physical barriers such as interruptions, noise, time constraints, etc, and psychological barriers such as feelings, prejudices, lack of concentration, memory, etc.

Listening to a complainant or an alleged harasser can evoke personal feelings and emotions which may affect your ability to remain impartial. It is necessary to remain neutral for active listening to be effective. Be sensitive about the types of questions you ask and how you ask them.

The use of appropriate questioning

Questions must be open and reflective, probing and summarising. Using the "funnel technique" in an investigation will help you to move from assumption to evidence (see Figure 19). Interviewers must avoid leading questions or statements, and try not to create hypothetical scenarios.

Figure 19.
The funnelling
technique

From assumption to evidence

[1]Questioning complainants, accused harassers and witnesses, using the funnelling technique

Complainant

In your own words, tell me exactly what happened . . .
How are you feeling at the moment?
Was the incident physical or verbal?
Did he/she/they touch you?
If so, where did they touch you and in what way?
Did he/she/they use inappropriate language?
What words were used?
Where did this happen?
Did this occur outside the workplace, inside the workplace or at a work-related event?
In what context was the behaviour?
What is your relationship with the accused?
How would they describe it?
Was it strictly business, or did it involve some form of socialising?
How long have you known the accused?

[1]Adapted from *Sexual Harassment in the Workplace* by Ellen J Wagner. © 1992 Creative Solutions, Inc. Reproduced by kind permission of AMACOM, a division of American Management Association International, New York, NY. All rights reserved. http://www.amanet.org

Has the accused ever done anything to you in the past?

How did you handle it then?

What did you say or do to indicate that you objected to the behaviour?

What is the atmosphere like in the area/department that you work in?

Is there a lot of joking, teasing or innuendo?

What is the team spirit like?

What role has your manager/supervisor played in this (only if manager/supervisor is not the accused)?

Are there any possible witnesses to the incident? Who could have heard or seen something relevant?

Have you spoken to anyone about the incident – at the time or since then?

Did you take any action yourself? If so, what happened?

Do you know of anyone else who has experienced something similar from the same person/people?

If so, do you know what happened?

How has the behaviour/incident affected you?

What would you like to see happen next? Or how would you like to see this resolved?

What would you feel comfortable doing next?

Are you satisfied with how this interview has been conducted?

What is your understanding of the next steps and how the investigation will proceed?

Would you like support, counselling or advice whilst the investigation continues?

Are you able to go back to your workplace comfortably?

The accused harasser/s

Do you know why I am here?

What would you like to say in response to the brief summary of events that I have just given you?

In your own words, tell me exactly what happened.

What actually occurred? What did the complainant say? What did you say?

Where did this happen?

Did this occur outside the workplace, inside the workplace or at a work-related event?

Who else was there?

Are there any aspects of the complaint that you agree with? What do you disagree with?

What do you not remember?

Is there anyone else who might have seen or heard something relevant to this discussion?

Who are they? What could they have seen or heard?

Did you talk to anyone about this incident? When did you do this? What is your relationship with that individual?

What kind of working climate is there in the department/team? Is there a lot of joking or teasing? Did the complainant ever join in?

Had the complainant's behaviour changed recently? When did this happen? Why do you think it happened?

Has your behaviour changed recently? When did this happen? Why do you think it happened? What do other members of the department/team think about this change in behaviour?

How would you describe your relationship with the complainant? Was it strictly business, entirely personal, or both?

How long have you known the complainant? How do you think the complainant would describe the relationship? Who else would be in a position to know its nature and be able to describe it accurately?

What are you prepared to do about this situation? How would you suggest resolving it?

Do you understand how this investigation will continue and who will ultimately decide how the situation will be resolved? Do you understand that no one in the organisation is permitted to victimise an employee making a complaint of harassment, and that the consequences for doing so are great?

Witnesses

Have you ever personally seen or heard anything to indicate that the complainant was being made uncomfortable at work, or that they found the working environment offensive?

What did you see or hear? Who was making things uncomfortable? In what way?

Did the complainant ever tell you about this incident? What did the complainant tell you? When did the complainant tell you this?

What type of relationship would you say existed between the complainant and the accused?

Was it strictly business, entirely personal or both?

What kind of relationship did the complainant have with the supervisor/manager? Was the supervisor/manager aware of the problem? How do you know? What did the supervisor/manager do about it? What details can you provide of that? Do you know when it happened, what time, where?

How did other members of the department/team behave toward the complainant?

What is the atmosphere like in the area/department you work in?

Is there a lot of joking, teasing or innuendo?

What is the team spirit like?

Have you had any problems or noticed any barriers whilst working in your team (eg progression, promotion)?

What exactly did you see or hear? What happened then?

Who else might know something about this?

How do you feel about the situation? What kind of relationship do you have with the complainant and the accused?

Do you understand the importance of not disclosing any of this conversation with anyone else? Do you agree not to disclose this?

(Questions adapted from *Sexual Harassment in the Workplace*, by Ellen J Wagner, AMACOM, 1992. © AMACOM)

When questioning, interviewers should avoid:

● blaming the complainant – *"Well, if he did that to you, why didn't you hit him where it hurts?"*

● judgemental statements – *"A manager at your level should have known better than to approach your employee in that way."*

● leading and multiple questions – *"Are you sure he meant it in that way, or was it just your imagination?"*

The investigator's role is to gather the facts and evidence, and not expand the accusations.

Reflecting and summarising information

Reflecting is a brief statement, in the interviewer's words, of what the talker has been saying. It is useful in helping the interviewer check out whether there is accurate understanding of what is being said, and gives the interviewee an opportunity to correct or adjust the understanding.

Summarising is similar to reflecting, the main difference being that summaries can be used to move the interview on to another area or in another direction. Summaries can be used to clarify, for both the interviewer and the interviewee, the most important points covered so far, and to sum up at the end of the interview.

Challenging conflicting messages sensitively

In the course of an interview, inconsistencies in the interviewee's evidence may appear. Challenging conflicting messages can help an interviewee clarify their situation, and confront difficulties that have not been apparent before. It will also help the interviewer get a more accurate picture of what took place and why.

Challenge sensitively any contradictory statements, inaccurate assumptions and inconsistencies between behaviour and expressed feelings or two different expressed feelings. For example:

"Earlier, you stated that you knew all about what behaviours constitute harassment, because they are in the policy booklet on harassment. Now you're saying that you didn't know that making jokes about someone's religion could be harassment. Can we clarify what is your understanding of harassment?"

Ensure that challenges are not seen as confrontational, as this may put the interviewee on the defensive and hamper the progress of the investigation. Challenging is not an interrogation technique – the interviewer must display empathy and not use challenging to express disapproval or frustration.

Appropriate use of body language

Interviewers and interviewees will send messages through their non-verbal behaviour. The interviewer needs to read the messages from the interviewee without distorting or over-interpreting them, and use appropriate body language of their own to assist them in the interview process.

Interviewers need to read (and *not* interpret):

● facial expressions
● bodily behaviour
● voice-related behaviour
● general appearance.

Dealing with emotions

The emotions displayed by interviewees can range from mild distress to extreme anger. Interviewers need to pick up the difference between the interviewees talking about their emotions and the emotions they are expressing as they talk. They also must be able to cope with, and handle, the expression of these emotions: for example, some people find it difficult to deal with tears, but it would not be unusual in an investigation for an interviewee to cry, particularly if the discussion is very difficult for them.

Alleged harassers may respond emotionally, not just by displaying anger and embarrassment, but by showing signs of shock and shame – particularly if they have not harassed or bullied intentionally and did not realise the impact of their behaviour on the complainant. In addition, dealing with witnesses may also be difficult. Some witnesses may feel guilty about not interjecting or speaking up sooner about the incident.

The interviewer must create an atmosphere which allows the interviewee space and time to express their emotions safely. If it is necessary, adjourn the meeting to allow this to happen. Manage uncomfortable silences by patiently waiting for the interviewee, and gently prompting them to continue when they are ready. Silences give both the interviewee and the interviewer the opportunity to collect their thoughts and plan the next steps. A "no blame" attitude should be adopted by the interviewer in order to help the complainant, alleged harasser and any witnesses cope with their emotions and complete the interview.

The role of the trade unions

Trade unions have an important role to play in the investigation process. Not only do they have to ensure that the process is conducted fairly, it is also their responsibility to ensure that individuals involved in harassment cases (complainants, alleged harassers and even witnesses) have their rights maintained, and that provision is made for their representation. This may present difficulties, as trade unions only represent their members. However, they must set good enough standards and promote best practice to encourage other staff representation groups to do the same.

When representing the complainant the following guidelines should be taken into consideration:

- A representative should accompany a complainant throughout the whole investigation process.
- Outline fully the complainant's rights in the process.
- Keep notes of meetings.
- Provide advice on different kinds of support (e.g. external advice and counselling).
- Keep the complainant fully informed.
- Help the complainant decide on their own course of action.

● Representatives may recommend that the complainant not continue working with the harasser throughout the investigation process.

Representing the alleged harasser

Unions have had to face the question of representing a member who is accused of harassment, whilst also maintaining the union's commitment to oppose all forms of harassment.

Most unions start with the premise that every member has the right to be represented, and will represent them at every stage during the investigation. Other unions may limit support by refusing the alleged harasser representation, but inform them of their rights in the situation. The following case study highlights the difficulties that unions face when not representing alleged harassers fairly.

Case Study

Harassers and Trade Unions

In *Fire Brigades Union v Fraser* (12 June 1997), the Employment Appeal Tribunal (EAT) upheld a finding that the union discriminated against its member by refusing to provide him with representation or legal assistance in connection with a complaint of sexual harassment made against him by another member.

George Fraser was a retained fire-fighter, employed by the Lothians and Borders Fire Brigade. He was a member of the Fire Brigades Union (FBU). In September 1994, he was suspended from duty pending investigation of allegations by a woman colleague of sexual harassment. In April 1995, when he was asked by the employers to attend an interview, the chairman of the union's branch, Mr Napier, told him that he would be able to advise and represent him. However, in May 1995, Mr Napier was told that the union's regional committee had decided to support the female fire-officer, and instructed Mr Napier not to give assistance to Mr Fraser. Subsequently, the union refused to pay for a solicitor to represent Mr Fraser at the disciplinary hearing. The disciplinary hearing resulted in dismissal of seven of nine charges of sexual harassment. The employers did not take action on the other two charges.

Mr Fraser brought proceedings against the union on grounds that it had discriminated against him contrary to s12(3) of the Sex Discrimination Act by refusing to afford him access to representation or legal assistance. Rule 25(3)(a) of the FBU's rules provides that "any member requiring legal assistance in relation to any matter arising in the course of his/her employment in the fire service, may make application through his/her branch secretary to the executive council which may grant such assistance in its absolute discretion as it thinks fit".

The union's equal opportunities policy document says, in respect of dealing with a complaint: "The FBU will try to give every possible support to any member who is suffering as a result of discrimination or harassment. The union wants to create a climate of confidence so that members do not feel they have to suffer in silence, but rather their complaint will be treated seriously. If the regional committee feel there is a case to be pursued then they will represent the complainant. The interests of the accused member in any action – whether this be to pursue a complaint against management through the grievance procedure or to pursue a complaint against another union member through the union's internal disciplinary procedure – can be represented by 'an accused friend' but they may not necessarily be formally represented by the FBU.

If the regional committee decide to support a member's complaint of harassment or discrimination, then the harasser may not be represented by the union."

The industrial tribunal upheld the complaint and found that it was unprecedented in the region for a member to be refused representation by an "accused friend" or to be denied legal assistance, regardless of the alleged misdemeanour. The union had withdrawn support, believing this was a serious case of harassment, but without proper investigation or following a fair procedure. It compared the treatment of Mr Fraser to the high degree of support received by the complainant, who was accompanied by union representatives to meetings and received legal advice. The tribunal said that the union, in its anxiety to send out "the right message" to its women members, had assumed that Mr Fraser, "as a man, was guilty as accused". It concluded that a hypothetical woman in a comparable position, as an accused harasser, would not have been treated in the same way and would have "received the usual representation in a time of difficulty".

Advice and representation for the purpose of disciplinary proceedings is one of the essential benefits of trade union membership. It is difficult to see how a policy to refuse assistance to a member accused of harassing another member can be justified simply by reason of the nature of the alleged offence committed, or indeed the union's preliminary assessment of the merits of the case. As the EAT itself says: "In many cases, the worse the trouble the member is in, the more he needs the union's support."

(Adapted from *Equal Opportunities Review*, No. 76, November/December 1997. Reproduced with kind permission from Eclipse Group Ltd)

When both the alleged harasser and the complainant belong to the same union, a conflict of interest is apparent. In such cases, it is important to ensure that both parties receive equality of representation, ie that the complainant is not disadvantaged by being represented by someone with little or no experience.

In any event, when a trade union is representing both the complainant and the alleged harasser, the same official must not represent both parties, and the trade union should make it absolutely clear that they are not condoning offensive behaviour by providing representation.

If a union member is found to be guilty of harassment, they will almost certainly lose the right to retain membership, and as some unions see harassment as a breach of membership terms, harassers will also lose the right of representation at a tribunal.

Outcome of the investigation and appropriate actions

Once the investigation is concluded, the employer must inform the complainant and the alleged harasser of its outcome.

There are three possible outcomes when rounding off an investigation:

1. **Complaint not validated**. The complaint may not be upheld if the evidence is regarded as inconclusive in any way.

   Possible actions:
   - Provide counselling for both parties.
   - If appropriate, conduct mediation sessions to help the parties resolve minor matters together.
   - Consideration should be given to transferring or rescheduling the work of the employees concerned rather than expecting them to continue to work together against the wishes of either party.

2. **Complaint validated – informal resolution recommended**. In most cases where harassment is established, resolving the issue on an informal basis is a preferable option, providing this is agreeable with the complainant. In less serious situations (for example, certain circumstances when behaviour is unacceptable, yet unintentional, and the harasser regrets his/her actions) it may be appropriate to resolve the situation with non–disciplinary measures, less serious disciplinary actions or a combination of the two.

   Possible actions:
   - Provide counselling for both parties.
   - Provide harassment awareness training for harassers, and in particular coaching for harassers who are at supervisory and management levels.

- Consider placing a note on the harasser's file with the basic details of the allegation.
- Issue a warning to the harasser that any repeat of the behaviour will be dealt with by disciplinary action.
- Offer to implement some changes in the complainant's work environment that may increase her/his level of comfort. This may mean moving the harasser (and this should always be considered in the first instance). Only offer the complainant the possibility of a transfer if she/he asks for it, or if moving the harasser is not feasible.

3. **Complaint validated – recommendation of disciplinary action**. It will be necessary to carry out disciplinary procedures when an investigation concludes there is sufficient evidence of unacceptable conduct. Examples of situations which may warrant disciplinary action are:

- when the harasser, based on the circumstances, understood, or should have understood, that his/her conduct was unwelcome, but persisted in meting out the behaviour
- when there was intimate physical contact that was unwanted and unwelcome
- when there was a repetitive pattern of behaviour targeted specifically at the complainant
- when there was a serious isolated incident targeted at the complainant
- when behaviours aimed at the complainant had the effect of loss of promotion, or involved coercion in relation to career benefits.

In these serious situations, an employer is expected to carry out discipline measures, up to and including dismissal if necessary.

Possible actions:
- An official reprimand that outlines dismissal if the harassment reoccurs.
- If the harasser is a supervisor or manager, he/she should be removed from his/her position and transferred to another that does not involve the responsibility of managing others.
- Suspension without pay.
- Dismissal from employment – the harasser must not be permitted to resign under any circumstances.

If the decision is to move the harasser away from the complainant, the new post should be on the same, or comparable, pay and conditions. If not, the harasser may have grounds for a case of constructive dismissal against the organisation.

All recommendations are based on a reasonable belief that discrimination occurred, not necessarily on reasonable grounds.

In all cases, it is essential that procedures for monitoring each outcome and action are established and reviewed on an ongoing basis, so that there is no repeat of the harassment or any retaliation.

Right of appeal

Any employee being disciplined has the right to appeal the decision by following the normal disciplinary procedures. However, in the case of harassment complaints, systems for appealing a decision require sensitive handling and objective judgement, because of the complex nature of the issue.

In *Sexual Harassment in the Workplace: An Employment Guide*, the Local Government Management Board (LGMB) state:

"Appeals, however legitimate, are likely to cause detriment to one or other party. Allowing appeals which involve repeat investigations may in practice expose an individual to 'double jeopardy'. In these circumstances, an employee who has been cleared of harassment will once again be subject to the above procedures. Appeals permitted as a result of procedural inadequacies may similarly undermine a successful complaint."

Taking action

To maintain impartiality, it is vital that the investigation panel play no part in the disciplinary process. Investigations and disciplinary actions must be kept separate, and should not be implemented by the same people.

Investigating incidents of violence

Incidents of violence will nearly always be handled by the police. However, internal investigations must take place to ensure that the employee(s) get the level of aftercare needed following the incident.

Employers have stringent legal obligations in this area – not only do they have a duty of care under the Health and Safety at Work Act 1974 to provide a safe place of work, they also have a statutory duty to report all injuries and dangerous occurrences under the Reporting of Injuries, Diseases and Dangerous Occurrences Regulations 1985.

For these reasons alone, investigations must be thorough and action taken swiftly, in order to minimise the likelihood of a recurrence of the problem.

Similar processes to handling a harassment or bullying investigation can be used; however, more concentration on recording the incident and assessing the risk involved needs to take place.

Conducting an investigation in action

The following case study shows how a complaint of harassment was handled by a personnel officer in the Royal Mail, an organisation commended by a tribunal panel for its excellent harassment procedures.

Case Study

Royal Mail Cardiff – Conducting an Investigation

Robert Mead, area personnel officer at Royal Mail, Cardiff, has years of experience in dealing with sensitive issues in the workplace.

In June 1992, not long after starting his new role in Cardiff, Mr Mead received a complaint of harassment. The manager told Mr Mead that "This person has always been a nuisance; however, he is clever and we have never been able to nail him." Although his gut feeling was unease, and he was not happy with what he had heard, his experience taught him never to make judgements based on preconceived ideas, and he went through the following process to find out the facts and deal with the situation.

Mr Mead asked the managers concerned to get statements both from the witnesses and the complainant.

Was this a real complaint of harassment or were managers trying to victimise the alleged harasser?

The complainant's manager interviewed her, and wrote a report of the incident to his line manager. This line manager interviewed the complainant again to clarify points which came out of the first report.

Interviews also took place with the alleged harasser. All the information, including the witnesses' statements, were sent to Mr Mead, who went into the department concerned and interviewed the witnesses himself. They were clearly upset about the incident, and it was revealed that others had suffered ill-treatment, but were afraid to complain.

After assessing all the evidence, Mr Mead suspended the alleged harasser on full pay pending the result of his investigation. It is important to note that suspension is not a penalty or an inference of guilt.

Mr Mead then began a thorough investigation process by interviewing the complainant. As his office was deserted (the complainant worked nights, and the interview took place in the evening) Mr Mead asked his assistant (who is female) to take notes. Mr Mead explained to the complainant his assistant's presence, and checked that this was acceptable before starting the interview. The complainant was happy with this.

"Would you like to talk me through what happened?" was his starting point. This, he said, gave the complainant a chance to relax and talk through the incident at her own pace. It also gave her the opportunity to open up and began to create an atmosphere of trust. The complainant began to relate her experience. "Is there any reason why he should behave like this?" Mr Mead asked. This helps to establish any background to the incident, and creates a clearer picture.

Mr Mead gently takes the complainant to phase two of the interview. "Let's go back to the written complaint" he suggests. The purpose of this is to check out any discrepancies in the complainant's statement. In this case Mr Mead found that there were none; however, he noted that there was a lewd comment made, which she was too upset to reveal to her line manager at the time.

"I note that a comment was thrown at you by the alleged harasser. I need to know what the comment was. Is there anything you wish to say to my assistant that you may be embarrassed about telling me? I will go out of the room if necessary." Mr Mead did not want to intimidate the complainant by his presence; however, because he had already set the complainant at ease, she was prepared to repeat the comment in front of him.

Phase three of the interview examines the statement of the alleged harasser. "Let's look at what he said – what do you think about this statement?" The complainant was honest in her response, disagreed with what was said and reiterated her version of the facts. Mr Mead then asked the complainant about other people who were involved (to confirm the facts in the witness statements).

Mr Mead, satisfied with the complainant's information, finished the interview by encouraging the complainant to report to her manager anything else that happens to her in the department as a direct result of making this formal complaint. (It is the manager's/employer's responsibility to protect the employee at work and prevent victimisation.) The complainant thanked him for listening to her.

Mr Mead began to build a picture in his mind about the character of the complainant. She seemed genuine, and was quite honest and open. If the complainant was part of a smear campaign against the alleged harasser, she had had plenty of opportunity to damage the individual's credibility by accusing him outright and without doubt of carrying out the incident. However, she was consistent and straight-forward in giving the facts, and had stated that although she was almost certain he had said the remarks, she did not see him say them.

Two copies of the interview record were signed by the complainant, and she was given the opportunity to attach a signed statement to the record of anything she disagreed with. The complainant was happy with the record, and did not need to do this.

The complainant's manager was interviewed next, and he corroborated the complainant's story. It is also confirmed that group harassment had taken place, that others had suffered from this and had made complaints. The manager tells of how he handled the initial complaints informally. He himself had witnessed previous minor incidents in the past and dealt with them immediately and informally.

Mr Mead also met with union representatives to inform them of what was happening. It is vital that unions are involved early in the process and are given updates as the investigation progresses.

The charge letter was sent to the alleged harasser. The letter was based on the five requirements of natural justice (outlined in the *Birchell v BHS* case), according to which the alleged harasser:

- was informed of the charges made against them
- was given the chance to prepare case
- was given the opportunity to state case
- should have the right to representation
- was given the right to appeal.

Correspondence to both the complainant and the alleged harasser was hand-delivered personally and/or via recorded delivery – to ensure that they were received by both parties.

Mr Mead interviewed the alleged harasser. The harasser was unaccompanied in the interview. Mr Mead reminded him of his rights to representation, and asked the alleged harasser if he fully understood the position he was in.

The harasser was asked if he was aware of and had seen Royal Mail's policy on harassment, to which he replied he had. The statement made by the complainant was given to the harasser. "What is your opinion of this?" asked Mr Mead.

The alleged harasser denied the allegations made, and was asked to give his version of the events. His version differed from that of the complainant's, and Mr Mead then compared the alleged harasser's statement with those of the other witnesses, and put to the alleged harasser the evidence which conflicted with his statement. Mr Mead did not mention any of the other complaints made against the alleged harasser, as they were dealt with informally and unofficially.

Mr Mead asked the alleged harasser to sign two copies of the interview record. The alleged harasser signed the record, although he added his own note disagreeing with a point in the record. This note was attached to the interview record.

Mr Mead also interviewed the other employees who allegedly took part in the incident. The three employees were interviewed separately, and the interviews were arranged in such a way as to avoid contact or discussion with each other. Although the three employees were possible conspirators, because no charges were made against them they had no right [to representation] and they were interviewed as witnesses to the incident.

After assessing all the information collected and gathered throughout his investigations, Mr Mead concluded that the harassment had indeed taken place, and recommended that the alleged harasser be dismissed.

The managers involved thanked Mr Mead and said that they believed morale had been raised instantly and employees felt that they could make a complaint, and it would be taken seriously.

Mr Mead says that tribunals have been impressed by the quality and thoroughness of Royal Mail.

Key learning points:

● Keep a totally open mind throughout the investigation, and whilst interviewing everyone concerned.
● Put people at ease, create a comfortable, relaxed atmosphere and try and probe. If the complainant sees your unease, he/she will be uncomfortable.
● Be objective – be careful not to be over-sympathetic with either party, particularly the complainant, who is normally the first person to be interviewed. By the end of the investigation you may have cause to change your view.
● Establish which are the key issues on which judgement is based, and which issues are supporting evidence.
● Keep a record of everything no matter how time consuming you think it is – dates are vital.
● If someone tells you about a telephone call or a reminder, put it in writing and add a small note on the file.
● Body language is important. As well as adopting a sensitivity in the use of your own body language, learn to interpret it in others in its right context.
● Remember, you must have enough information to support your view; it is not enough merely to have the view.
● Whilst interviewing, if a new door opens (ie a new area to investigate), close it down.
● Collecting evidence is like a jigsaw puzzle – look at the big pieces that can be put together first, and then the smaller pieces can be sorted out.
● If you carry out an investigation, and after all the interviews there is not enough evidence to take action or you are in doubt, do not be afraid to take the middle ground.

● The average length of time for an interview is 20–30 minutes.

His major learning point for other organisations is to ensure the system for dealing with harassment complaints is in place and complete before advertising it – because people will come forward with complaints and the system needs to be able to deal with them promptly and effectively.

Mr Mead says that because of his thoroughness and meticulous note-taking, his colleagues accuse him of paranoia. His answer? "I have never lost a tribunal case yet."

(Interview with Robert Mead, personnel manager, Royal Mail, Cardiff, 22 March 1995)

Reflection

Acting on complaints seriously, fairly and promptly is essential, as the way an employer deals with and conducts investigations of harassment, bullying and violence will be seen as a demonstration of an employer's commitment to stamping it out.

Organisations must ensure that, as part of the policy development process, they create investigation systems which are robust, and properly train staff in its procedures. This is the active part of creating a positive work environment – showing the company cares for the safety and well-being of employees.

References

Sexual Harassment in the Workplace, Ellen J Wagner (AMACOM, 1992).

Sexual Harassment in the Workplace: An Employment Guide, Local Government Management Board, 1993.

Tackling Harassment at Work, Labour Research Department (LRD Publications).

The Skilled Helper, Gerard Egan, 5th edition (Brooks/Cole Publishing Company, 1994).

CHAPTER 10

Taking legal action

This chapter will examine in detail the process of taking a case to an employment tribunal. The process is the same for both sexual and racial harassment cases. Also, if an employee, as a result of being bullied or suffering violence at work, resigns and claims constructive dismissal, this could result in an employment tribunal case.

Employers need to be aware that both the complainant and the alleged harasser may take the employer to a tribunal, and therefore employers should act fairly and reasonably to both.

Whilst it is important for employers and employees to be aware of what is involved in taking a case to the tribunal, it is important to note when considering taking action in this area that there is no substitute for taking sound legal advice. This can be obtained from a solicitor, law centre, Citizens' Advice Bureau (CAB), community relations councils, race relations offices or one of the specialised voluntary agencies like Rights of Women (ROW) or Women Against Sexual Harassment (WASH). It is important to get advice as soon as possible, as there are strict time limits for the bringing of an action, which are discussed below.

How to avoid tribunal action

Clear and effective harassment policies are the best way to ensure that individual employees will not feel the need to take legal action and employers will not find themselves in the position of defending costly, time-consuming tribunal proceedings.

Having the right policy framework will not only reduce the number of complaints but, where they do arise, will also provide a more satisfactory or immediate solution, and highlight the need for action before a tribunal should arise. A sound policy framework coupled with good practice within the organisation will also protect an employer against being held to be vicariously liable for the actions of its employees.

It is not sufficient just to have a comprehensive policy on paper. Where an employee does take legal action the tribunal will not only examine the harassment policies that existed in the workplace but will also consider the manner in which those policies were put into practice across the organisation.

In racial discrimination cases tribunals use the CRE's Code of Practice in Employment as a benchmark to evaluate the action taken by employers to prevent harassment. The Code of Practice contains practical guidance to employers for the elimination of discrimination in the workplace.

Where the recommendations of the Code of Practice have not been followed, this can be used by an aggrieved employee to show that the employer did not take reasonably practicable steps to prevent discrimination. The employer, therefore, may be liable under the Race Relations Act.

Guidance on the reasonably practicable steps that an employer can take in sexual harassment cases is contained in the European Commission Code of Practice on measures to combat sexual harassment. Although the Code is not legally binding on UK courts, in the case of *Grimaldi* v *Fonds des Maladies Professionelles* the European Court of Justice ruled that the national courts are bound to take the Code's recommendations into account in deciding disputes submitted to them where relevant.

The measures recommended by the Code of Practice include the following:

● As outlined in Chapter 8, a written policy statement which makes it clear that sexual harassment will not be permitted or condoned in the workplace, sets out what is considered inappropriate behaviour at work (explaining that such behaviour may be unlawful), and emphasises that managers and supervisors have a positive duty to implement the policy.

● A complaints procedure which gives employees confidence that all allegations of harassment will be dealt with seriously, expeditiously and confidentially, and which provides for appropriate disciplinary measures against employees found guilty of harassment.

● Provision of specialist training for managers and supervisors which identifies factors that minimise the risk of sexual harassment and familiarises participants with their responsibilities under the employer's policy and any problems they are likely to encounter.

Since tribunals should take the recommendations of the Codes of Practice into account, it follows that they will compare the preventative measures taken by employers with the Codes' recommendations. It is likely that they will find that an employer who has not followed the recommendations has not taken reasonably practicable steps to prevent harassment under the SDA or RRA.

Following the recommendations of the Codes of Practice will help substantially to reduce the number of tribunal cases that an employer should face, and will ensure that such actions have a good chance of being successfully defended. If anything, though, a good harassment policy may well encourage employees to make complaints, so legal action by employees in harassment cases can never be ruled out entirely.

Case Study

Taking Further Action

Babs was just 18 when she began to suffer sexual harassment from her boss. It took the form initially of lewd gestures, comments and being pestered for dates, eventually progressing to unwanted physical contact.

"I think he started on me because I was the youngest in the office and so he thought he could get away with it. He definitely singled me out: he would follow me when I was working and find a way to brush past me and touch me on the bottom. He was always commenting on what I was wearing and would tell me how my breasts were bigger than his girlfriend's.

The worst incident was when he invited me out to lunch and hinted very heavily that we could use his car to have our 'desert'."

The harassment continued for nine months, until Babs eventually made a complaint to her union representative, who advised her to give her boss another chance. The complaint went no further and no action was taken against her boss. Instead it was Babs who was asked to make allowances for the fact that her boss was not used to working with women!

After a brief respite the harassment resumed. Babs felt she had nowhere to turn to and started taking sick leave from work to avoid her boss, and when she was at work using any excuse she could find to stay out of his way. A month later her boss sacked her.

At first, being summarily dismissed came almost as a relief. Then a friend suggested that she get some advice from a solicitor about going to the tribunal. At first she had difficulty with money (full legal aid is not available for representation) and her legal bills were becoming excessive as the company lawyers fought hard to maintain their reputation. In the end, she received help from the EOC and the case got to a tribunal some 18 months after she left work.

"Apart from the nightmare of legal bills, the worst aspect of the case was the time it took to get to the tribunal. I always thought that they would settle the case, but their lawyers made life difficult for us at every turn. I was so nervous at the prospect of giving evidence, I was convinced that the tribunal would not believe a word I was saying. I braced myself for an ordeal. In the end it wasn't half as bad as I thought it would be. I had a lot of support from family and friends and by the time of the hearing I was so angry at the way I had been mistreated by the union and by the company that I was determined to say my piece."

Babs won her tribunal case and her employers were ordered to pay £8,500 in compensation. Her boss did not lose his job.

Dealing with complaints effectively

When an employee makes a complaint of sexual or racial harassment, this presents a number of sensitive issues for the organisation. Emotions frequently run high. Often it is difficult for those dealing with the complaint to be seen to be fair to both sides. How effectively complaints are dealt with is the acid test for any policy, however, and could mean the difference between an employee staying within the organisation to resolve the issue and resigning, being dismissed or going to a tribunal.

To reduce the risk that tribunal action will follow a complaint:

- be empathetic towards employees complaining about harassment
- ensure strict confidentiality at all times
- keep good records of the complaint and advise the complainant to keep full notes of incidents
- inform the harasser of the existence of the complaint
- conduct a full, fair and open investigation of the complaint.

Events that could lead to legal action being taken include:

- inadequate/inconclusive investigation
- not taking complaint seriously
- employee resigns claiming constructive dismissal
- employee is dismissed (and claims unfair dismissal)
- employee is selected for redundancy (and claims unfair dismissal)
- employee is victimised after making a complaint of harassment.

Settlements

The employer may decide that they wish to settle a case. In order to prevent a later application to a tribunal, a settlement should *either* be with the involvement of an ACAS conciliation officer *or* should follow the requirements of a "compromise agreement".

A valid "compromise agreement":

● must be in writing
● must relate to the particular complaint
● must ensure that the employee has received independent legal advice from a qualified lawyer
● must name the adviser, who should be covered by an insurance policy, entitling them to give advice.

Employment tribunals

Employment tribunals (formerly industrial tribunals) were first set up in 1964 under the Industrial Training Act to decide issues concerning employers' training levies. Their jurisdiction has increased considerably since then and now extends to matters relating to:

● contracts of employment (including breach of contract)
● unfair dismissal
● health and safety at work
● sex discrimination/race discrimination/disability discrimination
● equal pay
● redundancy
● maternity rights.

Tribunals sit at about 95 centres throughout the country. The tribunal panel consists of a legally qualified chair, usually a solicitor or a barrister of at least seven years' standing, and two lay members with practical experience of employee relations. For example, a tribunal hearing an unfair dismissal case will typically comprise someone representing an employers' organisation and another representing a trade union or workers' organisation. Hearings are usually in public and anyone who wishes to can go and listen to their proceedings.

For many people, going before a tribunal is synonymous with going to court and creates the same level of nervousness and anxiety. Tribunals are not like courts, however; they are much less formal, their procedures are more straightforward and user-friendly and they are completely devoid of wigs and gowns! However, tribunals have become increasingly legalistic over the years, and now model themselves more and more on county court procedures.

Tribunals are designed to provide quick, cheap and accessible justice. Unlike courts their proceedings are not governed by strict rules of evidence; you do not even need to be represented by a lawyer (though in most cases this is advisable) and members of the tribunal can ask questions of the applicant (the person bringing the case) and respondent (the person defending it).

Advantages of tribunals over courts
- Specialist knowledge which can be brought to bear on particular issues.
- Flexible procedures – no strict rules of evidence.
- No delay – decisions are usually arrived at quickly.
- More accessible and informal than courts.
- Self-representation is common in practice.
- Cheaper form of justice than courts – e.g. no issue fee payable.

Case Study

A Tribunal Experience

Abigail was a 32-year-old architecture student of Jamaican origin, who worked as a part-time barmaid to help pay her college fees. She was continually harassed by her boss, the bar steward, both racially and sexually.

"He went from being nice to me, giving me extra shifts when I needed the money, to being overly friendly, patronising and cloying. He would always compliment my hair, which would be in plaits or twists, and ask how I got it like that and how long it took. It got a bit monotonous, but I thought he was just interested. I suppose he thought he was paying me a compliment also when he said I was not like most lazy, ignorant Jamaicans who had nothing better to do than smoke ganja and listen to reggae music all day! Then one day he made an almost inaudible comment about some nature programme that had been on the night before, saying how he guessed all black women look better without their clothes. That was the start of everything. The space behind the bar was quite tight at one end and I noticed that whenever I was at that side he would take hold of me as he tried to squeeze past. His hands would be on my shoulders or waist and he would make a play of avoiding touching my breasts.

I really needed the work and so I guess I just put up with it for a long time. The last straw though was when he followed me down to the cellar and pushed me up against one of the barrels. I managed to push him away and I screamed at him that I had had enough and that he should leave me alone. The next day I was sacked for no other reason than that I had refused to give in to his advances."

Abigail decided straight away to get legal advice about going to a tribunal. She submitted claims of both racial and sexual harassment. Unfortunately she was given inaccurate and incomplete advice initially and by the time she began her tribunal case she was out of time and had to apply for an extension, which was granted.

The tribunal upheld the complaint as far as the sexual harassment was concerned, but had greater difficulty with the racial harassment. They held that the remarks her boss had made were not addressed to her directly and were not meant to be overhead.

The tribunal awarded Abigail £4,000 compensation, and her boss was fined £500 by the company, but kept his job. He claimed he was unable to pay, however, and she had to take enforcement proceedings against him. She was dissatisfied with the tribunal's overall decision. "They did not take the racial aspect of my case seriously, but I made the right decision and I would recommend anyone in my position to do the same thing."

Advice to employees thinking of taking legal action

If the harassment is reaching a level where grounds for tribunal action may exist, it is advisable to take certain preliminary steps which will facilitate the process:

● First, inform the harasser that their behaviour is unacceptable and causing distress and they should stop.
● Inform senior management of the conduct complained of and consider making a complaint.
● Confide in a colleague and/or inform a union representative.
● Keep a diary of incidents, noting dates, times, places, witnesses, etc. Note also any change in duties, hours or conditions of work.

The procedure for taking a case to a tribunal

The questionnaire

In race and sex discrimination cases, there is a special questionnaire procedure under the RRA s65 and the SDA s74 which gives an opportunity for the tribunal to obtain information about the treatment of the employee bringing the claim and about the workplace in general.

The questionnaire is drafted by the employee bringing the claim and it is best if this is submitted on the standard forms available from law centres, CABs or from the CRE or EOC (see overleaf).

RR 65

RACE RELATIONS ACT 1976

THE QUESTIONS PROCEDURE

CONTENTS

Guidance on the questions procedure

        Part I   — Introduction

        Part II — Guidance for the complainant

        Part III — Guidance for the respondent

Questionnaire of complainant

Reply by respondent (2 copies)

Appendix — Notes on the scope of the Race Relations Act 1976

A complainant should obtain TWO copies of this booklet, one to send to the respondent and the other to keep.
Before completing the questionnaire or the reply form (as appropriate), the complainant and the respondent should read Part I of the guidance and (again as appropriate) Part II or III.

Issued by   The Home Office and
              The Department of Employment

Figure 20.
The questionnaire

THE RACE RELATIONS ACT 1976 SECTION 65(1)(a)

QUESTIONNAIRE OF PERSON AGGRIEVED (THE COMPLAINANT)

Name of person to be
questioned (the
respondent)

To ....

Address

of ....

Name of complainant

1. I ....

Address

of ....

....

consider that you may have discriminated against me contrary to the Race Relations Act 1976.

Give date, approximate
time, place and factual
description of the treat-
ment received and of
the circumstances
leading up to the treat-
ment (see paragraph 9
of the guidance)

2. On

Complete if you wish
to give reasons,
otherwise delete the
word "because" (see
paragraphs 10 and 11
of the guidance)

3. I consider that this treatment may have been unlawful because

RR 65(a)

This is the first of
your questions to the
respondent. You are
advised not to alter it

4. Do you agree that the statement in paragraph 2 is an accurate description of what happened? If not in what respect do you disagree or what is your version of what happened?

This is the second of
your questions to the
respondent. You are
advised not to alter it

5. Do you accept that your treatment of me was unlawful discrimination by you against me?
    If not
    a   why not?
    b   for what reason did I receive the treatment accorded to me, and
    c   how far did considerations of colour, race, nationality (including citizenship) or ethnic or national origins affect your treatment of me?

Enter here any other
questions you wish to
ask (see paragraphs
12-14 of the guidance)

6.

*Delete as appropriate
If you delete the first
alternative, insert the
address to which you
want the reply to be
sent

7. My address for any reply you may wish to give to the questions raised above is *that set out in paragraph 1 above/the following address

See paragraph 15
of the guidance

Signature of complainant ....

Date ....

NB *By virtue of section 65 of the Act, this questionnaire and any reply are (subject to the provisions of the section) admissible in proceedings under the Act and a court or tribunal may draw any such inference as is just and equitable from a failure without reasonable excuse to reply within a reasonable period, or from an evasive or equivocal reply, including an inference that the person questioned has discriminated unlawfully.*

THE RACE RELATIONS ACT 1976 SECTION 65(1)(b)

REPLY BY RESPONDENT

Name of complainant

To ....

Address

of ....

Name of respondent

1. I..

Address

of ....

Complete as appropriate

hereby acknowledge receipt of the questionnaire signed by you and dated ....

which was served on me on (date) ....

*Delete as appropriate

If you agree that the statement in paragraph 2 of the questionnaire is accurate, delete this sentence. If you disagree complete this sentence (see paragraphs 21 and 22 of the guidance)

2. I *agree/disagree that the statement in paragraph 2 of the questionnaire is an accurate description of what happened.

I disagree with the statement in paragraph 2 of the questionnaire in that

*Delete as appropriate

If you accept the complainant's assertion of unlawful discrimination in paragraph 3 of the questionnaire delete the sentences at a, b and c. Unless completed a sentence should be deleted (see paragraphs 23 and 24 of the guidance)

3. I *accept/dispute that my treatment of you was unlawful discrimination by me against you.

a   My reasons for so disputing are

RR 65(b)

b   The reason why you received the treatment accorded to you is

c   Considerations of colour, race, nationality (including citizenship) or ethnic or national origins affected my treatment of you to the following extent:-

Replies to questions in paragraph 6 of the questionnaire should be entered here

4.

Delete the whole of this sentence if you have answered all the questions in the questionnaire. If you have not answered all the questions, delete "unable" or "unwilling" as appropriate and give your reasons for not answering

5.   I have deleted (in whole or in part) the paragraph(s) numbered ....
above, since I am **unable/unwilling** to reply to the relevant questions of the questionnaire for the following reasons:-

Signature of respondent ....

See paragraph 25 of the guidance

Date ....

(Reproduced by kind permission of the Employment Tribunals Service)

The questionnaire should be sent to the employer by recorded delivery within three months after the act of discrimination or within 21 days after the application to the tribunal has been made.

The aim of the questionnaire is to assist the employee and the tribunal in the formulation of the claim. The types of questions that would typically be asked of the employer would depend on how any major decisions affecting the employee were made; for example, reasons for issuing a written warning. Although the employer is not compelled to answer the questionnaire, if they deliberately fail to answer or do not answer fully, the tribunal is entitled to draw inferences from that fact.

Time limits

There are strict time limits within which a case must be brought before a tribunal. The application must be made by an employee to the tribunal within three months of:

● the last act of discrimination if the employee is working; or
● the date employment was effectively terminated if the employee has resigned or been dismissed.

To calculate the three month time limit take the effective date of termination, say 28 February, deduct one day then add three months, i.e. 27 May. In this example 28 May would be *outside* the time limit. It is not always easy to determine when time starts to run, but it will usually be from when a decision not to promote or appoint is taken or from when a warning is given, so it is important to be alert if tribunal action is being contemplated.

It is very important that these time limits are adhered to strictly, because a late application in most cases will be a non-application, as the tribunal does not have the jurisdiction to hear a case that is out of time without reasonable excuse. However, the tribunal can extend the time limit if it is "just and equitable in all the circumstances of the case". This can include a situation where the employee received inaccurate legal advice.

Although the time limits are strictly enforced, in exceptional circumstances the tribunal will allow a late application. For example, the time limit may be extended to account for a period where the employer was supposed to be dealing with the matter, but nothing in fact was done.

Form IT1 – the employee's application

The application should be made on form IT1 (Figure 21, overleaf). This form will ensure all relevant information is included, though it is also acceptable to make the application in the form of a letter or statement. IT1 forms can be obtained from job centres and most law centres, CABs and other advice centres.

INDUSTRIAL TRIBUNALS

Received at ITO

FOR OFFICE USE

Case Number

Code

Initials   ROIT

Application to an Industrial Tribunal

- If you fax this form you do not need to send one in the post.
- This form has to be photocopied. If possible please use BLACK INK and CAPITAL letters.
- Where there are tick boxes, please tick the one that applies.

1 Please give the type of complaint you want the tribunal to decide (for example: unfair dismissal, equal pay). A full list is given in Booklet 1. If you have more than one complaint list them all.

SEX DISCRIMINATION

4 Please give the dates of your employment

From   1 JULY 1994   To   29 FEBRUARY 1999

5 Please give the name and address of the employer, other organisation or person against whom this complaint is being brought

Name of the employer, organisation or person

THE CLUELESS COMPANY

Address

1 MAIN STREET
ANYTOWN

Postcode

Telephone   567 9128

2 Please give your details

Mr ☐   Mrs ☐   Miss ☑   Ms ☐

First names   BARBARA

Surname   HARRIS

Date of birth   2.3.77

Address

123 ACORN STREET
ANYTOWN

Postcode

Telephone   555 1234

Daytime Telephone   345 4312

Please give an address to which we should send documents if different from above

Postcode

Please give the place where you worked or applied to work if different from above

Address

Postcode

3 If a representative is acting for you please give details

Name   V FINE SOLICITORS

Address   45 THE HIGH STREET
ANYTOWN

Postcode

Telephone   678 7236

Reference

IT1(E/W)

6 Please say what job you did for the employer (or what job you applied for). If this does not apply, Please say what your connection was with the employer

ADMINISTRATIVE ASSISTANT
TO THE SALES DIRECTOR

Figure 21.
Form IT1

7 Please give the number of normal basic hours worked each week

Hours per week

30

8 Please give your earning details

Basic wage/salary

£ 800 : per MONTH

Average take home pay

£ 670 : per MONTH

Other bonuses/benefits

£ CHRISTMAS : per

9 If your complaint is NOT about dismissal, please give the date when the matter you are complaining about took place

10 Unfair dismissal applicants only
Please indicate what you are seeking at this stage, if you win your case.

☐ Reinstatement: to carry on working in your old job as before (An order for reinstatement normally includes an award of compensation for loss of earnings.)

☐ Re-engagement: to start another job or new contract with your old employer: (An order for re-engagement normally includes an award of compensation for loss of earnings.)

☐ Compensation only: to get an award of money

11 Please give details of your complaint
If there is not enough space for your answer, please continue on a separate sheet and attach it to this form.

I began my employment as office Junior to the Sales team, and was Promoted after 3 months to admin assistant. From that time on I was Subjected to Sexual harassment by the Sales Director Mr Mann. In the beginning he would frequently make rude gestures and explicit Sexual advances towards me. This involved touching me up and Pestering me for dates. When I complained to my Union Rep the harassment stopped but it resumed after a Short respite. I continued to reject his advances and he began to increase my workload and Put Pressure on me. He would unduly criticise my work, until on 29th February he told me I was Sacked. I consider that I have been unlawfully discriminated against on the grounds of my Sex.

12 Please sign and date this form, then send it to the address on the back page of this booklet.

Signed

B Mann

Date

5 - 4 - 99

IT1(E/W)

(Reproduced by kind permission of the Employment Tribunals Service)

The application must contain the following information:

- Employee's name and address (referred to as the "Applicant").
- Employer's name and address (referred to as the "Respondent").
- Grounds of the application (only a brief statement of the material facts is required at this stage).
- What relief is sought (i.e. what the employee wants the tribunal to do).

Form IT1 should be sent to the appropriate Regional Employment Tribunal which depends on the place of business of the respondent. The Employment Tribunal then send a copy of the IT1 to the employer (respondent) and also send them a notice of appearance.

Form IT3 – the employer's defence

If the employer wants to contest the action and set out a defence, they must enter a "notice of appearance" by returning form IT3 (see Figure 22). The employer has 21 days from the date of receiving the IT1 form to return form IT3.

Preliminary matters – before the hearing

Questions procedure

If the IT1 or IT3 does not set out the details of the case fully, either party can ask for further particulars of any allegation or claim made. If the replies given are not sufficiently detailed a further request can be made. Such requests however have limitations and should not be used as an attempt to conduct a trial of the issues on paper.

Discovery of documents

In order to prepare for the hearing, the employee will need to gather evidence which will often be contained in documents in the employer's possession. It is important for both parties to get as much information as possible about the other's case before the hearing, so that time and costs are not wasted once the tribunal is in session. This is done through a process called "discovery" and it is a crucial part of the information-gathering process in most tribunal cases.

Often there will be a voluntary exchange of documents between the parties, but if necessary the tribunal can order that relevant documents be disclosed to the employee. The order for discovery can be at the request of either party or by the tribunal itself. If an employer does not comply with an order for discovery, it could have damaging consequences for the defence, which may even be struck out in part or in its entirety.

THE EMPLOYMENT TRIBUNALS
NOTICE OF APPEARANCE BY RESPONDENT

In the application of

Case Number
(please quote in all correspondence)

* This form has to be photocopied, if possible please use Black Ink and Capital letters
* If there is not enough space for your answer, please continue on a separate sheet and attach it to this form

1. Full name and address of the Respondent:

Post Code:

Telephone number:

2. If you require documents and notices to be sent to a representative or any other address in the United Kingdom please give details:

Post Code:

Reference:

Telephone number:

3. Do you intend to resist the application? (Tick appropriate box)

YES ☐   NO ☐

4. Was the applicant dismissed? (Tick appropriate box)

YES ☐   NO ☐
Please give
reason below

Reason for dismissal:

5. Are the dates of employment given by the applicant correct? (Tick appropriate box)

YES ☐   NO ☐
please give correct dates below

Began on

Ended on

6. Are the details given by the applicant about wages/salary, take home or other bonuses correct? (Tick appropriate box)

YES ☐   NO ☐
Please give correct details below

Basic Wages/Salary	£	per
Average Take Home Pay	£	per
Other Bonuses/Benefits	£	per

PLEASE TURN OVER

for office use only
Date of receipt   Initials

Figure 22.
Form IT3

7. Give particulars of the grounds on which you intend to resist the application.

8. Please sign and date the form.

Signed   Dated

DATA PROTECTION ACT 1984
We may put some of the information you give on this form on to a computer. This helps us to monitor progress and produce statistics. We may also give information to:
* the other party in the case
* other parts of the Employment Department Group and organisations such as ACAS (Advisory Conciliation and Arbitration Service), the Equal Opportunities Commission or the Commission for Racial Equality.

Please post or fax this form to :

* IF YOU FAX THE FORM, DO NOT POST A COPY AS WELL
* IF YOU POST THE FORM, TAKE A COPY FOR YOUR RECORDS

Form IT3 E&W - 1/95

(Reproduced by kind permission of the Employment Tribunals Service)

Witness orders

Before the hearing date both parties need to organise who is going to attend as witnesses in the case. Again, people will often agree to attend, but if there is someone who is required to give relevant evidence who will not attend voluntarily, the tribunal can issue a witness order. If the witness fails to attend after receiving a witness order, this may also be regarded as contempt of court and if proven is liable to a fine of up to £1,000 or imprisonment. If you receive a witness order which you oppose you should write to the tribunal prior to the hearing stating why you cannot or should not attend.

Fixing the hearing

The tribunal sets a date for the hearing and each party is given at least 14 days' notice. Sometimes a pre-hearing review takes place to decide whether the employee qualifies to appear before the tribunal or to explore the chances of success. This is an informal hearing before the tribunal panel and may be held if either party or the tribunal itself requests it.

The hearing

There is no set procedure for employment tribunal hearings, but most have begun to model themselves on county court procedure They are however more informal and are conducted in plainer English than other court proceedings, with legal jargon kept to a minimum.

If unfair dismissal is claimed then the respondent will usually go first. A claim for discrimination however is usually opened by the applicant. In opening the case, the applicant must show how the case falls within the remit of the RRA or SDA. Then the applicant and witnesses called on the applicant's behalf will give evidence and be cross-examined by the respondent or their representative. The process is then repeated for the employer. Where a person is unrepresented, members of the tribunal can ask questions on their behalf.

Both parties will then make a closing speech, summing up the important points of evidence and drawing the tribunal's attention to the behaviour complained of and its effects. They will also address the tribunal on the issue of the level of damages sought.

Despite the relative informality of the proceedings, a tribunal hearing will be a traumatic experience for most people, particularly in discrimination cases. It is important that whatever the outcome an employee seeks help and support from colleagues or friends, again particularly in discrimination cases, where it is possible that the applicant could be the only black person, woman or disabled person involved in the case. In sexual harassment cases, and cases involving the

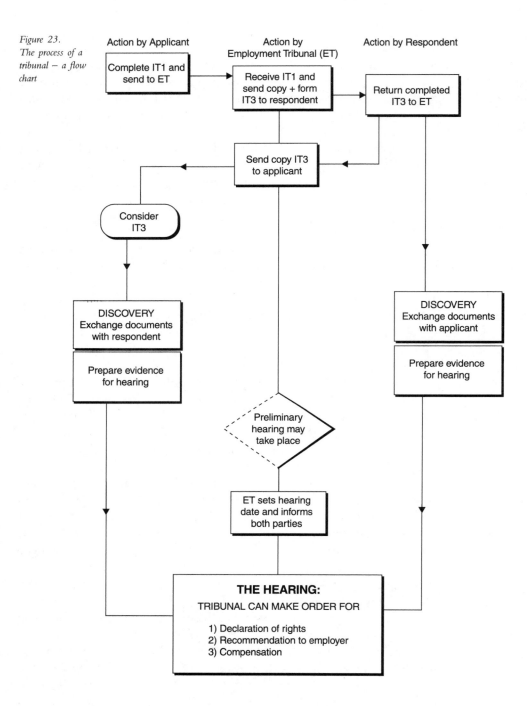

Figure 23. The process of a tribunal – a flow chart

Disability Discrimination Act, the tribunal can make an order prohibiting the identification of any person affected (e.g. the alleged
harasser, and the complainant) until a decision has been reached. In
cases involving sexual offences, the individual identities of those
affected can be restricted even in the tribunal's decision.

The decision

The decision of the tribunal panel is often unanimous, though it may
be by majority, which does not mean it is any less valid, but a dissenting
decision could form the basis of an appeal.

Parties will discover the outcome of the case very quickly, as the
decision of the tribunal is sometimes given on the last day of the hearing,
usually after a short adjournment. Alternatively, in more difficult cases,
if the panel is unable to decide on the day, they will deliver a written
judgement which is sent out to both parties by an agreed date.

If the tribunal decides that there has been unlawful discrimination
it can make one of the following orders:

● A declaration of the rights of the parties regarding the subject of
the complaint.
● A recommendation that the employer take specified action within
a specified time period.
● An order for compensation.

In discrimination cases, the main remedy will be to award compensation to the applicant. Compensation is divided into two parts:

1. Compensation for injury to feelings (the tribunal will take into
   account the behaviour complained of, the relative age, seniority and
   experience of the parties).
2. Compensation for loss arising directly from the discriminatory treatment (for example, lost wages, money lost through denied promotion, salary increase, etc).

The amount of compensation awarded in discrimination cases has
been the subject of much debate. It is important to remember that in
these cases it is often much more than just the feelings of the individual
concerned that are hurt. Often compensatory awards will take into
account the fact that the discrimination led to a dismissal or loss of
promotion, and the loss of earnings that resulted.

It is important to note that in discrimination cases there is now no
limit to the amount of compensation that can be awarded.

Examples of recent awards include Yeboah (£380k awarded against

The London Borough of Hackney) and Johnson (£20k awarded for injury to feelings against the Prison Service).

As well as compensation the tribunal can make a recommendation that the employer take certain measures within a fixed time period to remedy the effects of the discrimination or to prevent it occurring again, for example, adopting a comprehensive harassment policy. If the tribunal makes a recommendation and this is not complied with the applicant is entitled to an additional award of compensation.

Appeals

Either side can appeal the decision of an ET to the EAT. However, appeals will only be allowed if the tribunal has made an error in law, e.g. asked itself the wrong questions, come to a conclusion on the basis of no evidence or, exceptionally, behaved so unfairly that no reasonable tribunal would have behaved in that way.

Appeals must be filed within 42 days from the date the tribunal issued its extended written reasons for the decision. Either party can request extended written reasons whenever an appeal is contemplated.

Reflection

The aim of a tribunal is to deal fairly with complaints and appeals about issues of discrimination relating to harassment and bullying in employment. Although the process of tribunals can be lengthy, stressful and costly, tribunals are necessary to ensure that good employment practice is adhered to. Tribunal experiences send clear messages to organisations about the need to handle internal complaints of harassment and bullying seriously, consistently, and fairly, and will continue to set precedents for tackling discrimination in the workplace.

References

Employment Law: An Adviser's Handbook, Thomas Kibling and Tamara Lewis (Legal Action Group, 1994).

Employment Tribunal Procedure, Jeremy McMullen QC and Jennifer Eady (Legal Action Group, 1996).

CHAPTER 11

The process of education

This chapter looks at why it is necessary to educate the workforce and how this can be achieved, cites some of the approaches used in training and development, and gives examples of successful education initiatives.

The saying "Awareness is 90% of the solution" rings true when describing the role of educating the workforce about harassment, bullying and violence, and their effects. Increasing people's awareness is the best way to combat such unacceptable behaviour.

Why educate?

Education, training and development in the workplace is the key to organisational effectiveness. Without it, nothing positive can be achieved. Most organisations are keen to be described as "learning organisations", and initiatives such as Investors in People are being adopted to prove their commitment to the workforce. However, although attitudes to training and development have changed, it is still an area that is under utilised, poorly planned and driven by budget restraints rather than the need to support organisational values.

Investment rather than cost
Because training and development is often viewed as a cost or an expense, the amount that most organisations are prepared to invest is

minimal in comparison to the amount of corporate income earned. The inability to link training and development with profit and contribution to growth may be one of the reasons why very little attention is paid to measuring the returns that organisations can gain from investing in people, and making comparisons between investing in training to eliminate harassment, bullying and violence and the cost of getting it wrong (as outlined in Chapter 8).

Trevor Bentley, in his book *The Business of Training*, maintains that training creates future benefits for the individual as well as the organisation and therefore must be an investment. To measure benefits effectively, those responsible for training must carry out an investment appraisal which shows the return on training (the value and duration of the investment and the value and duration of the benefits received). They will also need to determine how improvements in individual performance affect profit.

With this in mind, the cost of not taking the effects of harassment, bullying and violence seriously also needs to be calculated. What potential return can be gained from investing in a training and development initiative to prevent offensive behaviour in the workplace, and what would we have to pay out if the organisation were to defend a series of tribunal claims?

$$\text{Equation: } (x) = \frac{\text{Total Training Investment}}{\text{No. of Employees}} \left[\begin{array}{c} \text{compared} \\ \text{with} \end{array} \right] (y) =$$

$$\frac{\text{Total Cost of Tribunal Claims}}{\text{No. of Complainants}}$$

The positive impact that harassment awareness can have should not be ignored. Investing in developing, educating and training employees in this particular area will bring about positive changes and benefits, some of which are listed below:

● A greater appreciation and understanding of harassment, bullying and violence at all levels in the organisation.
● The ability to set clear standards of behaviour, which can bring about desired behavioural changes.
● Organisational values become real and tangible.
● Supports a healthy change in the organisation's culture and climate.
● The organisation becomes more flexible and can respond appropriately to all types of change.
● A demonstration of the organisation's commitment to investing in the welfare of their employees by taking the whole issue of harassment, bullying and violence seriously.

● Improvements in the level of skill required to handle abusive behaviour effectively.

● Helps to turn policy into practice, and also meets certain legislative requirements.

We have already explored how harassment, bullying and violence can reduce organisational effectiveness, and complacency when developing education initiatives can be just as damaging to an organisation as a climate where unacceptable behaviour is the norm.

For any initiative to be successful, it is necessary to identify the following:

● The organisational context in which the training and development will be set.

● Clear accountabilities and responsibilities for making the initiative successful.

● A strategic and systematic approach for implementing the initiatives.

The organisational context

Those responsible for creating and implementing harassment training initiatives need to diagnose and analyse the climate, culture, structure and political issues that exist within their organisation, developing a strategy for dealing with them that will allow these initiatives to be effective.

Chapter 5 looked at the impact of power within organisations and Chapter 6 explored in depth the patterns of behaviour that reflect the organisation's culture, and how to analyse the culture and climate. Once this exercise is complete it should reveal the elements that must be taken into account when developing a strategy for getting training initiatives accepted. In this context the following questions should be considered:

● What problems connected with harassment, bullying and violence already exist within the organisation?

● What barriers and sensitivities towards harassment, bullying and violence – personal, individual and organisational – exist within the organisation? How can you overcome them?

● Is the timing right for the initiative?

● Given the current situation, will you need a short-term or a long-term training and development strategy?

● How do you demonstrate that the initiative will support and enhance organisational vision and values?

● Who will be the key stakeholders for the initiative and why?

● Who can make it happen and why? (Will they be genuinely committed, or will they pay political "lip-service"?)
● What level of resistance will there be to a harassment initiative? How can you overcome it?
● Politically, who stands to "gain" from seeing the initiative fail? Who are your "limiters" (people who will limit or block the amount of activity necessary to make the initiative a success)?
● At a senior level, who is known to perpetuate unacceptable and unreasonable behaviour, and who can be regarded as role models for acceptable behaviour?
● Who is borderline? How can you win them over?
● What about your personal role? How much influence do you have (or need) in order to make the initiative a success? Can you do this alone? What support might you need? Are you truly committed to making the initiative work, or is this just another "To Do" task or performance target?

Accountability and responsibility for educating the workforce

Employers

The heaviest responsibility falls on employers to educate employees on all issues relating to equality. The Codes of Practice operated by the EOC and the CRE recommend that employers train and raise awareness to ensure that everyone is familiar with the policy and procedures, and to gain the commitment of staff to make them work. Although there are clear guidelines in both Codes of Practice for areas such as recruitment and selection, at the moment, UK legislation only implies that harassment awareness should be included. The experience is very different in the US, as the following case study shows.

The US Experience
In the US, harassment training is required by law, and some states have specific legislation which provides for this. The State of Connecticut's Commission on Human Rights and Opportunities Act has the power to:
● (15)(A) require an employer having three or more employees to post in a prominent and accessible location information concerning the illegality of sexual harassment and remedies available to victims of sexual harassment; and
● (B) require an employer having 50 or more employees to provide two hours of training and education to all supervisory employees within one year of the effective date of this Act and to all new supervisory employees within six months of their assumption of a

supervisory position, provided any employer who has provided such training and education to any such employees after 1 October 1991 (enforcement date of Act) shall not be required to provide such training and education a second time. Such training and education shall include information concerning the federal and state statutory provisions concerning sexual harassment and remedies available to victims of sexual harassment.

(Adapted from "Harassment policies", *Equal Opportunities Review*, No. 46, November/December, 1992. Reproduced by kind permission of Eclipse Group Publishing)

Health and safety legislation and recent European Commission Directives place a clear responsibility on employers to create procedures and practices and provide appropriate training where employees are at risk with regard to personal safety.

Rather than have the requirement to educate imposed, it is far better for employers to create the internal motivation for training and development, as this will increase the levels of participation and commitment amongst employees to making them work.

Ultimate responsibility (accountability) rests with senior/top management for training and development activities. Whilst commitment is expected in the form of endorsement for initiatives, support must also come in ensuring that budgets remain realistic and intact, and that appropriate authority is given to those professionals responsible for implementation.

Whilst line managers have a responsibility to turn harassment policy into practice (see Chapter 8), connected to this is the need to safeguard every team member's right to attend training and development events. It is very easy to give work targets and deadlines priority over training events; however, as line managers are expected to identify the learning needs of those for whom they are responsible, they are also expected to help to manage their time to ensure those learning objectives are met. This is vital for those team members who have, for example, already been identified as having a specific problem with their behaviour and interpersonal skills, although their work performance may be good.

Line managers also have a particular responsibility to assure team members that they are both aware of, and trained to handle, complaints of harassment, bullying and violence. Because the level of responsibility required to turn harassment policy into practice is high, it is recommended that special, more intensive training and development is created for line managers. Suggestions for line management training will be explored later on in this chapter.

Trade unions

Trade unions also have a responsibility to increase awareness in organisations about harassment, bullying and violence amongst their members, officers and representatives. In respect of sexual harassment, the European Commission's Code of Practice on the Protection of the Dignity of Women and Men at Work states that:

"Trade unions could aim to give all officers and representatives training on equality issues, including dealing with sexual harassment, and include such information in union-sponsored or approved training courses, as well as information on the union's policy. Trade unions should consider declaring that sexual harassment is inappropriate behaviour and educating members and officials about its consequences is recommended as good practice."

This role is further extended to working in partnership with employers by becoming involved in policy development and ensuring members participate in training initiatives.

Officers and representatives of trade unions could adapt the roles of supporters/listeners in an informal procedure or investigators in a formal procedure, as a way of reinforcing union commitment to eradicating workplace abuse. They can also disseminate information and advice on union education initiatives to prevent harassment from occurring.

The Labour Research Department, an independent trade union-based research organisation, supplies trade unions with educational information. Its publication *Tackling Harassment at Work* is full of examples and case studies outlining union action aimed at eradicating harassment.

Figure 24.
Humour can be
appropriate

(Reproduced by kind permission of Phil Evans, cartoonist, and the Labour Research Department)

Specialist staff

Specialist staff such as HR practitioners or training and development managers have a professional responsibility to ensure that:

- training initiatives match organisational needs and are relevant
- the quality of the training is high
- commitment for initiatives is gained from all levels within the organisation
- evaluation and cost-effectiveness exercises are carried out.

In the case of training and development projects for harassment, bullying and violence, in view of the sensitive nature of the topic great care needs to be taken over the choice of those involved in delivering or facilitating training and consultancy. It is not unreasonable to expect high standards from those who will be responsible for meeting the learning objectives of the organisation.

Although helpful, it is not enough for a facilitator to have an interest in, or a vague understanding of, any issue connected to diversity. Whether an external or internal consultant, facilitator or trainer, the following criteria will assist in meeting the responsibility to provide the best possible learning opportunities for employees:

- A high level of expertise, demonstrated through knowledge, awareness and skills (for example, knowledge of discrimination law and other legislative frameworks, practical application of counselling skills in the workplace, awareness of innovative management development models, etc).
- A proven track record of involvement in successful projects (for example, for both internal and external specialists, a portfolio of work, good references and a reputable client list).
- Independence from any special interest group or "political" agenda.
- An understanding of organisational behaviour, strategic processes and policy creation.
- Experience of turning policy into practice.
- A sensitivity to equality and diversity issues generally.
- An ability to influence change at a senior level.

Personal responsibility

Individuals have a responsibility to participate in the training programmes provided for them by employers and trade unions. The process of raising personal awareness about abusive behaviour is similar to that of health and safety requirements – knowing about the policy is not enough – and being able to reduce the impact of having an accident at work is vital. Understanding the nature of harassment, and what constitutes it, not only reduces the chances of being a target, it ensures individuals develop a personal awareness that their own behaviour does not amount to the harassment of others.

Individuals also have a role in expressing their development needs to their line managers, particularly if they recognise areas where they find it difficult to challenge unacceptable behaviour, or need to develop skills in becoming more assertive. One-to-one meetings, performance reviews or appraisals are ideal for requesting and suggesting appropriate training courses.

A strategic and systematic approach

As mentioned previously, careful planning and research must take place in order to make training and development effective. Adopting a systematic approach to training and development enables organisations to respond proactively to changes that are inevitable, and reduces the risk of "knee-jerk" reactions to problems that may arise unexpectedly. The following case study highlights the consequences of attempting to implement an initiative without prior planning.

Case Study

To Fail to Prepare . . .

Carolyn, a senior personnel executive in a large public sector organisation, describes the difficulties she faced when attempting to introduce harassment and bullying policy and procedures:

"We were on the brink of having to defend the organisation in tribunal proceedings which, quite frankly, we would have been very lucky to win. Against the advice of my personnel department, a complaint of harassment was not investigated, and the perpetrator was not disciplined – even though the circumstances around the complaint would have led to a straightforward management decision for disciplinary action. As a result of our failure to deal with the complaint effectively, the complainant went straight to the EOC, who supported her claim of direct sex discrimination.

Rather than go through the whole tribunal process, the organisation admitted some liability, and offered the complainant another role in the organisation (away from the perpetrator) and a large compensation payment, with a no-publicity clause in the settlement. We also agreed to implement a new harassment and bullying policy and procedure, as well as awareness training, within six months.

The chief executive, who was angry about the action taken against the organisation, told me personally that he felt 'this was a lot of fuss over nothing'. He felt my department had turned into the 'thought police', and was encouraging more people to 'whinge' about their managers, rather than cope with their workloads and all that went with it. The chief executive only approved budget for general awareness sessions for every member of staff, and because he did not believe we needed one, refused to endorse the policy and complaints procedures, and did not allow additional budget for a specialist consultant to formulate a proper system for the organisation. My belief is that he and his top team deliberately procrastinated, and, after much toing and froing with frequent demands for changes or clarification of the plans, his final decision was made three months after proposals were first brought to him for approval.

Because of the time limit, quick awareness sessions were arranged, but as they did not form part of a wider plan, they did not have the desired lasting effect, as nothing else took place to reinforce the messages of the awareness sessions. More importantly, the resistance to this exercise was incredible (although, with hindsight, not surprising) – everyone looked at it as only happening because of the complaint in the member's department, and saw it as a lip-service. The grapevine worked very well too, with some employees speaking up at the sessions about the stalling tactics of the senior management team clearly showing their lack of commitment to this topic. 'They obviously don't care about us; and they are the ones who need it most' was the usual comment.

After the awareness sessions, numerous complaints of harassment and bullying were made about the senior management team, and as a result, a hefty, widely publicised series of tribunal cases were successful, costing the organisation £1.5 million.

Our main defence in the tribunal hearings was one of having learned from previous misdemeanours the need to educate the workforce, hence our investment in awareness sessions. Although this was noted by the tribunal chair, it was made clear to us that this did not fully represent a total commitment to eradicate harassment and bullying, and there did not seem to be any strategy. More notably, senior management commitment was not evident, and indeed the opposite was true – as the complainants produced evidence of senior managers preventing individuals from attending the training events.

The adverse publicity meant that our chief executive had a change of heart – the training exercise started all over again, properly timed and with policy and procedures backing it."

(Carolyn, senior personnel practitioner)

The creation of a training strategy arising from the initial audit and goal-setting exercise must be seen as part of an overall strategy for combating unacceptable behaviour. A training strategy designed to support an anti-harassment strategy has the following key elements:

The training purpose –	What is our overall aim and what do we want to achieve? What will be the end result?
Learning needs analysis –	Who knows what about harassment, bullying and violence? Identifying knowledge gaps, harnessing key strengths and matching individual learning needs to organisational learning needs.
The training plan –	How are we going to implement our purpose? Concentration on resources, consideration of appropriate timing, identifying who to train, deciding the best way to communicate the training programme, choosing appropriate approaches to training and development. Selecting monitoring and evaluation techniques.
The investment required –	Cost and returns exercise, and investigation into how to budget for it.

The training purpose and the learning needs analysis represent the research required to create the training plan. It is vital to conduct some form of research and planning in order that the strategy reflects what individuals need to learn, and what the organisation wants everyone to learn about harassment, bullying and violence to prevent its occurrence.

The training plan is the systematic element of the strategy, and must be carefully thought through before implementation.

A training strategy need not be elaborate (as Figure 25 illustrates).

Above all, training in the area of harassment and bullying must be seen to be integral to organisational development and part of the mainstream, not a special "quick fix" added in because of external pressures.

Figure 25.
A training strategy

Feb 1999

XYZ org.

Harassment & Bullying Project

DRAFT TRAINING STRATEGY

Overall aims:

To ensure that every member of staff, (including volunteers) is aware of our stand against unacceptable behaviour in this organisation. Also, to ensure that staff have the appropriate level of skill to challenge unacceptable behaviour if it arises.

Learning Needs Analysis

Conducted mini-survey of 100 staff, mix of management, admin. and clerical, and professional & technical grades.

Following key areas identified as learning gaps:

- Policy statement (all levels)
- Understanding of the nature of harassment and Bullying (all levels)
- Understanding the procedures (managers) - this includes links to Disciplinary and grievance procedures
- How do we challenge Harassment & Bullying? (all levels & volunteers)
- Managing conflict situations (managers and professionals).

NB

Very strong team environment amongst some depts. - working relations are good, however, not certain how to deal with conflict.....

Check against results of last years Staff Survey

②

Training Plan

Timescale: must be completed by June 2000.

Resources: Training & Development Unit (will give them full accountability)
Equality Working Group –
Possible external expertise –
dependent on budget meeting (25/4/99)

Who to train: & what to deliver: All staff – Short introductory sessions, and one day awareness
Snr – middle managers – Commitment gaining, procedural knowledge and general awareness course.
Key staff – train as investigators (criteria to be developed).
Key staff – train as supporters (selection criteria to be developed).

Communications: Staff briefing system, newsletter, and leaflets and posters. Issue policy statements as part of training courses. Also to customers & clients. Further research as to whether a confidential hot-line would be cost-effective. If yes, include in telephone training budget.

Investment Required

(Expand)

Allow £25,000 – subject to budget and requirement of external expertise.
Expected returns? Could measure morale (through staff survey) and levels of productivity.

Approaches to training and development

The bottom-line goal of any educational, training and development initiative connected with harassment, bullying and violence is that it must achieve specific value and behavioural changes to be effective. Training that addresses behaviour is key, as it will eventually influence a positive change in individual attitudes. For example:

● Changes in the use of negative language.
● Empathetic rather than scathing attitudes towards harassment.
● People become more understanding and appreciative of other cultures.
● Individuals are aware of the effect that their own behaviour can have on others.
● There is a higher standard of professionalism in the approach to colleagues and clients.
● The organisation as a whole has an environment which values positive and productive working relationships based on an enabling climate and the equal distribution of power.

The relationships between education, training and development as forms of learning are vital to the design of programmes for harassment, bullying and violence. Dictionary definitions of **educate** include *"to develop (bring up) so as to form habits, manners, intellectual and physical aptitudes; to train the mind and abilities of"*. **Develop** is defined as *"to unfold more fully or advance, bring out all that is potentially contained in or latent"*; and **training** is defined as *"instruction and discipline in, for some particular art, profession, occupation or practice; to make proficient by such instruction and practice, and to cause to grow in the desired manner"*. It is clear from these definitions that to improve behaviour and combat discrimination at organisational, interpersonal and personal levels, programmes have to be designed that integrate these different types of learning.

Full integration of education, training and developmental forms of learning means that harassment, bullying and violence programmes must contain the appropriate mix of knowledge, skills, and awareness and attitude topics (see Figure 26 overleaf) in order to achieve the desired value and behavioural changes regarded as significant to the organisation.

Knowledge topics would include the following:

● Theory behind harassment, bullying and violence – definitions and what they constitute.
● Understanding the organisation's policy, procedures and commitment to eradicating harassment, bullying and violence.

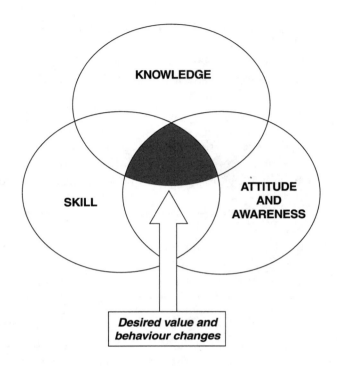

Figure 26. Key elements of harassment and bullying training initiatives

- Discrimination and health and safety law and its links with harassment, bullying and violence.
- Understanding links to the organisation's grievance and disciplinary process.
- What is expected of employees in terms of responsibility and standards of behaviours.

Increasing and building skill levels can cover a range of areas such as:

- How to identify harassment, bullying and violence.
- How to challenge it effectively.
- How to assist both targets and perpetrators.
- Personal safety issues.
- Recognising potentially violent and dangerous situations.
- How to reduce the possibility of violence escalating.

Attitude topics should address the following issues:

- General awareness of the effects of unacceptable behaviour.
- Why harassment, bullying and violence occur and the psychology behind them.
- Attitudes (both social and personal) towards sexual and racial harass-

ment, violence, bullying, harassment of disabled people, the harassment of gay men and lesbians, and other areas that are not normally discussed.
● Real-life case studies and experiences of harassment, bullying and violence.
● Examination of personal awareness of behaviour – unconscious signals through verbal and non-verbal language.

Training methods

As well as traditional training methods such as tutor-led sessions and group work, the following can be used to add variety to the learning environment:

● written case study scenarios
● scenario enactments and role plays (by trained actors)
● behaviour analysis and modification exercises
● videos
● real-life experiences related within small, confidential groups
● action- or focus-group learning
● team-led learning.

Striking the right balance when selecting methods for delivering harassment, bullying and violence courses can be difficult. Should lecturing play an important role in delivering serious messages? Is it appropriate to use humour? How far can we allow open discussions to go? What type of activities would be appropriate to use? How do we challenge prejudicial viewpoints and behaviour on a course? The solution to these issues lies in ensuring that programmes are designed to enable as much participation as possible, which allows the learners to take more responsibility for their learning. In addition, learning events must meet the needs of different groups of employees within the organisation by acknowledging levels of motivation, existing skills and knowledge, and their learning styles.

Whom do you train?

The most obvious answer to this question is everyone in the organisation. However, training every member of staff is not always easy to achieve, particularly when budget and time restraints, a lack of people resources, a resistance to change and the whole issue of abusive behaviour often appear as barriers.

The ideal scenario would incorporate a cascade approach to harassment, bullying and violence awareness, starting from top/senior management levels and trickling down or cascading right through other levels of the organisation, with continued senior management support throughout the entire process. Some organisations concentrate on giving senior management priority with training, whilst others have focused on providing front-line staff with training in areas such as how to deal with aggressive customers. Grouping different levels of staff is necessary in order that appropriate training programmes can be created and delivered effectively. However, this does not mean compromises can be made on the quality and clarity of the learning events. Indeed, it involves acknowledging that messages about harassment, bullying and violence will have to be delivered in different ways, according to the needs and priorities of each group.

Below is an example of a standard, one-day harassment awareness course aimed at all staff within the organisation, with the appropriate mix of knowledge, skills and attitude topics.

One-day Harassment Awareness Course

Aim

The programme is designed to increase participants' awareness and knowledge of harassment as a form of discrimination. It is also designed to help individuals challenge unacceptable behaviours and to ensure their own behaviour does not constitute harassment.

Objectives

At the end of the programme, participants will:

● have a greater awareness and understanding of what constitutes all forms of harassment and bullying
● understand the impact of their own behaviour on others, and how to challenge discrimination in others
● understand the relevant legislation as it applies to harassment and personal responsibilities within their organisation's policy
● identify issues arising from the programme that can be put into a personal action plan.

The programme

Setting the context

● Why a course on harassment?

What is harassment and what constitutes harassment?

- Unravelling some concepts and attitudes towards harassment.
- Discovering some broader definitions.
- Examining the behaviours that constitute harassment.
- Understanding the effects of harassment on targets and in the workplace.

Harassment legislation and the organisation's policy

- Summary of the legislation that underpins harassment.
- Overview of the organisation's policy.
- Understanding the formal and informal processes to resolve harassment.

Dealing with harassment – a case study

- Practical exercise dealing with harassment, using discussion and role-play techniques.

Action planning

- Participants will develop a personal action plan based on key learning points from the day.

The learning needs analysis would determine how relevant to the organisation the programme might be. It can also be adapted to meet the specific needs of the following groups of employees:

- senior and first-line managers
- front-line staff (those who come into direct and regular contact with customers and clients)
- HR practitioners
- groups of staff where a gender imbalance exists
- staff with specific roles within the policy process.

Senior and first-line managers

The key message that senior and first-line managers must understand is that accountability for eradicating harassment, bullying and violence in the organisation ultimately rests with them.

In addition to the standard programme, relevant topics would include:

● Taking harassment and bullying seriously – handling harassment informally and formally.
● Establishing an overview of management responsibilities within the organisation's policy.
● Challenging unacceptable behaviour and language in others.
● Setting standards of behaviour and improving working relationships.
● Checking your own behaviour and becoming a role model.

Front-line staff

Those staff who have regular contact with customers and clients need to be aware not only of how to project a positive image to customers and clients whilst being courteous, but also how to handle any unacceptable behaviour from their customers and clients.

In addition to the standard programme, specialist training for handling and avoiding aggression and violence in the workplace and dealing with the issue of personal safety must be considered to reduce the risk of abusive behaviour and attacks. Relevant topics would include:

● Understanding the extent to which aggressive and violent behaviour has increased in the workplace.
● Preventative measures to avoid aggression and physical attacks.
● Learning to trust their instincts and respond appropriately.
● Assertiveness and effective interpersonal skills.

HR practitioners

It is often assumed that anyone working in a personnel or HR role would automatically have the expertise to be able to handle issues of harassment, bullying and violence. This assumption means that HR professionals are often left out of training programmes. However, there is a particular need for HR practitioners to gain additional skills and knowledge in the area of abusive behaviour, so that they can confidently facilitate the process of creating strategies and policies and help senior managers take ownership of the issue.

In addition to the standard awareness programme, one-to-one or small group coaching sessions would be an appropriate way to give HR professionals the support mechanisms needed to implement strategies. Using a coaching model, the coach would explore with the coachee(s), in an open, confidential environment, possible goals and targets for the HR departments, whilst getting them to establish the reality and size of their objectives. Options for appropriate actions would be explored (such as how to keep the senior management team and/or stakeholders committed to harassment training plans) and an agreement on key actions and timed implementation plans would close the process.

Groups of staff where a gender imbalance exists

Some consideration must be given to how (in particular with sexual harassment) training will be delivered where women or men are in the minority within a team, department or the whole of the organisation, and negative behaviour is centred around their difference. (The same principle can apply to issues connected to race, disability, sexual orientation, etc.) It can be counter-productive to expect, for example, two female managers to attend a sexual harassment awareness course with eight male managers, reflecting a working environment dominated by men. Different issues will arise for men and women, and this can create a power imbalance and inhibit the learning process.

In such cases, sex discrimination legislation may allow for positive action measures to be adopted, such as women-only training courses, which will help to address specific skills and strategies to enable women to combat sexual harassment in a male-dominated environment.

Staff with specific roles within the policy process

Training for those with specific roles to play within the policy process would include:

● Investigation skills training (for those responsible for carrying out investigations in the formal procedure).
● Counselling/helping skills for supporters and advisers dealing with issues of harassment in the informal procedure.

Training in these areas may require specialist expertise. However, the amount of investment required would ensure that the organisation has groups of highly trained staff who would be capable of handling issues of harassment and bullying. Training in these areas would also ensure that ownership of a policy to combat abusive behaviour rests with everyone in the organisation and not just senior management and HR departments.

Other relevant areas of training

What is often seen in organisations that exhibit chronic, abusive behaviour patterns is the need to address a gap in basic management skills and practices amongst those responsible for leading and managing. Organisational audits and surveys reveal that managers rarely receive training to carry out their roles before being promoted or employed as a manager, yet are given resource and authority and assume responsibility for the welfare and progress of teams of people. This problem is widespread, even though access to management development has increased and the quality of training is high. Employers need to ensure that a good foundation in management skills and practice exists in those they select and promote into managerial positions – and take full responsibility for improving and maintaining high management standards of behaviour.

Expanding training programmes (for all levels of employees) to include the following skill areas would assist in supporting a harassment, bullying and violence strategy:

- counselling, coaching and mediation skills
- interviewing skills (which would include grievance and disciplinary procedures, recruitment and selection)
- performance appraisals/reviews
- motivation and delegation skills
- managing diverse teams
- meeting skills
- advanced interpersonal skills.

Assertion and empowerment training can help to increase confidence levels and arm employees with the additional skills needed to challenge abusive behaviour appropriately. It will also help employees to understand the impact of negative behaviours, and increase their ability to take personal responsibility for their own behaviour.

Dealing with resistance to training

There will always be an element of resistance to a training programme in harassment and bullying. Resistance to training is a form of resistance to change, and this can be overcome by ensuring that, where possible, employees are involved in the process of creating and choosing appropriate programmes, so that some level of ownership is achieved. The organisation also needs to be prepared to answer the question, "What is in it for me?" Giving employees time to consider and think through benefits by using a "drip-feed" approach (a little bit of information received on a regular basis) can also help to reduce some of the fear and insecurity they may be experiencing. The "three-line whip" approach (or making training compulsory) to ensuring that every employee attends training can also create walls of defensiveness and resistance, particularly in the area of equal opportunities training. Although it may be necessary to adopt this approach, every attempt should be made to encourage and persuade people to attend programmes of their own accord.

There are times, however, when it will be necessary to face the reality that not everyone has the motivation or the desire to change – expecting every member of staff to be on board with a training initiative at the same time is unrealistic. Efforts should be concentrated on ensuring that a majority of the workforce is or will be committed to the aim of eliminating abusive behaviour, and not on the few that may continue to resist, despite strategies deployed to change their minds.

Examples of successful education initiatives

Sharing experiences widens understanding, and is one of the best ways of gaining insight into what works well in other organisations, and how training and development initiatives have helped to combat harassment, bullying and violence. This part of the chapter outlines good, creative education initiatives that are considered as best practice examples that every organisation can learn from.

The first case study explores the method used in a development programme at a secondary school.

Case Study

Young Bullies in the Making?

Bullies can move from primary to secondary school – from playground to workplace – without ever understanding their own behaviour. Jennifer Cashman, of Positive Practice, describes the methods she used in local schools to address the issue of bullying:

"Working with a group of Year 7 pupils (identified by school staff as bullies or victims of bullies) in a secondary school in South London in recent years I used group discussion, role play, pair and small group exercises to encourage the group members to:

● experiment with alternatives to present behavioural patterns
● experience these problems from another perspective (ie reverse the bully and victim roles)
● identify areas/relationships experienced as problematic by the pupils
● confront those areas/relationships and consider the processes contributing to the difficulties experienced
● enhance their self-esteem through positive experiences
● build trust and self-confidence.

The group provided a supportive environment where pupils were able to explore their perceptions of themselves and their behaviour, examine the reasons for the behaviour and experiment with ways of changing and also widening the range of their coping skills.

A majority of the pupils identified as bullies acknowledged that their behaviour was unreasonable – but not until they had participated in discussion and role play from the victim's viewpoint. As a result the children resolved to tackle some of the issues surrounding their behavioural patterns.

Pupils identified as 'victims' were also often surprised during the experiments to witness mirror images of their own behaviour. Working from the premise that to change their behaviour would elicit different responses from their persecutors, each group member identified and practised behaviours and coping skills which they felt would help them to escape from their present 'victim' behaviour.

During the course of this group work many of the pupils began to recognise the 'vicious circle' of learning and teaching behaviour by example. During one discussion period it was suggested that we held a similar group for parents of group members and also include some teachers whose oppressive behaviour caused concern to many of the children involved.

An important learning process for the people taking part in this programme was that it is possible to break and change established patterns of behaviour and to experience an enhancement of confidence, trust and self-esteem both for themselves and those around them.

A comment from one 12-year-old summed it up fairly accurately when he said: 'I always thought I'd grow up just like my Dad, get what I wanted by threatening to flatten anyone who didn't agree with me. I didn't realise that wasn't what I wanted – it was just what I thought was *expected* of me.'"

(Jennifer Cashman, director, Positive Practice)

Assertiveness and interpersonal skills training is one of the most popular forms of personal development in UK workplaces. As previously mentioned, a programme concentrating on the development of interpersonal skills can greatly influence an individual's internal power and improve levels of self-worth. The following case study outlines how a specially designed personal development programme assists thousands of people with facial disfigurements.

Facing Reality

Changing Faces is a charity (established in 1992) which raises public awareness about the challenges people with facial disfigurements face every day. More importantly, Changing Faces assists people with facial disfigurements in raising their level of self-esteem, by focusing on the communications skills needed to deal with other people's reactions, through training. There are an estimated 400,000 people in the UK who have a severe disfigurement, blemish or scar which affects their ability to lead a normal life.

I asked James Partridge (executive director of the charity) to supply me with case studies of people with facial disfigurements who had been targeted with harassment and bullying. "Are these harassment examples? They happen so frequently that it is difficult to single them out as cases of harassment, rather than occurrences that people with facial disfigurement experience on a regular basis – maybe I have just accepted this behaviour as part of the scheme of things . . .," James said.

He did give me an example of a secretary who has a noticeable birthmark on the side of her face. She felt so harassed by the behaviour of her work colleagues that she was convinced her career prospects in the organisation were written off. The behaviour of her colleagues manifested itself through distance and shunning – she believed colleagues were moving away from her and not wanting to be close to her, because they were embarrassed, or put off, by her appearance.

This had the effect of making her feel very nervous and uneasy. The effects worsened, and after a long period of being subjected to this treatment, she became ill and her GP diagnosed that she was clinically depressed.

She was referred to Changing Faces, and the assertiveness training she received to help raise her self-esteem helped to take away the sting from her colleagues' behaviour. She learned to convey, "It's OK to sit next to me" rather than "Go away". She also identified someone in the workplace she could talk to at times when she needed support.

James described the rationale for devising the special programme of workshops for anyone affected by facial disfigurements. "Operations and plastic surgery aren't always the answer. Not everyone will have the option of surgery open to them, and although it can help to a certain extent, it may not remove a disfigurement completely."

In social interactions, we tend to focus on people's faces, and having a facial disfigurement can make normal interaction embarrassing and uncomfortable. We are constantly bombarded with assumptions about what is necessary for successful life – and one of them is good looks.

Sometimes, the behaviour of a facially disfigured person can unwittingly contribute to the feelings of inadequacy experienced as a result of being exposed to negative behaviour. James described the hostility and defensive behaviour adopted by those with facial disfigurements as "self-protecting", a mechanism developed to counteract negativity from others. "What we have learned is that the responsibility lies with us to increase our own social and communication skills so that we have more control over our social interactions, and thus feel more confident when being in the company of others." With this in mind, Changing Faces has developed a programme of workshops which, supported by counselling and one-to-one sessions, concentrates on improving social and interpersonal skills, and starts with the following foundation workshop:

Outline of a foundation workshop – the FACES process

F Finding: Participants are given the opportunity to share the experiences of living with facial disfigurement through discussions and practical exercises.

A Accepting: As a first step towards "coming to terms" with disfigurement, participants are led towards an understanding of social interaction problems and the way in which society's views can influence how they feel about themselves.

C Communicating: Participants learn more about the communication processes and how they themselves can influence the way they are received by those around them.

E Experimenting: In the workshop every participant has the chance to work on the specific situations that are causing them difficulties (eg starting a conversation, dealing with staring).

S Succeeding: Individual "action plans" are drawn up at the end of the workshop to help participants translate what they have learned into their everyday lives.

With the emphasis placed heavily on practicalities, the programme is highly participative, and adopts a pragmatic approach to creating realistic action plans for the future of every participant. Changing Faces also runs specialist programmes for children with facial disfigurements.

"We hope the social skills and strategies learned on the programme will help participants overcome their fears and face reality – so that they feel confident about contributing to the society they are part of" said James.

(Interview with James Partridge, executive director and founder of Changing Faces)

Short presentations, regular briefings and articles in company newsletters are alternative methods of raising awareness about discriminatory behaviour. The following article, taken from The Industrial Society's *Briefing Plus* publication, is a prime example of how the media can use its influence positively to issue an important message.

TIPS FOR MANAGERS
Rooting Out Racism

AN INCREASING number of unfair dismissal cases are being brought on the grounds of racial discrimination, suggesting that all is not well for ethnic minorities in the workplace. Statistics suggest people from ethnic minorities are more likely to face unemployment than their white counterparts, are the last to be hired and the first to be fired. So how can you beat discrimination in your own organisation's recruitment, selection and promotion procedures?

1   Awareness is important. If you are not aware of racism and how it manifests itself, and how serious it is, you cannot deal with it adequately. Awareness training is a very worthwhile investment.

2   Re-examine your practices, procedures and systems and make sure they do not, and cannot, discriminate against anyone.

3   Watch out for signs of racial harassment, and make sure staff know where to turn for help if they are victims. Workers who are targets of harassment may not always complain because they fear reprisals.

4   Set standards of behaviour for your staff, communicate them clearly (including them in induction of new staff), and ensure they are observed. For example, make it clear that racist language is unacceptable, spelling out how it will be dealt with.

5   Avoid stereotyping, which may lead to incorrect assumptions about standards of performance, behaviour and attitudes.

6   Be sensitive about cultural and religious observances.

7   Actively promote the benefits of working in a diverse group to all employees.

8   Get to know the community your organisation works in, and the different racial groups within it.

9   Evaluate your own management style. Ask yourself if your actions are open to misinterpretation, or if they perpetuate racist views and practices.

(Article by Cathie Louis from *Briefing Plus* June 1994, The Industrial Society)

One of the most worrying trends discovered when researching into abusive behaviour for this book was the rate at which aggression and violence are escalating in the workplace. There is an urgent need to increase awareness about abusive behaviour in the workplace, and people's ability to handle it. This last case study explores the work of a national charity committed to improving the personal safety of all.

Case Study

The Suzy Lamplugh Trust

In 1986 Diana Lamplugh set up the Suzy Lamplugh Trust after the disappearance of her daughter Suzy, an estate agent who went to meet an unknown client and never returned. Suzy's disappearance highlighted the risks that are faced by almost every worker, and also revealed the inadequacy of employers in protecting their staff.

The Trust's mission is "to create a safer society and enable all people to live safer lives". It achieves this by adopting a positive approach to tackling violence and aggression in society: undertaking research, hosting conferences, working closely with public sector and government organisations, and developing and delivering educational resources and training through a network of tutors and trainers throughout the country.

The work that the Trust has done to reduce the risk of violence in the workplace has earned it a good reputation amongst UK organisations for providing practical advice to employers and employees. The Trust has developed a series of programmes and workshops based on common-sense preventative measures to increase employees' personal safety skills in the workplace. Programmes range from flexible-learning packages, full and half-day training courses, to introductory talks and presentations, covering topics such as the facts about personal safety, defining violence and aggression, identifying and assessing possible risks at work, understanding reactions to fear, stress and aggression, tension-control techniques, non-verbal and verbal communication, and safety when travelling.

The Trust's resources also include a number of publications and videos for schools, children, young adults, disabled people and the general public, as well as those aimed at working women, employees and employers. In particular, the guidance notes for employers outline the main health and safety responsibilities, policy, procedures and how to create and maintain a safer working environment.

Below is an example of advice given in the booklet *Working Safely in Other People's Homes.*

Working in other people's homes

Aggressive and violent behaviour can be caused by people feeling that there is an intrusion into their private lives. The potential for violence against you in people's homes may depend on why you are there. On the other hand, the person may just have had a bad day and you are the last straw. Or he or she may have had a bad experience with a previous caller.

TAKE CARE:

▲ Always remember why you are there. It is their home, and you are going into it.

▲ You are invading their space.

▲ It is their territory and they are in command. Your job may represent a threat to this.

▲ Go in daylight if possible.

THINK BEFORE YOU GO:

▲ Do you have to go alone?

▲ Are there any records/reports available to you before you go?

▲ Do people know where you are going?

▲ Have you got someone to check in with (a friend/colleague/manager)?

▲ Do you have a telephone/ phonecard/money/telephone

numbers?

▲ Will you need a mobile phone, pager or other form of help to keep in touch?

▲ What is the location like?

▲ How are you getting there and back?

WHEN YOU ARRIVE:

▲ Remember you are the visitor.

▲ Say who you are, why you are there and show your ID if you have one.

▲ Check who you are talking to.

▲ Do not enter the house at all if the appropriate person is not available.

▲ Let them know (honestly) how much of their time you will need.

▲ Wait to be invited in or at least ask if you can go in.

▲ Acknowledge that it is their territory; let them lead the way; don't take over.

▲ You may decide not to go in or to leave immediately (eg if the person is drunk or aggressive). Listen to your instincts.

▲ Check as you go in how the front door locks.

▲ Take only what you need into the house.

▲ Take care with documents you may not want them to see.

▲ Study your surroundings. Look for an exit.

▲ Ensure you can get out quickly if necessary – don't get trapped. Try to sit nearest the door.

▲ Ask for dogs or other animals to be put in another room.

▲ Try not to react to bad, dirty or smelly surroundings.

▲ Remain alert. Watch for changes in mood, movements or expressions.

▲ Do not spread your belongings around. You may need to leave in a hurry.

▲ If you feel at risk – leave as soon as possible.

▲ If you are prevented from leaving or threatened, stay calm and try to control the situation.

▲ Do what you have to do to protect yourself.

(Reproduced by kind permission of The Suzy Lamplugh Trust)

For the Suzy Lamplugh Trust, acknowledging that every individual has the right to live life to its fullest lies at the heart of their philosophy, and is the driving force behind the Trust's campaigning activities for relevant legislation and the formulation of national strategies on personal safety issues. It is now presumed that Suzy Lamplugh was murdered and she has been declared dead. However, the Trust will continue to influence organisations and assist them in tackling aggression and violence in the workplace by reinforcing the lessons learned from Suzy's disappearance.

Reflection

Educating the workforce to develop positive working relationships by reducing incidents of harassment, bullying and violence must be viewed as a continuous process, and one which is integral to achieving desired behavioural changes amongst working colleagues. In *The Fifth Discipline Fieldbook* by Peter Senge, Richard Ross, Bryan Smith, Charlotte Roberts and Art Kleiner, organisations that need to change profoundly (in order to become learning organisations) have to experience a deep learning cycle, which consists of employees developing new skills and capabilities that may change people's understanding and abilities. As the new skills and capabilities develop, a deeper level of awareness and sensibilities is formed, widening people's perspectives and creating a greater sense of "team" rather than individual vision. Gradually, basic shifts in attitudes and beliefs occur, and the organisational culture changes – unconsciously and over a long period of time.

The role of good quality education, development and training should therefore not be underestimated, as it is indispensable when establishing and reinforcing an organisational culture where harassment, bullying and violence is not tolerated.

References

Preventing and Remedying Sexual Harassment at Work: A Resource Manual, Michael Rubenstein (IRS, 1992).

Training Your Staff, Jacquie Bamborough (The Industrial Society, 1994).

Training and Development, Rosemary Harrison (Institute of Personnel Development, 1990).

The Business of Training, Trevor Bentley (McGraw-Hill, 1990).

Tackling Harassment at Work, Labour Research Department (LRD Publications).

Nursing Standard, Vol. 8 No. 34, 18 May 1994.

Working Safely in Other People's Homes, The Suzy Lamplugh Trust, 1998.

The Fifth Discipline Fieldbook, Peter Senge, Richard Ross, Bryan Smith, Charlotte Roberts and Art Kleiner (Nicholas Brearley Publishing, 1996).

"Rooting out racism", *Briefing Plus* article, The Industrial Society, June 1994.

Conclusion

What of the future?

With the challenge of competing in global markets, the move towards ethical business standards and working partnerships with local communities, organisations in the UK must become more flexible and healthier if they are still to be considered as major players in the world business community.

Taking harassment, bullying and violence seriously is therefore a vital step in achieving organisational "fitness". Although this may sound like a cliché, a content and happy workforce *will* produce positive results for the organisation, whereas a climate that is rife with abusive behaviours will have a negative effect on the performance of the organisation (as we hope this book has already shown). To pay little or no attention to this fact will have devastating consequences for UK organisations.

Although there is clearly a need to revise current legislation, a balance is required. The issue is not to sensationalise harassment, or over legislate; it is to provide a clear, workable framework that makes it easier for organisations to tackle harassment, bullying and violence. Two major lessons can be learned here: namely, the US experience of legislative loopholes and the culture of litigation that has grown as a result; and the Swedish experience of producing a clear framework of legal guidelines for the issue of bullying and "Dignity at Work" in general. UK legislation does need to be clearer and more concise, but it should not be entrenched with complicated clauses that make it difficult for employers to meet legal obligations and must encourage employees to take responsibility for their behaviour.

Organisational responsibility also extends to the role played in local communities. Over recent years, the UK has reeled in the detrimental effects that the racist murder of Stephen Lawrence has had on the ethnic minority community. It can be argued that this issue will have an impact on institutional discrimination in organisations – not only will organisations be employing young people like Stephen who have great potential to offer because of their differences, they may possibly employ those who could be responsible for the crimes committed against Stephen Lawrence and others like him. Combating and tackling those who abuse power in the workplace will have a positive effect on the way employees behave in their local community and, eventually, on people's behaviour in society generally.

Frank Furedi in his book *Culture of Fear* argues that we live in a society preoccupied with abuse, danger, safety and survival. Furedi says that within this culture of abuse, an industry of bullying has been created: *"the inflation and trivialisation of bullying has turned virtually every peer-to-peer relationship which is stressful into an experience of abuse"*. Whilst this view may exist, it does not deal with the fact that abusive behaviour is on the increase, and strategies must be adopted in order to challenge it. Using labels to describe negative behaviours and raising the profile of abusive behaviour form a key part of giving people a wider perspective so that they can develop tools and options to handle it.

Tackling harassment, bullying and violence is not about promoting a culture of fear; it is about dealing with the reality of the shadowy side of human behaviour, and ensuring that individuals and organisations can take responsibility and confront the issues raised as a result.

The way forward

The way forward for organisations means ensuring that the commitment to address the issue of harassment, bullying and violence remains a high priority by adopting the following strategies:

● Constantly evaluating and monitoring the culture of the organisation, testing the temperature of the culture and reviewing policies so that they continue to meet the needs of the organisation.
● Setting standards of behaviours and continuing to appreciate differences in the workplace.
● Acknowledging the place of true empowerment in creating a positive working environment.

● Encouraging leaders, managers and strategists to be visible role models.
● Being tough on perpetrators, whilst helping them to change their behaviour, and encouraging targets and victims to take responsibility.
● Continuing to educate and develop the workforce, and networking with other organisations that are taking on the challenge of tackling abusive behaviour.
● Never underestimating the effects of not taking harassment, bullying and violence seriously.

As illustrated in the three circles diagram (Figure 27), addressing the needs of the individual as well as the organisation, whilst creating and planning appropriate strategies and policies, when combined, will create a "harassment–free" zone.

Figure 27.

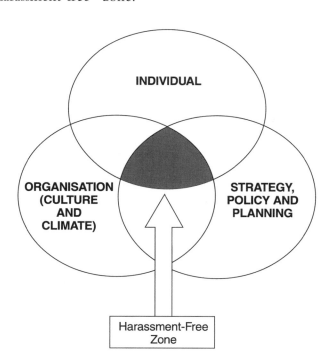

We hope that the book has helped you and your organisation start to meet the challenge of creating a positive and healthy work environment.

Reference

Culture of Fear: Risk-taking and the Morality of Low Expectation, Frank Furedi (Cassell, 1997).

Resources

Below is a list of addresses of organisations and other resources from which you will be able to gain further information relating to harassment, bullying and violence in the workplace.

GENERAL

Industrial Relations Services
18–20 Highbury Place
London
N5 1QP
0171 354 5858
Produces Equal Opportunities Review *and other publications and conferences on equal opportunities issues*

Industrial Society
Robert Hyde House
48 Bryanston Square
London
W1H 7LN
0171 479 2000
Campaigns, researches, trains, provides consultancy on employment, management and equal opportunities

Institute of Personnel and Development
IPD House
35 Camp Road
Wimbledon
London
SW19 4UX
0181 971 9000
Produces resources on personnel and salary setting

Labour Research Department
78 Blackfriars Road
London
SE1 8HF
0171 928 3649
An independent, trade union based research organisation, which
supplies information for the trade union and labour movement

Local Government Management Board
76–86 Turnmill Street
London
EC1M 5QU
0171 296 6600
Researches and produces reports on issues for local government

TUC Equality and Social Policy Department
TUC Congress House
23–28 Great Russell Street
London
WC1B 3LS
0171 636 4030
Provides useful publications on equal rights and social, health and
environmental protection issues

The Andrea Adams Trust
Maritime House
Basin Road North
Hove
East Sussex
BN41 1WA
01273 704 900
A national charity devoted to raising awareness of and tackling bullying

DISABLED PEOPLE
Changing Faces
1 & 2 Junction Mews
Paddington
London
W2 1PN
0171 706 4232
A campaigning and training organisation for facially disfigured people

Disabled Living Foundation
380–384 Harrow Road
London
W9 2HU
0171 289 6111
Provides information on employing people with disabilities

The Employment Service
152 Rockingham Street
Sheffield
S1 4EB
0114 203 3000
Distributes the Code on Employment of Disabled People

MENCAP
123 Golden Lane
London
EC1Y 0RT
0171 454 0454
A campaigning and information organisation for people with learning disabilities

Scope
6 Market Road
London
N7 9PW
0171 619 7100
An organisation for people with cerebral palsy

EX-OFFENDERS

Apex Trust
St Alphage House
2 Fore Street
London
EC2Y 5DA
0171 638 5931
Advice and consultancy on all issues regarding the employment and recruitment of ex-offenders

NACRO
169 Clapham Road
London
SW9 0PU
0171 582 6500
NACRO is the organisation for the care and resettlement of offenders and can advise on employment rights for ex-offenders. It has many local projects

HEALTH AND SAFETY, PERSONAL SAFETY AND VIOLENCE

Health Education Council
St Dunstan's House
201–211 Borough High Street
London
SE1 1GZ
0171 556 2191
Produces booklets and gives information

Health and Safety Executive
HSE Information Centre
Broad Lane
Sheffield
S3 7HQ
0114 289 2345

The Suzy Lamplugh Trust
Training Dept.
PO Box 17818
London
SW14 8WW
0181 876 0305
www.suzylamplugh.org
Information on personal safety – advice, training and resources

LAW AND EMPLOYMENT ISSUES
ACAS
180 Borough High Street
London
SE1 1LW
0171 210 3613

Department of Education and Employment
Caxton House
Tothill Street
London
SW1H 9NF
0171 273 3000
The Department of Employment and ACAS produce leaflets on employment rights

The Industrial Society
Employment law helpline 0171 479 2424
This helpline is for members of The Industrial Society only

LESBIANS AND GAY MEN
Lesbian and Gay Employment Rights (LAGER)
Unit 1G
Leroy House
436 Essex Road
London
N1 3QP
0171 704 6066
Produces regular bulletins on lesbian and gay employment rights and issues and can give advice to individuals facing discrimination at work

Stonewall
16 Clerkenwell Close
London
EC1R 0AN
0171 336 8860
A campaigning body for the rights and welfare of lesbians and gay men (will give advice and information about discrimination in the workplace)

RACE
Churches Commission for Racial Justice
Inter Church House
35–41 Lower Marsh
London
SE1 7RT
0171 620 4444
Provides information and advice on the Churches Campaign for Racial Justice

Commission for Racial Equality
10–12 Allington Street
London
SW1E 5EH
0171 828 7022
Produces guides to the Race Relations Act and many books and leaflets, and can provide advice on employment and discrimination issues

Institute of Race Relations
2–6 Leeke Street
Kings Cross Road
London
WC1X 9HS
0171 837 0041
Provides information and publishes books and resources

Runnymede Trust
133 Aldersgate Street
London
EC1A 4JA
0171 600 9666
Produces books and the journal Race and Immigration *(which has a very useful source section) ten times a year*

RELIGION – NORTHERN IRELAND
Fair Employment Commission
Andras House
60 Great Victoria Street
Belfast
BT2 7BB
01232 240020
Advice on and enforcement of the Fair Employment Act Northern Ireland

TRAINING RESOURCES

BBC for Business
Woodlands
80 Wood Lane
London
W12 0TT
0181 576 2361

WOMEN

Equal Opportunities Commission
Overseas House
Quay Street
Manchester
M3 3HN
0161 833 9244
*Produces guides to the Sex Discrimination Act and information
on employment rights, and can give advice*

Rights of Women (ROW)
52–54 Featherstone Street
London
EC1Y 8RT
0171 251 6577

Women Against Sexual Harassment (WASH)
5th Floor
4 Wild Court
London
WC2B 4AU
0171 405 0430
Confidential advice line and information about sexual harassment